Global Trends
in Real Estate Finance

Global Trends
in Real Estate Finance

Edited by

Graeme Newell

Professor of Property Investment
University of Western Sydney
Australia

Karen Sieracki

KASPAR Associates Limited
UK

✺WILEY-BLACKWELL

A John Wiley & Sons, Ltd., Publication

Blackwell Publishing was acquired by John Wiley & Sons in February 2007.
Blackwell's publishing programme has been merged with Wiley's global Scientific,
Technical, and Medical business to form Wiley-Blackwell.

Registered office
John Wiley & Sons Ltd, The Atrium, Southern Gate, Chichester, West Sussex, PO19 8SQ,
United Kingdom

Editorial offices
9600 Garsington Road, Oxford, OX4 2DQ, United Kingdom
2121 State Avenue, Ames, Iowa 50014-8300, USA

For details of our global editorial offices, for customer services and for information about how
to apply for permission to reuse the copyright material in this book please see our website at
www.wiley.com/wiley-blackwell.

Library of Congress Cataloging-in-Publication Data

Global trends in real estate finance / edited by Graeme Newell and Karen Sieracki.
    p. cm. — (Real estate issues)
  Includes bibliographical references and index.
  ISBN 978-1-4051-5128-3 (hardback : alk. paper) 1.   Real property. 2.   Real
property—Prices. I. Newell, Graeme. II. Sieracki, Karen.
  HD1375.G63 2010
  332.63'247—dc22

                                                                                      2009019839
A catalogue record for this book is available from the British Library.

Set in 10/13pt Trump Mediaeval by Macmillan Publishing Solutions, Chennai, India

Printed in Singapore by Ho Printing Singapore Pte Ltd

1   2010

The Royal Institution of Chartered Surveyors is the mark of property professionalism worldwide, promoting best practice, regulation and consumer protection for business and the community. It is the home of property related knowledge and is an impartial advisor to governments and global organisations. It is committed to the promotion of research in support of the efficient and effective operation of land and property markets worldwide.

Real Estate Issues

Series Managing Editors

Stephen Brown   Head of Research, Royal Institution of Chartered Surveyors
John Henneberry   Department of Town & Regional Planning, University of Sheffield
K.W. Chau   Chair Professor, Department of Real Estate and Construction, The University of Hong Kong
Elaine Worzala   Professor, Director of the Accelerated MSRE, Edward St. John Department of Real Estate, Johns Hopkins University

Real Estate Issues is an international book series presenting the latest thinking into how real estate markets operate. The books have a strong theoretical basis – providing the underpinning for the development of new ideas.

The books are inclusive in nature, drawing both upon established techniques for real estate market analysis and on those from other academic disciplines as appropriate. The series embraces a comparative approach, allowing theory and practice to be put forward and tested for their applicability and relevance to the understanding of new situations. It does not seek to impose solutions, but rather provides a more effective means by which solutions can be found. It will not make any presumptions as to the importance of real estate markets but will uncover and present, through the clarity of the thinking, the real significance of the operation of real estate markets.

Books in the series

Greenfields, Brownfields & Housing Development
Adams & Watkins
978 0 632 0063871

Planning, Public Policy & Property Markets
Edited by Adams, Watkins & White
9781405124300

Housing & Welfare in Southern Europe
Allen, Barlow, Léal, Maloutas & Padovani
9781405103077

Markets and Institutions in Real Estate & Construction
Ball
978140510990

Neighbourhood Renewal and Housing Markets
Edited by Beider
9781405134101

Mortgage Markets Worldwide
Ben-Shahar, Leung & Ong
9781405132107

The Cost of Land Use Decisions
Buitelaar
9781405151238

Towers of Capital: office markets & International financial services
Lizieri
9781405156721

Urban Regeneration in Europe
Couch, Fraser & Percy
9780632058412

Urban Sprawl
Couch, Leontidou & Petschel-Held
9781405151238

Real Estate & the New Economy
Dixon, McAllister, Marston & Snow
9781405117784

Economics & Land Use Planning
Evans
9781405118613

Economics, Real Estate & the Supply of Land
Evans
9781405118620

Development & Developers
Guy & Henneberry
9780632058426

The Right to Buy
Jones & Murie
9781405131971

Mass Appraisal Methods
Kauko & d'Amato
9781405180979

Economics of the Mortgage Market
Leece
9781405114615

Global Trends in Real Estate Finance
Newell & Sieracki
9781405151283

Housing Economics & Public Policy
O'Sullivan & Gibb
9780632064618

Mortgage Markets Worldwide
Ben-Shahar, Ong & Leung
9781405132107

International Real Estate
Seabrooke, Kent & How
9781405103084

British Housebuilders
Wellings
9781405149181

Building Cycles: Growth & Instability
Barras
9781405130011

Forthcoming

Transforming the Private Landlord
Crook & Kemp
9781405184151

Housing Markets & Planning Policy
Jones & Watkins
9781405175203

Affordable Housing & the Property Market
Monk & Whitehead
9781405147149

Housing Stock Transfer
Taylor
9781405170321

Real Estate Finance in the New Economic World
Tiwari & White
9781405158718

Contents

Contributors

Alastair Adair is Professor of Property Investment and Pro Vice Chancellor (Communication and External Affairs) at the University of Ulster. He holds a PhD in Urban Development from the University of Reading and is a Fellow of the Royal Institution of Chartered Surveyors. He is a member of the UK Research Assessment Exercise Town and Country Planning Sub-Panel 2008 and 2001. In 2008 he was awarded the Richard Ratcliff Award by the American Real Estate Society. Currently he is the Deputy Editor of the *Journal of Property Research* and is a member of the editorial board of four other international journals.

Jim Berry is Professor of Urban Planning and Property Development at the University of Ulster. He holds a Doctor of Philosophy and is a chartered surveyor and chartered town planner. Specific research interests at local, national and international levels include urban regeneration, real estate investment, property market performance and analysis of housing and planning policy. He is a member of the editorial board of the *Journal of Property Research*.

Lijian Chen is Managing Director and Head of Global Real Estate (GRE) – Greater China, UBS Global Asset Management. In this role, he is responsible for managing and developing the GRE business as well as the strategic initiatives in the region. He is a member of the Asia Pacific Management Committee of UBS Global Asset Management. Formerly, he was GRE's global head of research at UBS. He serves on the Board of Directors of the American Real Estate Society. He receives his PhD from MIT.

Simon Clark is Head of European Real Estate and a specialist in the taxation of real estate transactions at global law firm, Linklaters. With more than 30 years experience in the real estate sector, he is involved at a senior level with real estate industry bodies such as the Urban Land Institute, the British Property Federation and the Investment Property Forum's educational charity.

Ian Cullen is a co-founding director of IPD and head of systems and information standards. He is an economist with extensive experience of portfolio analysis and property market research. He took his doctorate at University College London where he started his career as a lecturer and researcher in urban analysis. At IPD, Ian is responsible for all technical aspects of the delivery of client information services, the production of real estate indices and related investment performance measurement systems. In addition, he has extended IPD's Index operations to cover Fund level indices and services, has developed a social housing benchmarking service in the Netherlands. Most recently he has built the world's first Pan-European and Global Property Indices, and put in place the infrastructure required to support the rapidly growing property index based derivative markets.

Tim Hackemann studied law at the German Universities of Giessen and Berlin and is tax advisor and attorney-at-law with Ernst & Young AG in Eschborn/Frankfurt. Since 1992 he is working on a variety of tax law matters and he specialised in Merger & Acquisitions, EU Law and cross-border transactions. He is also an expert for the German REIT. Furthermore, he is a regular speaker at conferences on international tax issues and commentator of double tax treaties respectively and co-author of the EPRA Global REIT.

Tony Key is Professor of Real Estate Economics at Cass Business School, City University London, where he heads a real estate group delivering undergraduate and postgraduate courses with an annual intake of 200 students. Prior to joining Cass, Tony was Director of Research for Investment Property Databank (1988–2002), and had previously worked for Centre for Environmental Studies and Property Market Analysis. He is a member of the editorial broads of the *Journal of Property Research* and the *Journal of Property Investment and Finance*.

Nicolas Kohl holds a master's degree in business administration from the European Business School Schloss Reichartshausen (EBS) in Oestrich-Winkel, where he graduated with distinction. During his studies, he also spent exchange semesters at the University of Florida and the Ecole Supérieure de Commerce de La Rochelle. Since May 2005, he worked as a research assistant and doctoral candidate for Prof. Dr Wolfgang Schäfers at the Chair of Real Estate Management of the IRE|BS International Real Estate Business School at the University of Regensburg. His research interests include real estate capital markets and corporate governance.

David Lorenz is the principal and founder of Lorenz Property Advisors – Chartered Surveyors (a strategic sustainability consultancy) and managing partner of AAAcon Asset Management GmbH, both located in Germany. He holds a degree in real estate economics, a Master of Science in Construction Management, and completed his doctoral studies on 'The Application of Sustainable Development Principles to the Theory and Practice of Property Valuation' at the University of Karlsruhe, Germany. David has several years of experience in valuation, asset management, investment advisory and project development and is actively engaged in research and education at the Chair of Sustainable Management of Housing and Real Estate at the University of Karlsruhe. He published numerous articles on the topics of sustainability in property investment, valuation and risk assessment. He is a professional member of the Royal Institution of Chartered Surveyors (RICS) and currently serves as Chairman of the RICS EU Advisory Group on Sustainable Property Investment and Management.

Thomas Lützkendorf is Head of the Chair of Sustainable Management of Housing and Real Estate at the School of Economic and Business Engineering at Karlsruhe University (Germany). He holds a PhD (1985) and Habilitation (2000) in the area of implementing sustainable development principles within the property and construction sector. Within the scope of various teaching, research and consulting activities he is concerned with questions relating to the integration of sustainability issues into decision-making processes along the life cycle of buildings as well as regarding the relationships between buildings' environmental quality and economic advantageousness. He is a member and scientific consultant of the 'round-table on sustainable building' at the German Federal Ministry of Transport, Building and Urban Affairs. In addition, Prof. Lutzkendorf is a founding member of the International Initiative for a Sustainable Built Environment (iiSBE) and actively involved in various standardisation activities at the national, European and international level.

Will McIntosh is Dean of the College of Business and Professor of Finance at the University of Cincinnati where he teaches real estate and alternative investments. Prior to joining the University of Cincinnati, Dr McIntosh served as Managing Director and Global Head of Research and Strategy for ING Real Estate. He has also served as Managing Director and Head of Research for AIG Global Real Estate Investment Corp. and Prudential Real Estate Investors. Dr McIntosh is a Past-President of the American Real Estate Society and the Real Estate Research Institute. He is also a former board member of the National Council of Real Estate Investment Fiduciaries and currently serves on the Research Committee of the Pension Real Estate Association. Dr McIntosh is a former Associate Professor of Finance and Director of the Center for Real Estate Studies at the University of Kentucky. He received his PhD in Finance from the University of North Texas and an MBA in Real Estate and a BS in Business Education from Eastern Kentucky University. He has published extensively in the area of REITs and real estate investment.

Stanley McGreal has researched widely into issues relating to housing, urban development and regeneration, planning, globalisation, property market performance and investment. Professor McGreal has been involved in major research contracts funded by government departments and agencies, research councils, charities and the private sector. Analysis of housing, urban renewal strategies and regeneration outputs in the property sector and the investment market have been a central theme of this research with particular implications for policy. Professor McGreal has over 300 published works. He has been an invited speaker at several conferences, holds membership of several editorial boards and serves on various international committees. He is Past-President of the International Real Estate Society and is currently Director of the Built Environment Research Institute at the University of Ulster.

Gary McNamara is Head of Property Derivatives at DTZ. He is a chartered surveyor and graduated with a BEng in Electronic and Mechanical Engineering and an MSc in International Real Estate both from the University of Reading. He helped to initiate the property derivatives offering within the DTZ and Tullett Prebon partnership in 2005 and has since been helping to develop the market globally through various means including published articles, presenting at conferences and advising on transactions with clients. Prior to this, Gary worked as part of the DTZ capital markets investment team and has also worked with DTZ in New Zealand and Australia. DTZ's strategic partnership with Tullett Prebon offers a versatile and comprehensive range of brokerage, research and advisory services to clients looking to integrate property derivative contracts into existing portfolio management, investment and hedging structures.

Olivier Mesmin is a Tax Partner at Baker and McKenzie SCP in Paris and is an attorney registered at the French Bar. He is a recognised expert in the field of real estate taxation and has – in his capacity as advisor of the FSIF (French Reit federation) – been closely involved in the design and implementation of the French Reit regime. He is also an active member of the European Public Real Estate Association (EPRA).

Thomas I. Mills joined UBS in 2003, and is currently based in Tokyo, Japan as the Head of Research in the Corporate Strategy Group of Mitsubishi Corp. – UBS Realty Inc., a joint venture between UBS Global Asset Management and Mitsubishi Corporation that manages two J-REITs listed on the Tokyo Stock Exchange. Prior to his current position, Tom served in UBS Global Asset Management's Global Real Estate group as head of APAC research and before that was head of European research. He received his undergraduate degree from Harvard College, and an MBA from the Haas School of Business, University of California, Berkeley.

Mohammad Ali Muwlazadeh is an Associate Professor in Urban Planning. He received his MA and PhD degrees from Indiana State University and the University of Glasgow respectively. His current position is a postdoctoral research fellow in the Faculty of Engineering, Science and the Built Environment (ESBE) at London South Bank University, UK. He was the chair of the Urban Planning Department at Chamran University in Iran.

As a town planner, he acted as the consultant and worked both in local and national government surveying and planning. His research interests focus on the urban land and housing policies, housing finance and real estate Islamic finance since 1992.

Neo Poh Har is currently pursuing her PhD at the National University of Singapore (NUS), where she also completed her BSc (Real Estate) and MSc (Estate Management) degrees. She has published in major real estate journals including *Real Estate Economics*. She is presently a senior research analyst in one of the top real estate companies in Asia. Prior to joining the industry, she was involved in a NUS funded research project on the growth strategies of Asian REITs.

Graeme Newell is Professor of Property Investment at the University of Western Sydney, Australia. Professor Newell is a Fellow of the RICS and a Fellow of the Australian Property Institute, having strong links to the property industry at an international level. He is editor of the *Pacific Rim Property Research Journal*, as well as being on the editorial board for a range of international property journals including the *Journal of Property Research* and the *Journal of Property Investment and Finance*. Professor Newell is actively involved in property investment research in Europe, having strong links to the RICS, EPRA and Investment Property Forum. He has numerous property research publications and research grants in areas including sustainability and the role of property in portfolios; he also regularly speaks at property industry conferences regarding strategic property investment issues. He has recently received major awards from both the American Real Estate Society and European Real Estate Society for his contributions to the development of property research and property education at an international level.

Joseph T.L. Ooi is an Associate Professor at the National University of Singapore (NUS). He has published in major real estate journals including *Real Estate Economics, Journal of Real Estate Finance and Economics, Journal of Real Estate Research, Journal of Property Research* and *Journal of Property Investment and Finance*. Joseph has received recognition from the Emerald Literati Network (two Outstanding Papers, a Highly Commended certificate and an Outstanding Reviewer award), the European Real Estate Society (Best Paper award) and the American Real Estate Society (four manuscript prizes and an Outstanding Reviewer award). Joseph is also a recipient of the prestigious NUS Young Researcher Award as well as the International Real Estate Society's 2008 Achievement Award for outstanding research, education and practice at the international level.

Ali Parsa is Rotary International Professor in Urban Planning and Business Development at the University of Ulster. He is also visiting Professor of

Urban Planning and Development at London South Bank University. He holds a PhD in International Planning and Construction from Newcastle University. His research interest includes analysis of real estate market structures in emerging markets, housing policy issues, Shariah compliant real estate investment and global real estate strategies of tall buildings. Ali is the Executive Director of Middle East Real Estate Society.

Tom Road is a real estate lawyer at Linklaters focussing on real estate merger and acquisition transactions.

Wolfgang Schäfers graduated in business administration from the University of Mannheim and received his doctoral degree from the European Business School Schloss Reichartshausen (EBS). He began his career at Arthur Andersen (today Ernst and Young) in Frankfurt, where he became partner and was responsible for the real estate corporate finance team. In 2002, he became Managing Director at Sal. Oppenheim, Europe's leading independent private bank, where he has been heading the real estate investment banking branch ever since. In addition, Prof. Dr Schäfers was offered a Chair of Real Estate Management at the University of Regensburg in October 2004. He is author and (co-)editor of diverse real estate publications, such as the 'Handbook Corporate Real Estate Management' or the 'Handbook Real Estate Banking'. Moreover, Prof. Dr Schäfers is a founding member of the 'Gesellschaft für Immobilienwirtschaftliche Forschung e. V.' (gif), a member of the European Real Estate Society (ERES) and a member of the editorial board of the 'Zeitschrift für Immobilienökonomie' (ZIÖ).

Karl-Werner Schulte was appointed the professorship of the Chair of Business Administration, in particular Investment and Finance, at the EUROPEAN BUSINESS SCHOOL International University Schloss Reichartshausen (ebs) in 1986. In 1990 he founded the ebs Real Estate Academy and has been its academic and managing director till 2006. Among his special honours are the presidency of the European Real Estate Society (ERES) and the International Real Estate Society (IRES). Since 2006 he has been responsible for promoting real estate education and research in Africa as an IRES Director. He has been elected as an Honorary Member of the Royal Institution of Chartered Surveyors. As a member of numerous advisory and editorial boards of renowned real estate companies and academic journals such as gif and IMMOEBS, Prof. Dr Schulte links practical and theoretical aspects of real estate. Many of his publications have become key literature of the discipline in Germany.

Karen Sieracki has been actively involved in property research and investment management for the past 25 years. She has her own research company,

KASPAR Associates Limited, working with a number of leading institutional clients and the property industry at large. She is Visiting Professor at the University of Ulster, and is External Examiner at London South Bank University. She is a member of the ULI European Policy Committee and the ULI UK Executive Council and chairs its Think Tank Forum. She sits on the Education Strategy Group and the CPD Events Group for the Investment Property Forum. In addition, she serves on the Editorial Boards of the *Journals of Property Research and Property Valuation* and is a Royal Institution of Chartered Surveyors APC Assessor.

Preface

Recent years have seen international property emerge as an increasingly important element in a property portfolio for a wide range of property investors, both in terms of nationality and type. This is reflected in 32% of the $1 trillion in global commercial property transactions in 2007 being cross-border, as well as global REIT markets now established in over 20 countries in the USA, Europe and Asia-Pacific. International property investment has clearly transformed the property landscape in terms of property players, products, markets and structures. The details below give a snapshot of these exciting international property investment developments, as well as a context for this book.

All major property players now have a diverse range of both listed and unlisted property products with different risk profiles to meet the global mandate for many property investors. The capital flows to property from pension funds, managed funds, both public and private property companies, private equity and syndicated vehicles in recent years have been significant; particularly as many investors saw themselves as underexposed to property. Private equity funds and sovereign wealth funds (SWFs) have also taken on an increasingly significant role, with SWFs such as Abu Dhabi Investment Corporation and GIC having substantial global property portfolios. As the avenues for property investment have increased, investment in property has been made more accessible to the individual.

Similarly, REIT markets have truly become global markets in the last 6 years. This has seen the traditional major REIT markets of the USA and Australia now accounting for only 64% of global REIT market capitalisation. This now sees over 500 REITs globally in 20 countries, with a market capitalisation of over £330 billion. Importantly, major REIT markets have now been established in France, UK, Japan, Singapore and Hong Kong, providing investors with extra listed property investment opportunities compared with only listed property companies previously. This has also driven the rapid growth in over 250 global property securities funds with strong international agendas. This diversity of property products has been further evidenced by the development of property derivatives and the use of sophisticated property financing products, including commercial mortgage backed securities.

Fundamental to this growth in international property investment has been the emergence of new property investment markets, as these emerging property markets have improved their economic competitiveness, market transparency, legal frameworks and financial structures. This has seen these emerging property markets become increasingly important to international investors, as they seek portfolio diversification and expected higher returns, resulting from the strong growth in available funds needing to be invested in property globally and the lack of local property investment opportunities. Property markets in China and India have become a high priority for global property investors, as well as the property markets in Eastern Europe, Russia, South America, Latin America and the Middle East. This sophistication is reflected in property investors now sub-classifying China, India and Russia into Tier 1, 2 and 3 property markets, as well as core, value-add and opportunistic property funds being established to reflect the different risk appetites for global property investors.

International property investment decision-making has been further enhanced by professional associations such as EPRA, INREV and APREA providing enhanced professional property developments and property networks in Europe and Asia. Similarly, the level of property performance information has improved considerably in recent years; for example, IPD now report direct property performance in over 20 countries. Property has now come of age after waiting on the sidelines for over 30 years. It is on the global investment table now and has the necessary infrastructure for its continued support and maintenance. These important developments have also resulted in property career opportunities in many of these property markets in key areas such as property fund management, investment banking, asset consulting and property research.

Overall, these exciting developments in international property investment and finance have seen a vibrant international property investment scene in recent years. However, the global credit crisis in 2007–2008 has clearly impacted on property at a global level and has seen significant reductions in property investment activity in 2008, as well as a significant deterioration in REIT markets at a global level. Property is an asset class which is capital intensive and which is inextricably linked to the capital markets. In particular, commercial property transactions are down 49% in the first half of 2008 compared to the first half of 2007, and REIT market returns for the last year (to August 2008) have seen significant under-performance in all REIT markets (e.g. Australia, Japan, UK, Singapore, France). Similarly, the debt markets for property (e.g. CMBS) have quickly stalled.

It is in this dynamic, but challenging, context of international property investment that we have put this book together on international property investment and finance. The key objective is to enhance our understanding of these global property investment and finance initiatives and issues that have shaped global property in recent years and that will continue to do so.

To achieve this goal, we have drawn upon the collective knowledge and wisdom of a diversified international portfolio of leading property academics and leading property professionals with extensive expertise in these key areas of global property investment and finance. They have each provided incisive chapters on a diverse range of the key ingredients in global property investment and finance that have helped shape global property investment now and into the future.

In putting this book together, we have not only focused on the various property products in these different markets, but we have also identified the key property processes that will continue to shape international property investment. Key areas include sustainability, corporate governance, Shariah finance and the challenges of preparing the next generation of property professionals in these property markets. It is a changing world, and property has kept pace with the challenging macro and micro conditions with innovation and adaptability.

We hope that this book provides an exciting context for the increasingly important role of international property in property portfolios; particularly as we move forward in resolving many of the property issues flowing from the current global credit crisis.

We would like to thank the authors who have kindly contributed to this important text; their insights into the key areas of international property investment and finance have added a real richness to this text. We give our special thanks to Stephen Brown, Head of Research at the RICS, who helped and encouraged us from the inception of the idea for this book to its final manifestation. Also, our thanks to Blackwell and IRES for facilitating this text.

We hope you enjoy reading this book and using it to inform property students, academics and the property industry and the investment community from institutions, advisors to the general public about the increasingly important role of international property investment and finance.

Graeme Newell and Karen Sieracki

Part I

Products

1

Global Real Estate Investable Universe Continues to Expand and Develop

Lijian Chen and Thomas I. Mills

Introduction

Investors today should expect to gain significant diversification benefits and achieve higher risk-adjusted returns by adding real estate to their multi-asset portfolios. Furthermore, when expanding from a purely domestic property exposure to a global real estate portfolio, there are additional benefits. For example, the effect of diversification is enhanced by the low correlation of real estate returns across regions, which strengthens the argument that real estate should be considered a separate asset class, competing squarely with stocks and bonds. In addition, the large size of the global investment universe provides a greater number and larger variety of potential investment opportunities and strategies.

An attractive way for investors to add global real estate to their portfolios is through public real estate investment trusts (REITs). Both the private and public global real estate investment universes have experienced substantial increases in value over the past decade. In particular, the market capitalization of REITs around the world has grown exponentially over the last 10 years, notwithstanding recent market corrections in many countries. The rapid REIT market expansion was mainly due to the steady creation of new REITs, the acquisition of new properties by existing REITs and increases in value of their property holdings. In order to illustrate this growth, we first present our most recent estimate of the size of core private real estate markets by region. Then, we discuss the dramatic growth of the global public real estate market and highlight several major REIT markets to illustrate several important and unique emerging trends. We attempt to demonstrate why we believe there is still plenty of room left for further market expansion of the public real estate investable universes. The high volatility seen in many REIT markets in 2007 and recent weakness in certain private real estate markets have not altered the fundamental case for global real estate. On the contrary, the recent market changes have created even more numerous and attractive opportunities for many investors.

Global core real estate universe: $8 trillion and growing

Our latest estimate for the global investable universe of core real estate, summarized in Figure 1.1, indicates that the total market value has increased from approximately $6.6 trillion at the end of 2004 to nearly $8.0 trillion as of the end of 2005, an increase of more than 20%. When data becomes available allowing a more current estimate using 2007 year-end data, based on the performance of private real estate over the past 2 years, we expect that the investment universe may have approached or even exceeded $10 trillion.

Our model for estimating the total value of core real estate in the investment universe first determines those countries that may be considered suitable for core real estate investment by institutional investors, based on such factors as size of the economy, political stability and the level of economic development. From that point, estimating the size of the investable

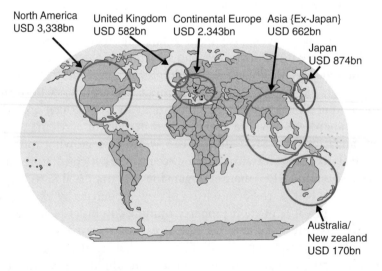

Figure 1.1   Real estate market size by region. *Source*: UBS Global Asset Management Real Estate Research as of December 31, 2005. This data does not include single-family homes.

real estate universe in each of the selected 27 countries entails considerable subjectivity and is not an exact science. At the asset level, it is not uncommon for two appraisers in the same market to disagree on the value of a specific building. Expanding this example across national borders and continents, there are potentially vast differences in valuation methods in different countries as well as significant variation in many real estate market-related definitions (e.g., quality, product type, sectors and market rents). Therefore, instead of such a bottom-up approach, we employ a top-down approach. We start with the largest 65 metro markets in the USA, where we have greater confidence in our estimate of total real estate value. Then, we use a simple econometric model to estimate the size of the investable real estate universe for the other countries. The results from our econometric model are checked for reasonableness and further improved by applying our knowledge of various markets. For example, we anticipate that the model would understate the value of the real estate universe in the cases of Hong Kong and Singapore, two densely populated areas with more than 10 times as many people per square mile as the most densely populated European country. Therefore, we fine-tune our estimates using a bottom-up approach, which leads to substantial upward adjustment of the size for Hong Kong and Singapore. Similarly, we increase the estimate for the UK by nearly a third based on the more reliable information on the amount of real estate owned by institutions in that country.

The estimation of real estate market size for any country remains largely a work of art. While we make no statement that the estimations presented herein are any better than those of our industry peers or friends in academia, we do believe that the estimates are reasonable approximations that allow a good understanding of the relative sizes of real estate markets in different countries and a good comparison of the aggregate size of the real estate universe with the equity and debt asset classes. The estimates shown are based on the data available from year-end 2005, and undoubtedly the market size has expanded significantly in the years since that time. Also important to note is that the relative value of real estate in each region is less likely to have changed drastically.

In most countries around the world that we consider potentially suitable targets for institutional investors' global real estate portfolios, private real estate prices have been rising. Other than the development of new properties or the addition of new countries and their core real estate stock to our list of core countries, such price increases are effectively the only way for the value of the real estate investment universe to rise. The increase in capital values in the USA has been tracked by the National Council of Real Estate Investment Fiduciaries (NCREIF), and for an indication of trends elsewhere, the Investment Property Databank (IPD) indices facilitate a comparison in many more countries. Of the 21 countries for which IPD maintains indices, there were only two countries experiencing negative capital value returns in the past 2 years: Germany in 2006 and 2007, and the UK in 2007. From a total return perspective, the UK in 2007 registered the only decline while Germany in both 2006 and 2007 saw the positive income returns more than offset the negative capital value returns. Clearly, the impressive performance of real estate investments has been one of the major contributors to the increase of market value worldwide.

Even more dramatic than the long-term increase in prices of real estate around the world and the associated increase in the size of the investable universe of core, institutional-quality property is the rise in equity market capitalization of publicly traded real estate and the proliferation and growth of REIT-like structures around the globe. Figure 1.2 depicts the dramatic increase of public real estate's market capitalization. Notwithstanding the decline in market capitalization from its global peak in May 2007 of $952 billion, the overall increase over the past decade is considerable. In the 5 years through the end of April 2008, the FTSE EPRA/NAREIT global listed real estate index increased from 224 companies and a market capitalization of $265 billion to 291 companies and a market capitalization of $786 billion, representing an increase in market capitalization of 197% over the period. Out of the $786 billion universe, approximately 40% was in North America, 40% in Asia and 20% in Europe as of April 2008.

Existing REITs have been acquiring properties, and their properties have gone up in value as private real estate prices have increased. In some markets, new public real estate companies have been created. For example,

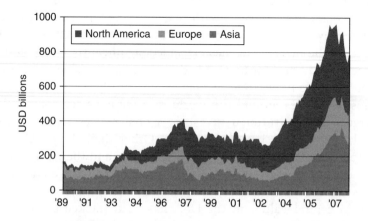

Figure 1.2 Growth of global REIT market capitalization: December 1989–April 2008. *Source*: UBS Global Asset Management Real Estate Research based on data obtained from FTSE EPRA/NAREIT.

in Japan, where the J-REIT market did not exist until September 2001, it grew to a sizable REIT sector of 42 J-REITs and a market capitalization of JPY 4.4 trillion (roughly $42 billion) by May 2008, an increase from 28 J-REITs and a market capitalization of JPY 2.8 trillion as of the end of 2005. While over the long run this growth has been substantial, in the 12 months to May 2008, the market capitalization of the J-REIT sector has declined from approximately JPY 6.7 trillion in May 2007, highlighting the potential high volatility associated with public markets. Partly due to the decline of J-REIT unit prices in 2007, only two J-REIT IPOs occurred in that year as many planned launches were withdrawn or postponed pending improvement of public market conditions. In other countries, REIT legislation has been put in place but rapid growth has not ensued, due in some cases to cumbersome structures or regulatory barriers. South Korea's REIT market experienced only modest growth initially after its introduction in 2001, but changes have been enacted that potentially allow REITs there to be more scalable and sustainable.

In the years ahead, more investors are expected to discover merits of investing in global real estate. The success of the REIT revolution worldwide has provided investors even greater opportunities to exploit the benefits of investing globally. It is foreseeable that in the near future more countries are likely to join the family of countries around the world that have adopted REIT structures, thanks in large part to the substantial expansion of the global REIT universe over the past decade or so.

Why have REITs succeeded?

Interest in listed real estate has continued to grow over the past several years despite the weakness in 2007. The number of countries adopting REIT structures has increased, and more countries are entering the debate and planning phase of adopting them. In countries where REIT structures already exist, their market capitalizations have generally been increasing. It should be noted that while listed real estate does not necessarily have to be in the form of a REIT, the trend reflects investors' preferences for REIT-like vehicles. Investors seeking exposure to real estate favor the high payout ratio of property operating income that REITs must distribute in the form of dividends. Investors also like it that REITs must invest nearly exclusively in real estate. Another attraction of investing in REITs is the benefit of tax transparency that virtually all REITs offer.

There are other benefits from investing in REITs as well as listed real estate in general, *vis-à-vis* private real estate. REIT returns have low correlations with those of other asset classes, and even with private real estate indices, offering potential diversification benefits from adding REITs to a mixed-asset portfolio. Also, investors have come to view them as fairly liquid investments. REIT markets have, in many countries, reached a sufficient size, and their trading volumes have become large enough, that once decisions on company selection are made, investments in REIT shares can be executed in a timely manner. Because shares can be bought and sold more easily than private real estate can, shifting allocations from one property sector to another, and from one country to another can be done relatively quickly at reasonably low cost. Further, a relatively large amount of capital can potentially be spread over more companies by investing globally, achieving nearly instant diversification and high liquidity. It is for all of the above reasons that listed real estates, and REITs in particular, are steadily attracting more investors around the world. In most cases, REITs, in particular, have the additional advantage of having relatively high dividend yields due to the requirement that most of their earnings must be distributed to shareholders as well as paying no tax at the corporate level (shareholders generally must pay taxes on the dividends).

The tremendous demand for REITs and REIT-like products led to substantial declines of dividend yield spreads of REITs over 10-year government bond yields from 2004 to 2006. Following the decline in REIT share prices in many countries in 2007, dividend yields in many markets once again look very attractive relative to government bonds. In certain countries, dividend yields are relatively high in comparison with government bonds. In Japan, for example, as of May 2008, the average REIT dividend yield was 4.7%, a 310 basis point spread over the 10-year government bond yield, an increase from a spread of 110 basis points a year earlier. In other countries, spreads over government bonds have rebounded from negative territory. In the USA in September 2006, the average 3.9% REIT dividend yield was approximately 70 basis points below the 10-year treasury yield, but in April 2008 the 4.72% dividend yield represented an approximately 95 basis point positive spread. With higher dividend yields, it is important to note that REITs have once again become one of the most attractive investment sectors.

REITs have registered impressive total returns this decade worldwide. In local currency terms, the global FTSE EPRA/NAREIT index returned −10.8% in 2007, but in the 5 years through the end of 2006 the average annual return of 23.3% significantly exceeded the annualized return of 8.7% generated by global equities as measured by the global FTSE index over the same period.

The future evolution of REITs globally is likely to continue benefiting from two key trends. First, investors are increasingly drawn to the high dividend yields relative to general equities and the stability of the underlying asset class. Second, governments around the world are seeing REITs as a way to improve the relative competitiveness of their listed real estate markets. The REIT sector will likely enjoy a strong tailwind for many years to come.

REIT proliferation: thriving in 18 countries and counting

Despite having been created as long ago as 1960 in the USA and then introduced in the Netherlands, Australia and New Zealand in the late 1960s and
the early 1970s, by 1994 REIT structures existed in only these four countries, and the introduction of REITs was being considered in one more. Since
1994, however, the number of countries with REITs or REIT-like structures
has grown to at least 18 as of July 2007, and legislation was either in place
or under consideration in at least another 12 countries (Figure 1.3).

REITs and REIT-like structures continue to spring up around the globe.
Take Hong Kong as an example. In 2005, Hong Kong successfully delivered
the Link REIT, which became the largest REIT IPO in the world when it
issued shares with an aggregate value of HKD 22 billion ($2.8 billion). In
the late 2005, all of the first three Hong Kong REIT IPOs, raised a combined total of HKD 25.8 billion ($3.3 billion). By the year-end 2005, the
Link REIT alone had a market cap of more than HKD 31 billion due to a
rapid increase in its share price following its IPO, indicative of the success of the nascent structure. Even though the HK structure does not offer
any additional tax incentive, the market's strategic influence in Asia has
attracted both local and foreign real estate companies to consider taking
advantage of the opportunity to list in Hong Kong. Within a month of the
Link REIT IPO, the Hong Kong Stock Exchange experienced two additional successful listings of REITs: prosperity REIT and GZI REIT. The latter owns properties in Mainland China.

There were initially limits on Hong Kong REIT ownership of properties
outside of Hong Kong, which contributed to the decision of at least one
company, Fortune REIT, to list in Singapore instead of Hong Kong, despite
owning retail properties located in Hong Kong. However, in order to make
Hong Kong a more competitive and attractive market for REIT listing, in
the summer 2005, the government relaxed restrictions on property ownership, allowing Hong Kong REITs to own property outside of Hong Kong
(such as in Mainland China). This made possible the previously mentioned
launch of GZI REIT, a Hong Kong REIT owning properties in Mainland
China, in the late 2005. Rules and policies instituted by governments to
guide the development of a REIT sector are clearly one of the most important factors impacting the growth of the sector.

Besides the success in Hong Kong, France is another country where
REITs have succeeded. Since its introduction in 2003, the French Société
d'Investissement Immobilier Cotee (SIIC) structure has fostered a sector
that has grown to a market capitalization of more than $50 billion as of July
2007. The French experience also appears successful in terms of its pricing
of listed property companies relative to the value of the real estate owned by
them. For the 13 years prior to the introduction of the SIIC structure, listed

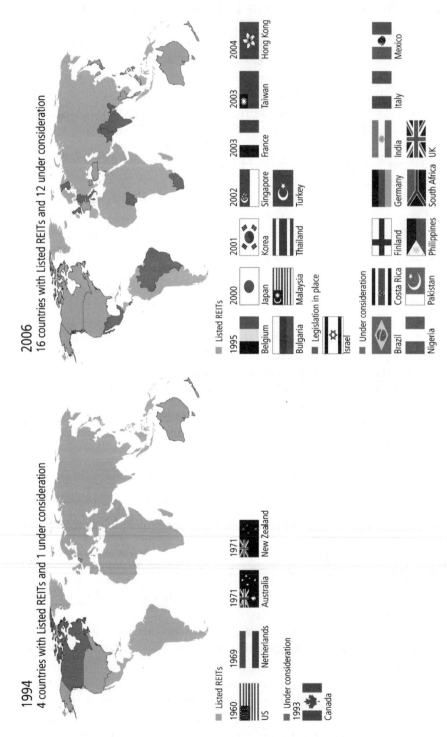

Figure 1.3 More countries adopt REIT structures. *Source:* UBS Global Asset Management Real Estate Research as of June 2006.

property companies in France traded at an average discount to net asset value (NAV) of approximately 25%, but by mid-2004 the sector was trading at a premium to NAV of ~8%. The structure has recently been revised to make it even more attractive for companies wishing to sell properties to SIICs. Similar to the UPREIT structure in the USA, which allowed sellers of properties to defer taxes on gains by accepting shares in the REIT buying the properties, the new rules allow capital gains on sales to SIICs to be taxed at a reduced rate. This change may encourage the transfer of assets from corporations that own and occupy their own real estate to SIICs, providing an additional source of growth for the market.

Two additional countries to introduce REITs recently were the UK and Germany, which added significantly to the total market capitalization of REITs globally. Both introduced REIT structures in 2007, retroactive to the beginning of the year. The governments of both countries were concerned about structuring the market so that tax revenues were not reduced. A major issue is that if a foreign entity acquires real estate in either the UK or Germany, taxes would be paid on the rental income stream. If that entity were to invest through a REIT, the income stream would become a dividend income stream and often taxed at a lower rate under withholding tax agreements, possibly at 0%. This potential loss of future tax revenue is something that concerns most governments, and impacted discussions of new REIT regime introductions in some countries. The UK REIT sector suffered from somewhat unfortunate timing, as 2007 was a year of REIT price declines generally worldwide. Nevertheless, by July 2007, there were some 11 UK REITs with a total market capitalization of approximately $58 billion. As of November 2007, some 17 UK REITs existed, and all of the major listed real estate companies had converted. The first German company to convert to REIT status was Alstria Office, in October 2007. Before the German REIT legislation was enacted, the Initiative Finanzplatz Deutschland (IFD) estimated that the listed real estate market in Germany could reach as much as EUR 127 billion by 2010. With the pullback in 2007, this may now look rather optimistic, but there is likely significant room for future growth.

In certain markets there is also cross border investment in which REITs in one country own significant amounts of property in another. For example, there are Australian listed property trusts (LPTs) that own properties in the USA and Japan. Such cross border investment would most likely serve as a source of growth even if the number of countries with REIT structures remained static or increased only sluggishly, which has not been the case in recent years.

Our estimate of the size of the commercial real estate market in Europe is just over $2.9 trillion (as of the end of 2005), and the UK and Germany together make up more than $1.1 trillion, or nearly 40%, of the total. Globally, approximately 90% of all commercial real estate is located in markets where REIT structures exist, following the addition of Germany and the UK to this group,

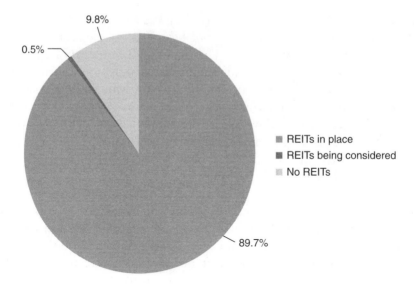

9.8%

0.5%

■ REITs in place
■ REITs being considered
▨ No REITs

89.7%

Figure 1.4   Share of investable real estate universe with REIT structures. *Source*: UBS Global Asset Management Real Estate Research data as of July 2007.

as shown in Figure 1.4. Given the sheer size of those two markets, the introduction of REIT structures had a significant impact on the global REIT universe.

In Figure 1.2 we show the market capitalization of listed property companies in the three regions of Asia-Pacific, Europe and North America. Figure 1.5 in turn depicts the breakdown by country within each region as of April 2008, as well as the relative sizes of each region, as the relative areas of each circles correspond to the market capitalizations of its respective region. This illustrates the relatively small market sizes of markets in Europe outside the UK, and also the rather dominating size of the US market, both within the North American region and in the global context. In addition, the market capitalization of Asian listed real estate companies is now nearly as large as that of North American companies.

The larger markets are generally characterized by higher daily trading volume, hence providing higher liquidity. In contrast, smaller, yet growing, REIT markets tend to have only limited liquidity. Several REIT markets remain small and have yet to show much potential for scalability. For example, with 19 REITs listed as of July 2007, all of Bulgaria's REITs had market capitalizations below $200 million. Thus far, the sectors in South Korea and Taiwan have not seen significant growth since inception. However, despite recent rapid expansion, there is still room for considerable growth in many listed real estate markets around the world, which will be elaborated below.

Another important trend to note is that the property-sector compositions of many REIT markets are very different. The US market is relatively

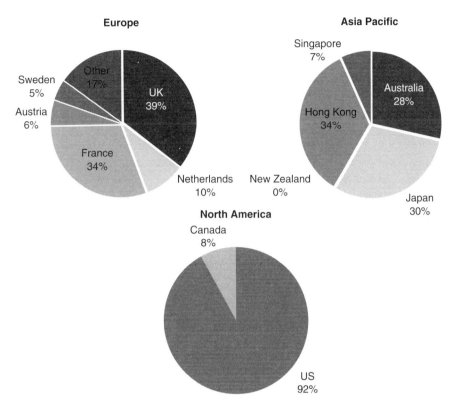

Figure 1.5 REIT Market capitalization by region with country weightings. *Source*: UBS Global Asset Management Real Estate Research based on data obtained from FTSE EPRA/NAREIT.

evenly composed of several key property sectors, including office, industrial, retail, and residential. Japan's REIT market is dominated by the office sector. It is clear that most REIT markets are still rapidly evolving, adding new sectors and changing the sector mix. Many REITs started with portfolios representing multiple property types (i.e., diversified across sectors). Increasingly, however, REITs have become more specialized, focusing on a single property sector.

The line between public and private real estates can be less starkly delineated than it might seem at first. Ownership forms between public and private real estates can change, also affecting the relative size of public and private markets at the margin. A large number of private companies have become public companies for a variety of reasons, including access to capital. Conversely, several companies have recently moved in the opposite direction. In the USA, a number of public REITs have been taken private, and the total transaction volume of such public-to-private deals rose from $3.8 billion in 2004 to $13.0 billion in 2005, and in the early 2007 a single deal, the privatization of Equity Office Properties, involved a port-folio valued at approximately $40 billion. In December 2005, the indus-trial REIT Centerpoint Properties agreed to be acquired by a joint venture, which included among its investors the largest pension fund in the USA: California Public Employees Retirement System (CalPERS). The sale trans-acted at a price of $50 per share, or significantly above the Green Street Advisors' NAV estimate of $31.75, although only a 9.1% premium to the pre-announcement closing price. In each such case of public real estate being taken private, the buyers presumably believed there was a chance for arbitrage between the two ownership types, or that if they were merely acquiring the real estate at market prices, the size of the portfolio and the chance to acquire it all in a single, if complicated, deal made it worthwhile. The Centerpoint Properties deal illustrates some additional reasons why an investor might be willing to pay more for a company than the underlying properties are worth on the private market, as Centerpoint owns a consid-erable amount of land available for future development and a platform to manage the assets and undertake future acquisitions and development. In the sense that real estate capital markets permit arbitrage of price ineffi-ciencies in the underlying assets of public companies, public and private real estates seem to be interchangeable. The acquisition of Equity Office Properties by private equity fund Blackstone in February 2007 was con-cluded at $55.50 per share, and the Green Street Advisors' NAV estimate at the time was $56.00. Blackstone's initial offer was for $48.50 per share, but they were forced to raise it when another bidder submitted a higher offer. Interestingly, within 2 weeks of reaching an agreement, Blackstone had in turn sold off 109 properties in the portfolio for approximately $19 billion. A portfolio of seven Manhattan properties was sold within 2 days. These events once more illustrate how quickly the overall size of the public and private real estate markets can expand and contract. Therefore, when dis-cussing the evolution of the REIT sector, it often makes more sense to focus on longer term trends and structural changes.

Early growth cycle: only the tip of the iceberg

Despite the significant long-term growth of public real estate markets around the world, we believe that we have experienced only the early phase of a growth cycle. Many favorable factors have continued to develop that we expect to help maintain the current momentum. First, real estate, as a distinct asset class with several attractive characteristics, has only recently begun to gather wider recognition from institutional and private inves-tors worldwide, especially many large institutional investors in emerging economies (e.g., China and India) and even certain developed economies (e.g., Japan and South Korea). In the coming years, we are likely to see many Asian institutional investors, following their European and American counterparts, start investing a substantial amount of capital in real estate. Japanese institutional investors' strategic allocations to real estate on average accounted for only 4.7% of their overall portfolios in 2007, according to a survey conducted by Russell Investments. This represented an increase from 3.4% in 2005, and the allocation was expected to increase to 5.7% by 2009. Nevertheless, the 2007 figure for Japan was significantly below the 6.7% strategic allocation in the USA, 8.9% in Europe and 9.6% in Australia. Furthermore, in China, a new wave of capital could soon be heading for domestic and global real estate investments once pension funds, insurance companies and banks are permitted to invest in the real estate asset class.

Second, from the perspective of optimal asset allocation, many investors are still significantly under-allocated to real estate in their mixed-asset portfolios. Even in the USA, many institutional investors hope the values of their actual real estate investments can be increased to match their allocation targets, which often reach 10% or more. According to a survey of the largest 50 public pension systems in the USA by the newsletter *Real Estate Alert*, real estate holdings for these systems increased 33% to $144.3 billion in 2007. Perhaps even more indicative of the strong demand from pension funds in the USA is that additional $73.9 billion had been committed to specific advisors but not yet invested as of the end of 2007. Adding these commitments to the total real estate holdings of the pension funds would bring (if fully invested) the aggregate allocation to real estate up to 8.3% from the current 6.3% of invested assets according to the survey. In response to such potential demand, more and larger investment vehicles have been created in both the public and private real estate sectors. In addition, the breadth and the depth of the global real estate investable universe are so substantial that it is likely to take several more years before we should start to be concerned about oversupply of private investment vehicles, especially those that are structured to invest on a global basis, or become concerned about saturation of public real estate markets.

The proliferation and growth of REIT and REIT-like structures around the world has still utilized only a small share of the potential pool of securitizable real estate assets in many countries. Using relevant national GDPs, broad stock index market capitalizations, and our estimates of investable real estate market size as benchmarks, Figure 1.6 shows the relative sizes of four listed real estate markets as of the end of 2005 (the latest date for which we have a real estate investable universe estimate). Although the US REIT market capitalization was by far the largest of those in the four countries shown in terms of absolute value, it equaled approximately 2.4% of GDP and 2.7% of the market capitalization of large-cap stocks.

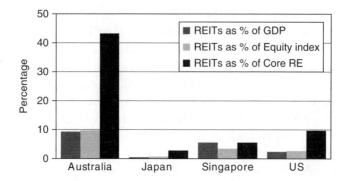

Figure 1.6 REIT equity market capitalization as share of GDP, stock markets and core real estate. *Source*: S&P, UBS Global Asset Management, EIU.

These relative shares were lower than those in Singapore, where REITs were only recently established, equaling approximately 5.6% and 3.5% of the country's GDP and the Straits Times Index market cap, respectively. The J-REIT market in Japan was by all three measures the least developed of the four countries analyzed. The market capitalization of REITs in the USA was equal to 9.7% of the total market size of core real estate in the country, a greater share than in either Singapore or Japan. However, on all three measures, Australia stands out as the country where the LPT sector was the most significant one in relative size. Perhaps the most noteworthy is that the market capitalization of the LPT market was more than 40% of the total core real estate market universe. This high percentage of real estate owned by LPTs is partly behind the recent trend in Australia for LPTs to acquire properties overseas. If the development of the Australian LPT market is a good guide, it suggests that REITs in Japan and Singapore, and even in the USA, still have considerable potential for growth.

Relative risk and return

Real estate investment spans much of the risk-return spectrum. As depicted in Figure 1.7, there is a wide spectrum of real estate investment strategies that range from core investing at the low-risk-low-return end to opportunistic strategies at the high-risk-high-return end. Public real estate investment, either REITs or other listed real estate operating companies (REOCs) are positioned between the two ends, given their generally perceived risk-and-return characteristics. Our placement of REITs is in the middle of the spectrum, yet above core real estate. REITs normally employ more leverage than core private funds, tend to be riskier and are expected to generate higher returns. But they are generally considered to be less risky than value-added real estate. One value-added strategy worth

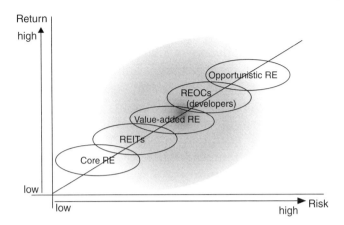

Figure 1.7 Real estate on the risk-return spectrum. *Source*: UBS Global Asset Management Real Estate Research.

noting is to invest in properties that are not considered core at the time of acquisition for various reasons, such as having significantly below-market occupancy, requiring substantial capital improvements, or being located in distressed markets but with promising recovery potential. Through successful execution of upgrading and repositioning strategies, the value-added properties can potentially be improved to achieve core status and be sold to investors in core real estate. Similarly, undesirable market dynamics such as a prolonged economic downturn and the deterioration of environmental quality, for example, could transform a core asset into a non-core one.

The above framework serves only as a general guideline and is certainly subject to debate. One could argue that positions for different strategies could vary from country to country. For example, REITs in some countries tend to have far less debt than others, sometimes due to regulatory limits, and are thus less risky than more highly levered REITs. In addition, certain REITs with high leverage, with unproven, risky strategies, specializing in less conventional property types, or any combination of these factors, might well be considered much riskier than an open-end fund focused on a value-added strategy. Moreover, not all REOCs are riskier than REITs, although it is generally true that they tend to have more volatile earnings and lower dividend payouts. In contrast, opportunity funds, free to use high debt levels, deploy creative strategies that might include acquiring non-performing loans backed by real estate, or investment in high-tech real-estate-related startups, and, usually having little liquidity for their closed-end units, are clearly at the high end of the spectrum. These funds can be attractive to those investors with greater tolerance for risk and who are attracted by a strategy often to target returns in excess of 20% per annum.

We began this chapter with our estimate of the size of the real estate investable universe, and clearly that is a moving target. Any attempt to quantify the size of the universe is always a work in progress. What is important is that we believe there exists sufficient depth and breadth in the universe for further expansion and innovation to absorb additional inflow of capital without quickly resulting in "irrational exuberance" in the global real estate investment. The real estate investable universe may have reached a period of stability given various uncertainties in the current global economic environment. But further growth will likely resume in the near future as opportunities and strategies seem to be boundless. And there is little doubt that over the medium to long term, the share of the investable universe that is in the control of public REITs is set to continue rising globally.

A new chapter for global real estate investment has emerged in the past few years. However, much of the story remains to be written. On the one hand, we may anticipate the content of some future chapters by borrowing pages from the history books of the stock and bond world, such as the further advancement of the REIT industry and the development of property derivative markets. On the other hand, given the unique attributes of the real estate asset class, we can envision that some chapters will likely feature the industry blazing new paths and learning and growing by trial and error along the way. Global real estate investment has definitely come of age, and the industry is continuing to advance, aided in no small part by the increases in size and sophistication of REIT markets around the world. It is expected to become more sophisticated, mature, innovative, transparent, disciplined and accountable to investors, and even better positioned to compete for capital with stocks and bonds.

Notes

1. Details on the market size estimates and other global real estate issues can be found in two papers, "Global real estate going mainstream" and "Global real estate investment – volume II: The world is becoming flatter," published in 2004 and 2006, respectively, and available on the internet at www.ubs.com/realestate.
2. At the time of the publication of this book, both the authors of this chapter would be transferred from their previous research roles to new business operation roles within UBS Global Asset Management. Due also to substantial personnel changes that have occurred since the first version of this chapter was written, the authors regret that it has become very challenging to update all exhibits used herein. However, they have done their best to update it where possible so as to improve its currency. Also, they have endeavored to add more insights from the vantage points of their current business roles.

2

The US Real Estate Investment Trust (REIT) Market

Will McIntosh

Introduction

In recent decades, the USA has witnessed a rapid integration of the real estate and capital markets. Both equity and debt investments in real estate can be publicly traded, primarily through real estate investment trust (REIT) and commercial mortgage backed securities (CMBSs) vehicles. With the transparency that accompanies growth in public trading, the risks, rewards, and diversification benefits associated with public real estate have become more widely known and understood.

It has taken the US approximately five decades to produce the structural model for REITs that exists today. The modern REIT structure is now sufficiently mature to attract the interest of global markets. While the Netherlands (1969), Australia (1985), and Canada (1994) were early adopters of REIT-type structures, more recently we have seen the creation of similar structures in Japan (2000), France (2003), Hong Kong (2003), the UK (2007), and now Germany.

In this chapter, we will review the history of the US experience with REITs, review the investment performance of the US REIT market, and provide some speculation on the future of the REIT vehicle.

The evolution of US REITs

The historical roots of REITs reside in New England where the development of the Massachusetts trust took place during the 19th century. Since state laws at the time precluded a corporation from owning real estate except as needed for business, the trust was developed as a legal entity to facilitate investment ownership of real estate. Many of the key features of REITs today were embedded in that early structure, including limited liability, share transferability, and the avoidance of double taxation on earnings.

A major blow to the use of this trust structure for investment in real estate was delivered in 1935 when the trusts lost their favorable tax status. For the next 25 years, the structure was in direct competition with other taxable investment vehicles plus a new creation, mutual funds.

In 1940, the Investment Company Act created the closed-end mutual fund vehicle. These funds were given tax-favorable status and became very adept at recruiting capital. The real estate trusts, which were now tax-paying at the trust level, experienced difficulty in attracting investors.

US REITs: creation to 1993

The adoption of the REIT Act of 1960 was intended to create a mutual fund vehicle for real estate. It returned the favorable tax status lost earlier by the Massachusetts trust. In order to qualify for the favorable tax treatment, requirements were stipulated on structure, asset composition, income composition, and dividend distribution. Over time the requirements have been modified and today they include the following.

Structure requirements.

- A REIT must be a corporation, trust or association.
- A REIT must be otherwise taxable as a domestic corporation.
- A REIT must be managed by one or more trustees or directors.
- Ownership must be through transferable shares or certificates.
- Ownership must be held by 100 or more persons.
- Five or fewer individuals may not own 50% or more of the shares.

Asset composition requirements.

- At least 75% of a REIT's assets must consist of interests in real property, cash or government securities.
- Securities of a taxable REIT subsidiary (TRS; created in 1999) must account for no more than 20% of the value of a REIT's total assets.

Income composition requirements.

- At least 75% of a REIT's gross income must come from interests in real property (rents and mortgage interest), and gains from disposition of real property interests including shares of other REITs.

- At least 95% of a REIT's gross income must come from items above plus dividends, interest, gains from disposition of securities and hedging income.

Dividend distribution requirements.

- A REIT must distribute 90% of taxable income to take the dividends paid deduction.

Since the REIT structure was intended for passive investment in real estate, REITs were not permitted to actively turn over properties or to directly manage them. As a result, most REITs used advisory firms for management and investment policy purposes.

There are three main types of U.S. REITs: equity REITs, mortgage REITs, and hybrid REITs.

- An equity REIT engages in buying, managing, and selling real properties. Some equity REITs also engage in development activities. Over time, equity REITs have specialized by property type. A few diversified equity REITs still invest across property types.
- A mortgage REIT engages in lending activities that are secured by real estate collateral. The mortgage REIT will hold whole loans or other debt obligations tied to real estate. Mortgage REITs tend to specialize in either residential lending or commercial lending.
- A hybrid REIT simultaneously invests in both the equity and debt side of the real property markets.

Much of the early interest in REITs was focused on mortgage REITs. Banks, thrifts, and insurance companies were precluded from making construction and development loans. However, mortgage REITs could make such loans.

At the same time, Regulation Q of the Federal Reserve capped the interest rates that commercial banks could offer on savings account deposits. As interest rates climbed, institutional deposits migrated to Europe. The mortgage REIT thus became one means to raise funds competitively for long-term commercial mortgage lending.[1]

The rapid expansion of mortgage REITs during this early period came to an abrupt halt with the economic stress of 1973. Rising interest rates produced widespread mortgage defaults and builder bankruptcies. Mortgage REITs suffered severe losses and interest in the REIT vehicle shifted sharply to the equity REITs.

In 1981, the Economic Recovery Act dramatically enhanced the ability of partnerships to shelter ordinary income as depreciation periods were

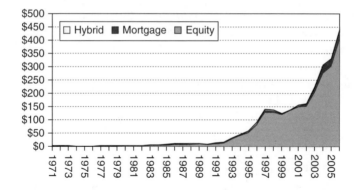

Figure 2.1   US REIT market capitalization ($B) 1971–2006. *Source*: NAREIT.

greatly reduced. Real estate limited partnerships became the vehicle of choice because of their ability to pass through operating losses, and investors flocked to the vehicle producing a boom in the construction of new structures. REITs, due to their inability to pass through losses, were unable to compete effectively in this environment.

As the negative consequences of the earlier Act became apparent, the Tax Reform Act (TRA) of 1986 was passed. This Act brought an abrupt halt to the real estate boom launched just 5 years earlier as the ability for partnerships to flow losses to personal tax returns was lost. At the same time, several enhancements were made to the REIT structure. Most notably, REITs were now allowed to manage their assets directly rather than through an independent contractor. Although the TRA of 1986 set off a major real estate bust, it laid the groundwork for the REIT structure to return to a most favored status among investors in real estate and for the market to boom as shown in Figure 2.1. But there were still a few developments needed.

Many large private portfolios of real estate, some held by institutions and some held by private investors, remained to be brought to market. Two large portfolios came to market in 1991: KIMCO Realty in November and New Plan Realty Trust in December. These transactions served as a signal to the market that large private portfolios could be successfully taken public.

In November 1992, Taubman Centers completed its initial public offering using a new structure, the UPREIT structure, illustrated in Figure 2.2. This device permitted a partnership to bring its portfolio to market without immediately triggering a taxable transaction event. So long as the partnership held its operating partnership units and the properties remained in the partnership, the taxes on any gain were deferred.

Prior to the passage of the Omnibus Budget Reconciliation Act (OBRA) of 1993, the investment by a pension fund in a REIT was treated as the

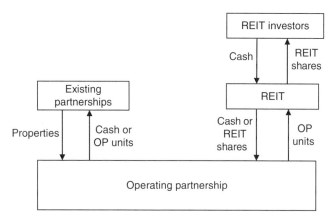

Figure 2.2 UPREIT structure.

investment of a single investor. As REITs attempted to comply with the 5/50 rule, whereby no combination of five shareholders can own more than 50% of the stock, many adopted provisions that restricted the investment of any one investor to <10% of outstanding shares. Given the relatively small capitalizations of REITs and the restriction to 10% of that capitalization, pension funds were not major REIT investors. OBRA permitted a pension fund to count all of its investors in the fund as individuals for REIT purposes. This dramatically shifted the interest of pension funds in REIT shares.

US REITs: the Modern Era

The wave of IPOs that occurred during 1993 and 1994, as depicted in Figure 2.3, was the result of a convergence of stimuli to both demand for REIT shares (pension funds) and supply of owned real estate (UPREIT structure). By 1990, the combined impact of the savings and loan crisis, the TRA of 1986, overbuilding during the 1980s, and regulatory pressures on bank and insurance lenders, resulted in a depression in the real estate industry.

With the advent of the UPREIT structure and increased interest by institutional investors that now benefited by allocating a larger portion of their funds toward real estate, the number of IPOs soared. During 1993 and 1994 several large portfolios transitioned to the public market. According to NAREIT, there were 95 IPOs for an aggregate equity investment of $16.5 billion during this 2-year period. By 1995, the REIT market had exhausted the advantageous market conditions that existed in the early 1990s, and the number or REITs that could be restructured into UPREITs was quickly drying up.

The significant drop in the value of commercial property during the early 1990s prompted many private real estate companies to decide that

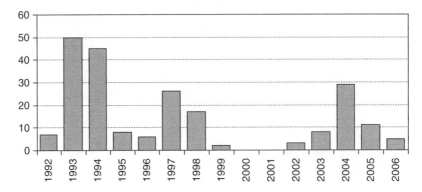

Figure 2.3   REIT initial public offerings (number). *Source*: NAREIT.

the best and most efficient way to access capital was through the public markets using REITs. Further, since 90% of a REIT's taxable income must be redistributed, it was difficult to acquire the necessary capital to grow. The pressure to grow and obtain desirable financial returns made taking real estate portfolios public a natural choice. Despite the explosive number of IPOs during the early 1990s, the REIT market was still in its infancy.

While pension funds gained increased ability to invest in REITs, insurance companies gained an incentive to divest owned real estate. In January 1994, the National Association of Insurance Commissioners raised the reserve requirement for owned real properties. Consequently, several insurance companies began reducing direct property holdings to avoid the associated higher required reserves, thus causing the steep drop in IPOs between 1994 and 1995.

The second wave of IPOs shown in Figure 2.3 is attributed to the Taxpayer Relief Act of 1997, where President Clinton on August 1997 signed into law the REIT Simplification Act of 1997. This allowed a REIT to provide a small amount of non-customary services to its tenants without disqualifying the other rents collected from them. Changes were made which permitted the creation of timber REITs. Further, the US Treasury Department amended its tax treaty negotiations position, which enabled most non-US shareholders to pay only 15% in taxes on REIT ordinary dividends. The influx of foreign capital thus encouraged REITs to go public. As the turn of the century neared, the international financial crisis and an enormous appetite for dot. com firms caused the REIT market to cool off and IPOs subsided for a while.

By 2004 the average REIT had reached $1billion and the vehicle was again seen as a stable investment option for both institutional and individual investors alike. Around this time a change in the US and UK tax treaty gave British pension funds the ability to invest in US REITs without any taxes being withheld on REIT dividends. This influx of British investment was accompanied by the passage of the American Jobs Creation Act in which two of the primary provisions eliminated a discriminatory barrier to foreign

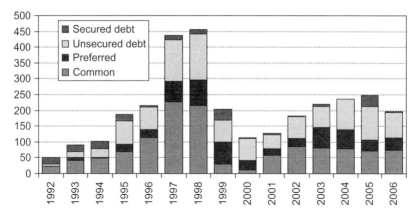

Figure 2.4 REIT secondary offerings (number). *Source*: NAREIT.

investors buying publicly listed REIT stock and allowed a REIT to either fix a mistake or pay monetary penalties for most violations of the REIT tax rules, instead of facing possible loss of REIT status as under prior law.

Larger REITs

Following the 1993–1994 wave of IPOs, the subsequent growth in REIT capitalization was fueled largely by secondary offerings. This is seen by the increased number of offerings (depicted in Figure 2.4) between the years 1992 and 1998, with 1997 and 1998 being peak years. According to NAREIT, there were 443 secondary common share offerings ($32.4 billion), 146 secondary preferred share offerings ($13.3 billion), 277 unsecured debt offerings ($23.0 billion) and 28 secured debt offerings ($6.4 billion) in the these 2 peak years. Around the turn of the century, the number of IPOs and secondary offerings dropped, as did the growth rate in the US REIT market capitalization. Given the bust of the tech bubble in the early 2000, investors were eager to partake in more stable investments. Thus REIT shares were valued higher in the public market than the private, resulting in a stimulus between 2000 and 2005 that increased the number of secondary offerings.

REITs had been outperforming the returns of major indices for some time prior to their inclusion in major public indices. In the latter part of 2001, the S&P opened its S&P 500 and other indices to REITs. This gave REITs a new image of stability and credible performance among small investors which funneled capital into the REIT market fueling an unprecedented growth in the US REIT.

As a result of the growth through secondary offerings plus internal growth over the period, the average REIT capitalization went from $170.2 million in 1993 to $2.4 billion at the end of 2006 (Figure 2.5). Because of their much larger capitalization than the pre-1992 REITs, they are much

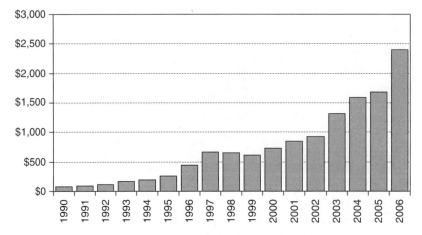

Figure 2.5   Average REIT capitalization ($M). *Source*: NAREIT.

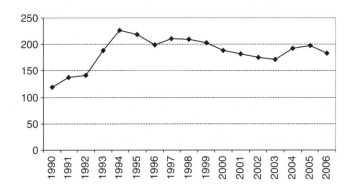

Figure 2.6   Number of REITs. *Source*: NAREIT.

more liquid and as such are also more interesting to institutional investors. It is thought that the increased public investment has led to a better
management of REITs due to the required transparency set forth by the
Securities and Exchange Commission and demanded by the market, or
face ill favor with immediate negative consequences.

Also contributing to the average growth of REITs was a very active
merger and acquisition history. During the period from 1995 to 2006,
a total of 115 REIT IPOs occurred. Yet, during the same period, the actual
number of REITs declined by 36 as seen in Figure 2.6. Many new portfolios
of property were brought to market at the same time that existing public
portfolios were combined producing larger REITs.

As REITs went public, they became increasingly transparent which
caused the marketplace to differentiate between well-run and poorly managed REITs. The range of yields being paid on REIT stock began to widen
as the market penalized the lower-performing REITs with higher yields and

rewarding the well-run REITs with premiums to net asset value (NAV). This condition led REITs with limited growth opportunities and capital market access to consider the option of merging with stronger performing REITs. The following are the additional performance-related reasons used by some REITs to consider mergers.

- *Rebalancing debt/equity ratios.* At the time of their IPO, many real estate companies had a low debt-to-market capitalization ratio. After going public however the need to finance growth and even operations led REITs to take on increased levels of debt.
- *Expanding operational capabilities and enhancing growth.* A good way to secure essential management talent.
- *Increasing market dominance or obtaining geographic diversity.* Keeping pace with investors' expectations often proved difficult for REITs with a lack of excess capital, lack of opportunity, increased competition, or a lack of management depth.
- *Providing an exit strategy for those who no longer wish or able to operate a public company.* The SEC and IRS place reporting responsibilities on publicly traded REITs that is not suited for all real estate operators.
- *Providing better liquidity opportunities for investors.* Owning a share in a mid-size REIT does not provide the same level of liquidity as many other publicly traded companies. The larger the REIT however the greater the number of investors, which leads to more liquidity for existing shareholders.

Active management

When Congress created REITs in 1960, the REIT was precluded from the active management of its assets. Advisory firms emerged to perform the function. Then, in 1986, REITs gained the right to directly manage properties rather than use an independent contractor. Still, the REIT was limited to only providing customary services to their tenants.

With the passage of the REIT Modernization Act of 1999, REITs were permitted to own up to 100% of the stock of a TRS that could now provide non-customary services to REIT tenants. The taxable income earned by the TRS would not disqualify tenant rents to the REIT for purposes of meeting the gross income tests.

Market acceptance

For a number of years, REITs were not viewed by the investment community as operating enterprises. As such, they were precluded from admission into several of the major indices of market performance, including the S&P 500 Index.

The nature of REITs as operating entities was given increased stature with the issuance of IRS Revenue Ruling 2001–2029 (June 4, 2001). This ruling concluded that REITs dooperate an active business. While the ruling had the effect of permitting a corporation to qualify for a tax-free spin-off of a REIT, it also put the markets on notice that REITs were operating entities in the eyes of the IRS.

When trading closed on October 9, 2001, Equity Office Properties Trust was added to the S&P 500 Index, the first REIT to be so recognized. It was followed shortly thereafter by Equity Residential Properties (November 1, 2001), Plum Creek Timber (January 16, 2002), and Simon Property Group (June 25, 2002).

Currently, there are 11 REITs included in the index despite the loss of Equity Office Properties Trust from the list due to its acquisition by the Blackstone Group (February 9, 2007).

The investment performance of REITs

Over the past 20 years, equity REITs produced an average annual return of 11.3%. This performance trails that of the S&P 500 index slightly with similar volatility. During the same period, mortgage REITs have produced substantially lower returns with much higher volatility. A summary of Annualized total returns for the three types of REITS and other indices is shown in Figure 2.7.

Before 2003, the volatility of REITs as measured by the standard deviation of returns was 12% and below that of the S&P 500 (15%) and the NASDAQ Composite Index (26%). As Figure 2.8 shows, the past few years of REIT returns became nearly twice as volatile as the S&P 500 and even more volatile than the tech-heavy NASDAQ. Over the long term however, REIT returns have been less volatile than both the S&P 500 and the NASDAQ returns.

The higher volatility in recent years is attributed to several factors. With historically low correlation to other stocks, REITs attracted strong interest

	1 Year	3 Years	5 Years	10 Years	20 Years	σ
All REITs	34.4%	23.8%	22.5%	13.8%	11.3%	17.8%
Equity REITs	35.1%	25.8%	23.2%	14.5%	13.1%	16.5%
Mortgage REITs	19.3%	2.8%	17.5%	8.5%	7.2%	32.7%
Hybrid REITs	40.9%	15.9%	24.6%	9.0%	7.5%	27.1%
S&P 500	15.8%	13.6%	6.9%	10.0%	14.2%	16.6%
Russell 2000	17.8%	15.3%	12.4%	13.2%	14.7%	18.6%
10-yr Tr. yield	4.7%	4.4%	4.3%	4.8%	6.1%	1.6%

Figure 2.7 Annualized total returns. *Source*: NAREIT, volatility based on 20-year annual returns.

on Wall Street following the tech wreck earlier this century. While the REIT class has grown tremendously over the past decade, it is still a relatively small asset class – equal to roughly the market capitalization of industrial conglomerate General Electric, for example. Thus, as more institutional investors have shown greater appreciation for the portfolio attributes of commercial real estate securities and have invested larger pools of capital into REITs, prices have become more volatile. As REIT price volatility rises, REITs have become increasingly appealing for hedge funds and short-term-minded traders who helped perpetuate the trend. The attractiveness of REITs in portfolio diversification has not subsided however and remains appealing especially for long-term investors.

Of equal relevance in portfolio construction is the ability of an asset to provide diversification benefits. US equity REITs have a relatively low correlation with broader equities, bonds and private real estate (Figure 2.9).

It is interesting to note the very low and negative correlation between US equity REIT returns and the yield on 10-year US treasury notes. While interest rates are expected to influence property capitalization rates and property capitalization rates are expected to influence REIT returns and values, the connections are obviously not strong.

Just as REITs provide diversification to a portfolio of stocks and bonds, they also can provide diversification benefits to a portfolio of private real estate. The correlation of US equity REITs with the portfolio of real estate represented by the NCREIF index is very low, as illustrated in Figure 2.10. Even when the appraisal-based NCREIF returns are unsmoothed, the correlation is still relatively low.

Given the mutual fund characteristics of REITs, an expectation might be that REIT share prices would trade on average very close to the NAV

	Oct 1990– Sept 2003	Oct 2003– Sept 2006	Oct 1990– Sept 2006
S&P 500 ®	15%	8%	14%
NASDAQ	26%	14%	25%
NAREIT	12%	16%	13%

Figure 2.8 Volatility of REITs versus other stock indexes. *Source*: FMRCo. (MARE) as of 30 September 2006. Source: NAREIT, volatility based on 20-year annual returns.

	Equities	Bonds	Public RE
Equities	1		
Bonds	0.16	1	
Public RE	0.21	0.07	1
Private RE	0.07	−0.32	−0.02

Figure 2.9 Correlation with Stocks and Bonds 1986–2006.

Quarterly returns

	3 Years	5 Years	10 Years	20 Years
Equity REITs	0.18	0.20	0.09	0.03
Mortgage REITs	−0.06	−0.29	−0.30	−0.06
Hybrid REITs	−0.05	−0.23	−0.18	−0.11

Figure 2.10   REIT correlation to private real estate. *Source*: NAREIT, NCREIF.

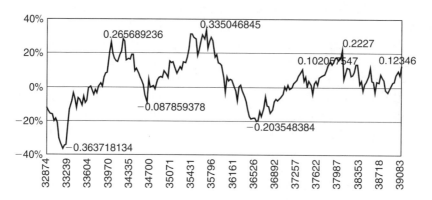

Figure 2.11   Share price premium to NAV. *Source*: Green Street Advisors.

of the underlying assets. As it turns out, the share prices of equity REITs have rotated around their NAV as depicted in Figure 2.11. However, the average over time tends to slightly exceed the actual underlying sum of asset values. This validates the value added by REITs moving from passive holders of property to more active managers of property with additional operating activities such as those now permitted through TRS. It should be noted that comparing the market capitalization of a REIT to NAV boils down to a comparison between the capitalization rate used in determining the value of the real estate and the market perception of what the underlying asset is worth. As such, a comparison to NAV is simply a ballpark indicator of how much the asset underlying the stock is over- or undervalued.

The future of REITs

REITs go global

After 40 years of experience with the US REIT vehicle, the acceptance of the structure globally has accelerated during the first decade of the 21st century. Countries that recently adopted REIT legislation include Japan (2000), South Korea (2001), Singapore (2002), France (2003), Hong Kong (2004), and the UK and Germany (2007). The REIT structure is also being put in place in Italy. This demonstrates that the structure has reached a level of maturity that

Country/Region	Total real estate (US$B)	Share of total	Total securitized real estate(US$B)	Share of total securitized	Implied total assets owned by listed RE companies (US$B)	% of High grade RE
North America	6,615	31%	554	35%	849	13%
Continental Europe	7,159	34%	249	16%	370	5%
United Kingdom	1,544	7%	120	8%	159	10%
Japan	2,816	13%	165	10%	228	8%
Hong Kong/China	1,108	5%	248	16%	292	26%
Australia	475	2%	113	7%	155	33%
Other	1,566	7%	145	9%	199	13%
Total World	**21,282**	**100%**	**1,595**	**100%**	**2,252**	**10.6%**

Figure 2.12 Size of REIT universe. *Source*: ING Clarion and ING Clarion Real Estate Securities.

will support rapid expansion in the transfer of private real estate to public vehicles over the near term. Figure 2.12 provides a perspective on the global REIT market by comparing each country's REIT holdings.

The movement of private real estate to public holdings increases the transparency of the underlying asset. While this has obvious benefits to equity investors in the asset, it also benefits debt investors. The globalization of REITs is also expected to produce globalization of unsecured debt financing by REITs plus continued expansion of structured finance vehicles like CMBS.

As global markets expand, an increase in cross-border investing by US REITs is expected. The early REITs to go cross-border have been and will likely continue to be in the retail and industrial property types as the REITs strive to serve the needs of their global tenants for space. A further stimulus will occur in those economies that accumulate sums to invest that exceed the volume of institutional properties in the domestic economy, such as the Netherlands and Australia.

Private to public migration continues

While the global growth of REITs will naturally result in shifts from private holdings of real estate to public holdings, there are other factors that will also contribute.

Although the recent trend in the US real estate market is to take public companies private, there is still substantial opportunity for growth in public holdings. It is estimated that only 10–12% of US property is in public vehicles. A substantial block of real estate continues to be held by owner-users. As this connection is broken over time, more property will be released to the market.

Many economies around the world still have substantial holdings of real estate held by the government. The continued transfer of these assets to private ownership will also feed the real estate markets and, in turn, the REIT markets.

The global population ages

As a population ages, the investment goals of the population shift from a wealth building model to one more focused on income generation. REITs become more desirable due to the significant role of the income return in the overall return to the asset. While this shift in emphasis makes sense for the individual investor, it is also relevant for institutional investors that must provide pension benefits to this aging population.

The continued transition of pension funds from a defined benefit model to a defined contribution model, coupled with the expansion in a variety of other tax-efficient savings vehicles, will stimulate the demand for mutual funds, including real estate mutual funds holding REIT shares.

Consolidation

As the REIT industry continues to mature globally, there will be waves of new firms coming to market followed shortly thereafter by periods of consolidation. Throughout the typical size of REITs should continue to grow. While the early mergers were focused more domestically, the future of mergers will have more of a global perspective.

Speculation on the future of the US REIT market

The increased number of mergers and acquisitions (M&A) in recent years as well as the privatization of several major REITs indicates a shifting trend in the REIT market. Figure 2.13 lists the REITs taken private since

REIT	Buyer	Sale price (not including debt assumption)	Premium to stock price month (before deal)
CarrAmerica realty	Blackstone group	$2.6 billion	120.60%
Meri star hospitality	Blackstone group	$1.1 billion	9.40%
Bedford property investors	LBA realty LLC	$435 million	20%
Arden realty	GE real estate	$3.1 billion	−2.30%
Town & country trust	Morgan stanley/onex	$929 million	35.20%
Center point properties trust	Cal east industrial investors	$2.5 billion	12.40%
AMLI residential properties	Morgan stanley	$1.2 billion	19.20%
Capital automotive REIT	DRA advisors	$2.2 billion	−3.10%
CRT properties	DRA advisors	$903 million	21.20%
Gables residential trust	ING clarion	$1.4 billion	18.80%
Prime group realty trust	Lightstone group	$209 million	13.30%

Figure 2.13 REITs taken private since 2005. *Source*: SNL Financial. www.thestreet.com.

2005 along with the buyer, sale price, and stock price premium. It is interesting to note that the average premium to stock price is slightly <15%.
The willingness of buyers to bear this premium appears to be the result of
the increased value of REITs in the private sector. This speculation is supported by the decreased number of IPOs and the secondary offerings reaching record lows. Further as the premium to NAV becomes negative REITs
are attracting less capital in the public market than they are worth. The
recent trend away from publicly traded REITs will eventually be reversed.
Currently REIT stocks are undervalued which will eventually reinvigorate
investor enthusiasm for REITs.

> The recent subprime mortgage crisis in the USA is likely to affect the
> US REIT market, the extent to which is not easily quantifiable. It is
> unfortunate that the mainstream media and the financial press fail to
> distinguish between the commercial and residential markets. US REITs
> however face a bigger problem of lost support among dedicated and
> non-dedicated investors. While the loss is marginal at present, there is
> an increased movement of dedicated REIT investors to look overseas
> for higher growth and a broader opportunity set. While the outflow of
> capital from the US market is not substantial; it does compound the
> current lack of investor enthusiasm. In their July 2007 US Quarterly
> Report, Prudential Real Estate Investors indicate that REITs have lost
> their appeal with growth and momentum investors who see continued
> multiple contraction and slower earnings growth in the next 2 or 3 years
> to be highly likely. However, REIT share prices are not cheap enough to
> attract the interest of value investors.

With REITs trading below NAV, a volatility greater than the S&P 500
and other indices, yields below 10-year treasury bonds, and decreasing
earning multiples, it is not all to certain where the US REIT market is
heading. It is likely, however, that REITs will continue to be privatized.

Note

1. In 1980, the Depository Institutions Deregulation and Monetary Control Act
   was passed by Congress and this terminated the Regulation Q ceiling on savings
   account interest rates effective in 1986.

3

Progress on REIT Regimes in Europe

Simon Clark, Tim Hackemann, Olivier Mesmin
Matthias Roche, and Tom Road

Introduction

This chapter will briefly set out recent major developments in existing REIT regimes in Europe and will discuss some of the developments that are expected to take place. It will not go into great technical detail, but rather will focus on crucial legal and regulatory issues and the latest developments. A brief explanation of the impact of European law on the REIT regimes will be given in the last section.

Even though the general framework of the various REIT regimes is to a large extent identical, there are nevertheless many technical differences among the various regimes. Many of the requirements for benefiting from a given REIT regime are motivated by governments' fear of abuse and their concerns about the loss of tax base.

Because many of these regimes are becoming more and more similar, the various REIT systems are slowly becoming harmonised. Perhaps a uniform European Union (EU) REIT regime may not be as far away as it seems.

Developments in France: SIIC 2/3/4 and the OPCI

The French SIIC

The French REIT/SIIC[1] regime was introduced in 2003, and certain amendments/improvements have been made since then. The main advantage of this tax regime is that it exempts quoted property companies from corporate income tax, provided these companies meet the obligation to distribute most of their income.

An SIIC is a non-transparent vehicle, with a corporate income tax exemption for qualifying activities. Qualifying activities are (i) the purchase or development of buildings with a view to leasing them and (ii) participation in corporate subsidiaries or partnerships having the same activity. Non-qualifying activities, such as trading activities, are fully subject to tax. When a company makes an election for the SIIC regime, an exit tax at a rate of 16.5% is triggered.

The conditions for the application of the SIIC regime are fairly flexible and simple compared to similar European REIT regimes. An SIIC must be quoted and is subject to a distribution obligation. Since 2007, there is a minimum 15% free float requirement, which is to be appreciated only on the first day of the effective entry of the company into the SIIC regime. An SIIC has to distribute 85% of its rental income and 50% of realised capital gains. It is worth noting that an SIIC is not subject to any formal gearing limitations (debt-to-equity ratio or the like). It has however to be underlined that two new provisions aimed at avoiding situations where SIICs are controlled by one single stockholder or held by non-taxable entities were introduced in 2007.

- As from 1 January 2007, the election for the SIIC regime is conditioned upon the SIIC share capital not being held for 60% or more by one single stockholder or a group of stockholders acting as one. This condition is to be met by SIICs existing prior to 1 January 2007 on 1 January 2009 at the latest. This 60% test may however be temporarily ignored upon certain circumstances (such as tender offerings).
- As from 1 January 2007, an SIIC is liable to a specific corporation tax at a rate of 20% assessed on its distributions taken out of tax-exempted results and distributed to those of its stockholders, other than individuals, which directly or indirectly own 10% or more of its share capital and are not liable to corporation tax in respect of the dividend received.

The French SIIC regime is relatively tax efficient for foreign investors who invest in French real property. Dividends distributed by an SIIC to a foreign shareholder are subject to withholding tax, whereby the rate of withholding tax (25%) is often reduced under tax treaties to 15%. Moreover, foreign EU-quoted property companies may also benefit from the SIIC status in respect of their French properties, provided the foreign company maintains a French permanent establishment to which the French assets (or the shares in the French property companies) are allocated. Based on treaty provisions, a repatriation of profits by the French branch to the foreign head office is possibly not subject to tax. Various foreign-quoted property companies have already opted for the SIIC regime.

Among the new provisions of the SIIC regime introduced in the past years, the major one provides for a temporary tax regime encouraging the outsourcing of real estate assets to SIICs (the so called 'SIIC 3 regime').

SIIC 3 regime

If an ordinarily taxed company switches to the SIIC regime, it is subject to an 'exit tax' in respect of the unrealised capital gains on its properties. The exit tax is levied at a 16.5% rate rather than at the ordinary French corporate income tax rate (33 1/3%). In order to promote the use of the SIIC regime, France has introduced a very beneficial regime from 2005 under which third parties may contribute real estate to an SIIC.[2] Under the new rules, corporate income tax is levied at a rate of 16.5% plus additional social taxes (17.05% in total) on net capital gains resulting from the contribution or sale by a corporate taxpayer of properties[3] or shares in real estate companies to an SIIC to a qualifying SIIC subsidiary. The SIIC that benefits from such a contribution or which has acquired assets under this regime must covenant to keep the building for 5 years. When the asset is acquired by a qualifying SIIC subsidiary, such subsidiary must in addition covenant to remain within the SIIC regime for 5 years. Non-compliance with any of these two covenants entails a penalty corresponding to 25% of the contribution/sale value of the building. This penalty is payable by the SIIC or its subsidiary as the case may be.

The scope of the SIIC 3 regime is very broad. In order to benefit from the reduced capital gains tax rate of 17.05%, the only requirement is that the vendor be subject to corporate income tax, whatever its activity or real purpose of business. Short-term gains realised by real estate brokers or property developers are, however, outside the scope of the regime. It is believed that the SIIC 3 regimes have contributed to the creation of a number of new SIICs during the past years.

Finally, it is important to note that this SIIC 3 regime is temporary. It was due to expire on 31 December 2007 and has been extended until 31 December 2008.

OPCI: 'the non-listed SIIC'

The OPCI,[4] a new type of non-listed real estate investment vehicle, has been introduced by the order of 13 October 2005 and further regulations. The first OPCIs were created in October 2007.

The OPCI may take the form of a tax-transparent fund with no legal personality (Fonds de Placement en Immobilier – FPI) or a limited liability company (Société à Prépondérance Immobilière à Capital Variable – SPPICAV), which is exempt from tax, subject to distribution obligations. Under both forms, the subscribers can request the repurchase of their units by the OPCI on the basis of the net asset value. An OPCI will need to be managed by an AMF-approved manager (i.e. a manager subject to French regulatory supervision). Unlike the SIIC, an OPCI is generally subject to specific rules such as dispersion of assets, liquidity requirements, gearing limitations. Such rules are, however, relaxed or even not applicable to the simplified form of the OPCI (OPCI RFA[5]), designed for certain qualified investors.

The OPCI RFA is an interesting 'club deal' investment vehicle, which benefits – under the SPPICAV form – of the SIIC 3 legislation described above. That is to say that a corporation that contributes or sells real estate assets or shares in real estate companies to a SPPICAV or a qualifying SPPICAV subsidiary may enjoy the reduced 17.04% corporation tax rate on the capital gain realised on such occasion under the same conditions as those applicable when the contribution or sale is to the benefit of an SIIC or a qualifying SIIC subsidiary. As a result, a number of investment funds have incorporated an SPPICAV RFA for the purpose of acquiring French real estate assets. So far, the great majority of existing OPCIs are incorporated under the SPPICAV RFA form and are pure club deal investment vehicles. Only two publicly traded OPCIs have been established as of July 2008.

The following are the main differences between the OPCI and the SIIC.

– An SIIC is a listed vehicle while an OPCI is not listed and may or not be publicly traded.
– SIIC shares may be traded above or below net asset value depending on stock market performance, while the value of an OPCI unit is solely linked to the assets' value.
– As far as an SIIC is concerned, the liquidity for the stockholder depends on the stock market, while the OPCI unit holder may ask for a repayment of its units based on the liquidation value of the OPCI at any time.

This last characteristic led the French stock exchange authorities to be very cautious in delivery agreements to publicly traded OPCIs, considering that real estate assets are not as liquid as financial assets.

The German REIT

After long and exhaustive discussions, the German REIT (G-REIT) legislation finally went over all parliamentary hurdles and became law on 1 June 2007, with retroactive effect as of 1 January 2007.

Key conditions

The G-REIT legislation provides for the following parameters:

• The G-REIT must be a stock corporation with both its legal (statutory) seat and its management seat in Germany. A dual-resident corporation will not qualify for G-REIT status.

The G-REIT must be listed at a recognised EU or EEA stock exchange. It must have a share capital of at least 15 Mio EURO.

- The G-REIT must distribute at least 90% of its net income.
  Distribution must cover ordinary income and capital gains (the latter may qualify for placement in a reinvestment reserve).

- The G-REIT may not have a single shareholder with a 10% or more direct shareholding.
  This G-REIT requirement is more generous than the one in the UK REIT, where the 10% requirement covers both a direct and an indirect shareholding.
  This feasibility of this requirement and, in particular, its control and monitoring, have been and are still subject to very intense discussion on the German capital markets.
  The 10% rule is seen as one of the major, if not the most important, elements in the G-REIT structure with regard to protecting Germany's right to levy tax on dividends distributed to any non-resident investors in a G-REIT structure (for more details, see the section entitled Taxation of shareholders).

- The G-REIT must have a minimum of 15% of its share capital in free float, and an individual shareholder may not own 3% or more of the G-REIT's share capital (in order for it to count as free float). At the time of listing the G-REIT must have a free float of 25%. Private G-REITs are not allowed.

- The G-REIT must meet a 75% asset test; that is at least 75% of the assets on its balance sheet must comprise real estate that meets the qualifying criteria. Residential property which was constructed prior to 1 January 2007 does not constitute qualifying real estate.

- The G-REIT must also meet a 75% income test; that is it must generate 75% of its gross income from leasing and letting its real estate assets.

- The G-REIT must not qualify as a real estate dealer. It must hold its real estate long term. The qualification as real estate dealer is given if more than 50% of the assets (determined at a fair market value) are sold within a 5-year period.

- The G-REIT must have a debt-to-equity ratio of 55:45 in regard of its qualifying assets (75% rule). The remaining 25% assets can be fully debt financed.

- The G-REIT can own its real estate portfolio directly or through a partnership structure (no de-minimise or maximum interest limitation). The partnership will not automatically be tax exempt (trade tax).
  Foreign real estate can also be held through a domestic foreign corporate subsidiary, which must be owned at 100% by the G-REIT and which is not tax exempt.

- Development activities for the own portfolio of the G-REIT are permitted. Development and management activities on behalf of third-party real estate must be placed in a (fully taxable) subsidiary corporation which must be owned at 100% by the G-REIT. Activities not relating to real estate (such as ring-fenced versus non-ring-fenced activities in the UK) are prohibited.

Taxation of the G-REIT

If the G-REIT meets the above criteria, it will be fully exempt from corporate income tax, the solidarity surcharge and trade tax.

Exit taxation

With a view to support the introduction of G-REITs, the G-REIT law provides for a favourable tax treatment in connection with the establishment of a G-REIT. This exit taxation applies to the real estate held by a real estate corporation, which wants to convert into a G-REIT provided such real estate meets certain holding requirements. Alternatively, it applies to the sale of real estate by a business to a G-REIT or pre-REIT. Again, certain holding patterns must have been followed.

If real estate qualifies for the exit tax, only half of the capital gain is subject to taxation.

To qualify for exit taxation, the respective transaction must have been consummated prior to 1 January 2010.

Other considerations

- The REIT-AG will lose its status at the end of the third year of identical breach or continuous violation over five consecutive years of the following different qualifying requirements:

  - 75% immoveable assets test;
  - 75% gross earnings test;
  - 90% distribution test;
  - 55% loan test;
  - 15% free float test;
  - 10% shareholding test.

- On a failure of the listing requirement the REIT-AG loses its status at the end of the preceding year.
- If the REIT-A G commences a trade or business it loses its status in the year the trading limits are exceeded.

Taxation of shareholders

Because of the G-REIT's tax exemption, all its distributions will be subject to full taxation at the shareholder level. A distinction must be made between resident and non-resident shareholders.

G-REIT dividends are fully taxable at the resident shareholder level, regardless of whether they are sourced by ordinary income or by capital gains.

Any capital gains realised on the sale of shares in the G-REIT will also be subject to full taxation.

Any tax withheld by the G-REIT is creditable or refundable at the resident shareholder level, depending on individual circumstances such as tax rate, losses, and so on. A reduced withholding tax rate may apply for tax-exempt resident taxpayers (such as non-profit organisations, public bodies, and so on).

Beginning 1 January 2009, the 25% flat taxation on capital income generated from investments privately held by an individual taxpayer will also apply to G-REIT dividends.

Non-resident shareholders are subject to individual or corporate taxation on their global income in their country of residence. Germany, as the source of the dividend income from the G-REIT, has only a limited taxation right on such dividend income.

To ensure that Germany retains the right to levy a reasonable level of tax and to make sure that a foreign corporate investor does not generate income that is not taxable in Germany (white income), the 10% rule has been introduced with regard to the level of the shareholding so that Germany retains its right to levy a withholding tax of 15%.

Final comments

The REIT structure was successfully introduced in Germany with legal effect from 1 January 2007. Looking at the detailed provisions of the G-REIT law regarding the structure of a G-REIT, how it works, and its tax ramifications, they are attractive and are workable in practice.

It is not because of the G-REIT law, that up to now (July 2008) only two G-REITs were listed at the German stock market. The market conditions for an IPO were not attractive during the recent past so that also REIT transactions were put on hold.

The UK REIT

Following the enactment of the Finance Act 2006, the launch of the UK REIT occurred on 1 January 2007. This enabled existing listed companies to convert to REIT status and new REITs to be incorporated and listed, provided the various conditions set out below are satisfied. Regulations and informal guidance have also been prepared which flesh out the details of the code set out in the primary legislation.

Key conditions

The following are the key conditions to becoming a UK REIT can be broadly summarised (for convenience, references will be made to a vehicle, although there can be REIT groups).

- The vehicle (or the principal company of the group) must be a UK tax resident, widely held and listed on a 'recognised stock exchange', with a simple share and loan capital structure.
- The vehicle must be substantially a property investor with 75% 'balance of business' tests (income and capital); at least three investment properties must be held although the definition of 'property' includes separate rental units (i.e. a shopping centre with more than three retail units would qualify). Owner-occupied property does not qualify. Development for investment is permitted (subject to a tax charge in certain cases if a sale takes place within 3 years of practical completion).
- Ninety per cent of the otherwise taxable income (but not capital) profits of the property investment business must be distributed within 12 months of the end of the relevant accounting period.

Taxation of the REIT

The tax treatment for the UK REIT itself is that it is exempt from UK tax on the income and capital gains produced by the property investments. The exemption is tightly defined so that it will not, for example, extend to the sale of group companies owning investment properties rather than the properties themselves. There is no obligation to distribute capital gains. Cash proceeds of sale held for up to 24 months after the sale are treated as the equivalent of the property for the purposes of the 75% (asset value) balance of business test.

The UK tax authorities have given themselves broad powers to counteract 'tax avoidance' transactions carried out by UK REITs and in extreme cases to cancel UK REIT status.

The UK REIT may carry on non-exempt activities (up to a 25% limit set by the balance of business tests). However, it will pay corporation tax on the profits from such activities (as from 1 April 2008, the rate will be 28%). In addition, the UK REIT will suffer tax penalties if it

- Pays a dividend to a shareholder holding 10% or more
- Has interest expense such that its gross income falls short of a 125% coverage ratio

Both of these provisions come from a desire to protect the UK Treasury from tax leakage. The 10% threshold is at the point where treaties reduce UK withholding tax below 15%. Interest will usually, of course, be p aid free of withholding tax. Neither provision is affected by the residence of the recipient of the payment, which is relevant from an EU law perspective.

The entry charge

In order to secure UK REIT status, an 'entry charge' has to be paid amounting to 2% (or 2.19% if the statutory facility to spread the charge over 4 years is taken) of the market value of the investment property assets, that is those which will obtain the benefit of the tax exemption. The charge does not, therefore, apply to assets held as trading stock. Acquisition by a UK REIT of a non-REIT will also lead to a requirement to pay the 2% charge on the investment property held by the non-REIT. The obtaining of UK REIT status produces a rebasing of the property for tax purposes so that historic contingent capital gains are extinguished, in addition to tax exemption being secured for the future.

Taxation of shareholders

For shareholders, distributions will be divided between income from the exempt and the taxable parts of the business. Distributions from the exempt side will be treated for UK tax purposes as if they were a special class of property income and paid subject to a withholding tax at the basic rate of income tax (20% as from 6 April 2008). Regulations permit certain shareholders to recover or avoid this withholding tax. Bilateral tax treaties may reduce the rate (by reference to the dividend article). Distributions from the taxable side of the business will be treated like normal UK dividends (no withholding tax will apply).

Comments

The new rules have been relatively well received and many of the major listed property investment companies (16 in total) have converted to UK REIT status since 1 January 2007. However, there has only been one 'new' REIT IPO (local shopping REIT). Although market conditions are regarded as a contributing factor, the REIT regime has also come under scrutiny for working best for the conversion of existing listed companies rather than newly incorporated companies.

Suggestions have been made to address this bias and ideas have focussed on reducing the potential costs a newly incorporated company incurs in becoming a REIT, including reducing or deferring the stamp duty land tax and/or entry charge payable. The justification for this is that, unlike the conversion of an existing company, a 'new' REIT does not benefit from the eradication of latent capital gains as a result of the rebasing that occurs on joining the REIT regime, as the base cost of a newly incorporated company's property assets should already reflect current or recent market valuations. In addition, it will also have paid 4% stamp duty land tax on the property acquisitions it has recently made. There has also been lobbying for an unlisted REIT (or at least for a listing on AIM to be accepted) for those companies that would otherwise become REITs but for the heavier costs associated with listing on the London Stock Exchange.

A further aspect of a healthy REIT regime is that it should facilitate, or at least not discourage, M&A activity. To date, the only public activity has been the announcement by Land Securities to demerge itself into three separate entities in due course. Consideration of the new regime in this context has focussed attention on ambiguity in the legislation and guidance in respect of the tax treatment of a target REIT company in respect of a takeover by a non-REIT. It was unclear whether HM Revenue & Customs had a discretion to rewrite the tax history of the target REIT following a takeover. The principal concern was that if the legislation was intended to give HM Revenue & Customs such a discretion, then purchasers would most likely lose the benefit of the rebasing of the target REIT's assets to the market value as at the end of the REIT's last full accounting period. However, HM Revenue & Customs have recently confirmed that it was not the intention of the legislation to give such a discretion and that consequently a non-REIT purchaser of a REIT would be able to sell the REIT's assets without suffering a significant capital gains charge.

A further topic of discussion has been the tax treatment of dividends from a REIT's non-UK subsidiaries holding non-UK property. Currently, dividend income from such subsidiaries is not tax exempt under the REIT regime. This has been viewed as a barrier to the UK REIT being a vehicle of choice for global real estate investors who would generally hold their foreign property through local SPVs. However, the government has recently published proposals for reforming the taxation of UK companies' overseas profits generally. The upshot of the proposals could be that UK companies are exempt from paying tax on dividends from non-UK subsidiaries, leading to the possibility that UK REITs might be a better vehicle for non-UK investment.

Finally, a summary of the UK REIT market would not be complete without reference to the current difficulties experienced by the commercial and residential property sectors and the global credit problems. It is unfortunate that the launch of the UK REIT market more or less coincided with the arrival of these market conditions, as the share prices of UK REITs have in particular suffered. Many REITs are now trading at significant discounts to net asset value with their share prices considerably lower than they were during the run-up to their conversion to REIT status. Whilst pre-conversion exuberance may have accounted for some of the pricing over optimism the more fundamental cause is the revaluation of the underlying assets and income streams, and the recent performance of the UK REITs has served to highlight their new status as more transparent vehicles for investment into those assets.

EU law and REITs: what are the issues?

Introduction

The basic principles of EU law are quite simple and require only common sense to be understood. The EC Treaty's aim is to create a true common market without 'economic frontiers' to hinder cross-border business. This common market is to be achieved by means of the EC Treaty freedoms of which the free movement of capital is the most important one for REITs. A common market for REITs in the EU entails the removal of cross-border tax barriers between the EU member states. The basic idea is that whether an investor invests in his domestic market or in another EU member state should not make a difference (from an economic point of view).

Where cross-border investments are treated less favourably than domestic investments, this difference in treatment enters the 'danger' zone, meaning that the different treatment could form a prohibited restriction of the free movement of capital (or the freedom of establishment). As follows from the above, it should be simply a matter of common sense for the legislators in the EU to determine whether their REIT systems are in line with EU law. Until the issue of the EU compatibility of REITs is resolved, the REIT or its investors should safeguard their rights under EU law by filing requests for equal treatment in a cross-border investment situation.

European REIT regimes and potential infringements

Currently, the REIT regimes in the EU contain quite a few potential infringements. Many of these were analysed in the EPRA report of August 2005 entitled 'European REIT regimes and the impact of the EC Treaty freedoms'.[6]

To sum up, prohibited restrictions seem to exist in various European REIT regimes with respect to the following:

- withholding tax burden;
- REIT requirements;
- shareholder restrictions;
- listing requirements; and
- asset level/activity test.

We will briefly discuss a few examples of these restrictions below.

A difference in withholding tax treatment for domestic dividend distributions and cross-border dividend distributions occurs in various Member States: for instance, the application of an exemption in the domestic situation and an actual withholding in the cross-border situation.[7] In general, the cross-border situation should receive equal treatment. This means a lower or no withholding tax burden in the cross-border situation.

In order to be eligible for REIT status, most Member States require a company to be incorporated under domestic law. Furthermore, the REIT often needs to be a tax resident according to the applicable domestic legislation. The fact that some Member States do not allow foreign legal entities or non-residents to opt for REIT status creates an economic disadvantage in a cross-border situation; in disallowing such an option, the Member States would seem to be protecting their domestic markets. Such a protectionist approach may constitute a prohibited infringement of the free movement of capital.

Certain REIT regimes impose different rules on resident and non-resident shareholders. If the rules for non-resident shareholders are less favourable than those for resident shareholders, we may be looking at a prohibited infringement.

We are currently experiencing that the EU Member States are starting to look at EU law compatibility of their (REIT) legislation, further to recent EU case law. Hence, we may conclude that EU case law has a greater harmonising effect than the combined political efforts from the European Member States.

Acknowledgement

This chapter is an updated version of a paper presented at the 2006 EPRA conference. The permission of EPRA to use and update this paper is gratefully acknowledged.

Notes

1. Sociétés d'investissements immobiliers cotées.
2. This regime will also apply to other publicly traded property vehicles and to SPPICAVs (form of OPCI).
3. Or of rights attached to a financial lease agreement, or certain real estate rights.
4. Organismes de Placement Collectif Immobilier.
5. OPCI à Règles de Fonctionnement Allégées.
6. Available at www.epra.com
7. The Dutch legislator has acknowledged this for distributions to foreign pension funds and has made public a proposal in which foreign EU pension funds are effectively granted an exemption from Dutch withholding tax, just like their Dutch counterparts.

4

Listed Property Trusts in Australia

Graeme Newell

Background to LPTs

The listed property trust (LPT) sector has been a very successful property investment vehicle in Australia over the last 30 years. This chapter reviews the development of LPTs, profiles their status and highlights key strategic issues that are impacting on the further development of LPTs in Australia. It also highlights the impact of the current global credit crisis on LPTs.

In Australia, LPTs are the equivalent of US REITs and were established as a listed property investment vehicle over 35 years ago. Until 1990, there was a lack of significant growth, with institutional portfolios being dominated by direct property holdings. The property market recovery in the early 1990s saw institutional investors search for liquidity – a major catalyst to LPT growth with both supply side and demand side appeal. Over this subsequent 15-year period, LPTs have become a mature, sophisticated, highly successful indirect property investment vehicle, with an outstanding track record and significant commercial property assets, being available to both general investors and institutional investors. Australian LPTs are the second largest REIT market globally (£53 billion at December 2007) exceeded only in size by the US REIT market (£153 billion at December 2007). The Australian property market is considered to be the world's most transparent property market (Jones, 2006). LPTs are an important ingredient in this high level of property market transparency in Australia.

Importantly, LPTs offer the following features often not available with direct property.

- high liquidity;
- high divisibility;
- low entry and exit costs via stockmarket listing;

- proper disclosure regarding stockmarket guidelines;
- access to 'trophy' property assets;
- access to quality sector-specific and diversified portfolios;
- high yields;
- tax transparency;
- professional fund management skills and expertise;
- efficient market place;
- ability to spread risk;
- non-valuation based performance reporting.

LPT regulatory framework

LPTs are a property investment vehicle listed on the Australian stock-market. LPTs invest in income-producing properties (e.g. office, retail, industrial), with the main goal of obtaining rental income. The standard Australian stockmarket regulations and the Managed Investment Act provide the regulatory environment for LPTs.

LPTs are tax transparent and do not pay company tax if they distribute 100% of their taxable income (post-depreciation) to the LPT shareholders. There are no limits on gearing, with international property investments acceptable. Whilst the traditional LPT structure was for external managers, recent years have seen most LPTs move to an internal management model (via stapled securities) to allow for non-property investment activities such as property development and other aspects of funds management.

LPT profile

At December 2007, the LPT sector had total assets of over £62 billion, comprising over 3000 institutional-grade properties in diversified and sector-specific portfolios (Property Investment Research, 2007a). LPTs currently account for over £52.7 billion in market capitalisation, being the third largest sector on the Australian stockmarket and now represent over 10% of the total Australian stockmarket capitalisation, compared to only 5% of the total Australian stockmarket capitalisation in 2000. LPTs also account for over 85% of property exposure on the Australian stockmarket – significantly above the equivalent global level of 31% (AME Capital, 2008).

Figure 4.1 shows the growth in LPT market capitalisation since 1987. Significant growth has occurred since 1992, which has seen the LPT market capitalisation grow from only £3 billion to its current level of over £52.7 billion; this sees Australian LPTs as the second largest REIT market in the world, accounting for 15.7% of global REIT market cap. Currently, there are a range of LPTs, including diversified LPTs (38% of LPT sector market

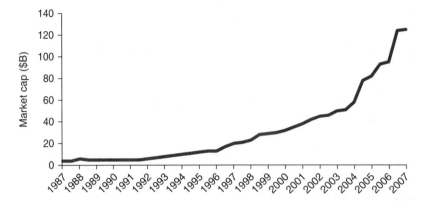

Figure 4.1   Growth in Australian LPT market capitalisation: 1987–2007. $1 = £0.4412 at December 2007. *Source*: Author's compilation.

Table 4.1   Leading Australian LPTs: December 2007.

LPT	Market capitalisation	Number of properties
Diversified		
Stockland	$12.21B	192
GPT	$8.48B	85
Mirvac	$6.16B	60
DB RREEF	$5.86B	198
Office		
Macquarie Office	$2.79B	41
Commonwealth Property	$2.50B	29
ING Office	$2.04B	24
Retail		
Westfield	$40.79B	121
CFS Retail Property	$5.25B	24
Macquarie CountryWide	$2.18B	244
Industrial		
Goodman	$8.31B	543
ING Industrial	$2.77B	539

Source: UBS (2008) and PIR (2007a).
$1 = £ 0.4412 at December 2007.

capital), office LPTs (8%), retail LPTs (44%) and industrial LPTs (10%). Unlike US REITs, Australian LPTs do not have residential property in their portfolios.

Table 4.1 presents an overall profile of the leading diversified and sector-specific LPTs in the LPT sector at December 2007. There are 34 LPTs in the top 300 companies on the Australian stockmarket, with 50 LPTs in total at December 2007. The largest LPTs include Westfield (£18.0 billion market capital), Stockland (£5.4 billion) and GPT (£3.8 billion), with Westfield being the world's largest REIT – being nearly double the size of

Table 4.2 Major Australian LPT fund managers: 2007.

LPT fund manager	Total assets	Percentage of total LPTs (%)
Westfield Group	$49.3B	28.5
Macquarie Bank	$16.1B	9.2
GPT Group	$11.1B	6.2
Stockland Trust Management	$10.8B	6.2
DB RREEF Funds Management	$9.0B	5.2
Colonial First State Global Asset Management	$9.0B	5.1
ING Management	$8.5B	4.9
Mirvac Group	$8.5B	4.9
Centro Properties Group	$8.4B	4.8
Goodman Funds Management	$7.7B	4.4
Total	$138.5B	79.1

Source: PIR (2007a).

the second largest global REIT (Simon Property Group: £9.8 billion). Other LPTs that are in the leading global REITs are Stockland (#8), GPT (#18), Goodman (#21), Mirvac (#30), DB RREEF (#34) and CFS Retail (#39). This sees Australian LPTs comprising three of the world's top 20 REITs and seven of the world's top 50 REITs.

Some LPTs have in excess of 100 commercial properties in their portfolios (e.g. DB RREEF, Goodman, Westfield, Macquarie CountryWide, Stockland) via local and international property exposure. Several LPT fund managers have a range of LPTs (e.g. Macquarie, ING), with the top 10 LPT fund managers accounting for 79% of the LPT market as shown in Table 4.2.

Currently, LPTs account for approximately 7% of institutional asset allocations and account for over 45% of all institutional-grade property in Australia. As Australia accounts only for 2% of the world's commercial property, this sees Australia as one of the most securitised property markets in the world, with 51% of the property market being securitised. LPT stocks are held by the major institutional investors, with both local and offshore property securities funds having significant levels of LPTs. LPTs are highly liquid stocks, having an average monthly LPT turnover of 9.7% of the total LPT market capitalisation in 2007 (UBS, 2007, 2008); this compares with an average monthly turnover of 3.8% in 1999. International investors (via global property securities funds) have significantly increased their allocations to LPTs, with international investors now accounting for over 22% of LPT holdings. Typical benchmark allocations for Australian LPTs in these global property securities funds are 13%, using the FTSE EPRA/NAREIT Global Real Estate Index.

LPTs have performed strongly compared to the other major asset classes over the last 10 years, with LPT risk levels being significantly below stockmarket risk, reflecting the defensive characteristics of LPTs. Sector-specific LPTs have also typically outperformed the corresponding direct property sector. These LPT performance analysis issues are discussed more fully in the next section.

Typically, LPTs are not highly geared compared to other stocks in Australia, with an average gearing of 35% at November 2007, although these debt levels have increased significantly in recent years, e.g. LPTs had an average of only 15% gearing in 1997. LPTs with international property exposure tend to be more highly geared, compared to those LPTs with domestic property portfolios. The yields for LPTs (currently 6.2%) make them attractive yield-focused investment alternatives to 10-year bonds, although there has been significant yield compression for LPTs in 2005–2007 (Figure 4.2). The LPT sector also trades at a significant premium to NTA; this is unlike most other securitised property markets and reflects the quality of LPT management and growth prospects.

LPT and stockmarket performance in Australia is correlated (r = .60 over 1985–2007), and it has been shown that there is no long-term market integration between LPTs and the stockmarket. This evidence of market segmentation suggests that there are diversification benefits from including LPTs in an investment portfolio, particularly in conditions of increased stockmarket volatility. Both diversified and sector-specific strategies have been shown to be equally effective for LPT portfolio diversification (Newell and Tan, 2003a), with LPTs also showing evidence of superior property selection and market timing (Peng, 2004). The establishment of an LPT futures market in August 2002 further enhanced the stature of LPTs, with institutions being able to use LPT futures as an effective risk management tool for hedging their LPT exposure (Newell and Tan, 2004).

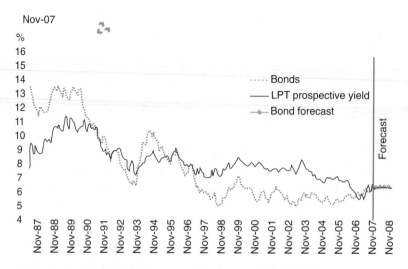

Figure 4.2   Australian LPT yield gap profile. *Source*: PIR (2007b).

Another key factor in the development and maturity of the LPT sector has been the establishment of benchmark LPT performance indices on the Australian stockmarket, as well as the production of LPT sub-sector performance indices by UBS for the leaders, office, retail, industrial and diversified LPT sub-sectors since 1993. This has recently been supplemented by additional LPT sub-sector indices by UBS for stapled securities LPTs and international LPTs, reflecting the emergence of these new key LPT sectors in recent years.

The re-badging of Australian LPTs as Australian REITs (or A-REITs) has also been implemented in 2007–2008. This is to make the Australian investment terminology for REITs consistent with that seen in all other REIT markets globally and has been strongly supported by the property industry in Australia.

Overall, LPTs have been seen to be a world-class indirect property investment vehicle, offering a range of attractive investment features and access to quality commercial property portfolios for institutional, international and general investors.

LPT performance analysis

Further evidence of the investment stature of LPTs is shown in Table 4.3, with the investment performance of LPTs compared to the other major asset classes. Over each of the 1-, 3-, 5- and 10-year holding periods, LPTs were seen to perform strongly, being in the top two performing asset classes in each case, and being the best-performed asset class over the last 10 years. Importantly, over the last 22 years, LPTs were the best-performed sector in 36% of years, only exceeded by shares being the best- performed sector in 41% of years. In particular, LPTs outperformed shares in 55% of years over 1985–2006; as well as LPTs being the best-performed asset class in 8 of the last 11 years (Table 4.4). This strong performance by LPTs reflects the significant growth and maturity of the LPT sector in the last 10 years. Importantly, sector-specific LPTs have also typically outperformed the corresponding direct property sector over these various holding periods (Table 4.5).

Table 4.3 Australian LPT performance analysis: September 2007.

Asset class	Average annual total return (%)			
	1Y	3Y	5Y	10Y
Direct property	17.27 (3)	15.72 (3)	13.97 (3)	12.18 (3)
LPTs	20.13 (2)	20.76 (2)	19.29 (2)	14.67 (1)
Shares	33.58 (1)	26.39 (1)	22.45 (1)	13.46 (2)
Bonds	3.12 (4)	4.96 (4)	5.06 (4)	5.59 (4)

Source: IPD/PCA (2007).

Table 4.4   Major Australian asset rankings: 1985–2006.

	Direct property	Shares	Bonds	LPTs
1985	2	1	3	4
1986	4	1	3	2
1987	1	4	2	3
1988	1	2	4	3
1989	2	1	3	4
1990	3	4	1	2
1991	4	1	2	3
1992	4	3	1	2
1993	4	1	3	2
1994	1	4	3	2
1995	4	1	2	3
1996	4	2	3	1
1997	4	2	3	1
1998	3	2	4	1
1999	2	1	3	4
2000	3	4	2	1
2001	2	3	4	1
2002	2	4	3	1
2003	2	1	4	3
2004	3	2	4	1
2005	2	1	4	3
2006	3	2	4	1

Source: Author's analysis.

Table 4.5   Australian LPT sub-sector performance analysis: September 2007.

Asset class	Average annual total return (%)			
	1Y	3Y	5Y	10Y
Direct property	17.27	15.72	13.97	12.18
Office	19.95	15.21	11.91	10.80
Retail	15.45	16.34	15.88	13.33
Industrial	13.01	13.25	13.34	13.22
LPTs	20.13	20.76	19.29	14.67
Office LPTs	19.00	18.90	16.00	11.60
Retail LPTs	17.60	20.00	19.40	15.90
Industrial LPTs	15.60	30.90	26.00	18.20
Diversified LPTs	25.20	19.40	19.10	14.60
International LPTs	17.30	18.00	15.60	16.30
Stapled LPTs	21.70	21.60	17.60	14.30
Shares	33.58	26.39	22.45	13.46
Bonds	3.12	4.96	5.06	5.59

Source: IPD/PCA (2007) and UBS (2007).

As well as delivering strong total returns, LPTs also have a risk profile significantly less than the risk level of the stockmarket. In particular, over 1985–2006, the LPT risk level of 11.4% was only 63% of the stockmarket risk level of 18.2%, reflecting the defensive nature of LPTs. On a risk-adjusted performance analysis basis, LPTs were the best-performed

Table 4.6   Australian LPT portfolio diversification: September 2007.

	LPTs	Shares	Direct property	Bonds
LPTs	1.00			
Shares	0.60	1.00		
Direct property	−0.09	0.00	1.00	
Bonds	0.35	0.13	−0.27	1.00

Source: IPD/PCA (2007).

asset class (Sharpe index of 0.49), compared to shares (second; Sharpe index of 0.33), direct property (third; Sharpe index of 0.27) and bonds (fourth; Sharpe index of 0.23). The beta for LPTs was 0.40, further reflecting the defensive characteristics of LPTs, compared to the overall stockmarket.

In assessing the portfolio diversification benefits of LPTs, Table 4.6 presents the inter-asset correlations over 1985–2007. With the correlation between LPTs and the sharemarket being $r = 0.60$, this reflects some degree of portfolio diversification benefits. Importantly, this correlation between LPTs and shares has decreased significantly in recent years; in particular, the correlation over 1985–1992 of $r = 0.71$ has reduced to $r = 0.24$ over 1994–2006. This demonstrates enhanced portfolio diversification benefits by LPTs in more recent years. LPTs and direct property were not correlated ($r = -0.09$) over this period, reflecting their performance being seen as separate and distinct property investment vehicles, with LPTs being seen as a hybrid of direct property and stockmarket performance.

Similarly, it has been shown that the addition of LPTs to a portfolio of shares, bonds and cash sees enhanced risk-adjusted mixed-asset portfolio returns for LPT levels in the portfolio of up to 20% (Newell and Tan, 2003b).

Overall, concerning performance analysis, LPTs have been shown to deliver strong risk-adjusted returns, as well as portfolio diversification benefits. Whilst past performance is not necessarily an indicator of future performance, the results for Australian LPTs present a strong picture regarding the strategic contribution of LPTs to investment portfolios in Australia.

Recent issues in the strategic development of LPTs

The LPT sector has undergone considerable development and structural change in recent years, including increased levels of international property, increased levels of debt, incorporating property development activities via the use of stapled securities structures, a reduced number of LPTs via significant mergers and acquisitions and use of emerging property sectors. The potential impact of these structural changes is to increase LPT risk levels and see LPTs as more sensitive to interest rates and less reflective of property market conditions, and reduce the traditional defensive nature of LPTs and their benefits in a portfolio. Importantly, LPTs have also recently seen a changing investor profile, particularly from the rapidly expanding global property securities fund sector.

These changes in the LPT sector have largely focused around the following key issues, all of which have significant strategic implications concerning the future development of LPTs.

Increased levels of international property

With LPTs accounting for over 45% of all institutional-grade property in Australia, the lack of local investment opportunities has seen LPTs seeking international property investments in recent years. Other motivating factors for LPTs seeking international properties in their portfolios have been diversification benefits, growth in investment funds, better returns and lower cost of capital. Beginning with Westfield America in 1996, international property in LPT portfolios now accounts for 39% of LPT total assets, with industry surveys indicating these levels of international property are expected to increase to 50–60% of LPT total assets over the next 3 years. In 2005, LPT international property acquisitions accounted for 79% of all LPT property acquisitions.

As seen in Table 4.7, international property has been included in LPT portfolios as stand-alone 100% international LPTs (e.g. Macquarie DDR, Babcock & Brown Japan Property Trust) or merged with local property (e.g. Westfield, Macquarie CountryWide, DB RREEF, Macquarie Office). This now sees 60% of LPTs in the ASX200 having international property in their portfolios. The initial focus of this international exposure by LPTs was US retail and US industrial, but this has now further expanded to include European commercial property (e.g. GPT, Macquarie CountryWide, APN European Retail, Rubicon Europe Trust, Westfield) and Asian commercial property, particularly in Japan (e.g. Babcock & Brown Japan Property Trust, Rubicon Japan Trust). Further significant developments into Europe and Asia by LPTs are expected in the future, although current property market uncertainty and tighter conditions in global credit markets may slow these developments in the near future. Evidence of strong performance by the international LPT sector relative to the other LPT sectors over the last 10 years is shown previously in Table 4.5.

While international property introduces the additional risk factors of currency risk, political risk and economic/investment risk, LPTs have typically used joint venture structures with local market participants, accessed transparent property markets, used skilled management teams and hedged rental income streams for up to 10 years as effective risk management strategies. Other foreign exchange (FX) risk management strategies used by LPTs include cross-country swaps and off-setting FX borrowings to cover both capital and income risks management of these international property

Table 4.7   Country profile for international LPTs in Australia.

LPT	Australian assets (%)	US assets (%)	European assets (%)	Asian assets (%)	NZ assets (%)
100% international portfolio (12 LPTs)					
APN European Retail Trust	–	–	100	–	–
Babcock & Brown Japan PT	–	–	–	100	–
Centro Shopping America Trust	–	100	–	–	–
Galileo Japan Trust	–	–	–	100	–
Mirvac Industrial Trust	–	100	–	–	–
Macquarie DDR Trust	–	100	–	–	–
Mariner American Property Income Trust	–	100	–	–	–
Reckson NY Property Trust	–	100	–	–	–
Rubicon America Trust	–	100	–	–	–
Rubicon Europe Trust Group	–	–	100	–	–
Rubicon Japan Trust	–	–	–	100	–
Tishman Speyer Office Fund	–	100	–	–	–
Merged domestic/international portfolio (12 LPTs)					
Centro Properties Group	67	30	–	–	3
DB RREEF Trust	79	19	–	–	2
GPT	73	4	23	–	–
ING Office Trust	67	30	3	–	–
ING Industrial	85	–	15	–	–
ING Community Living	50	46	–	–	4
Macquarie CountryWide	23	74	–	–	3
Macquarie Goodman	93	–	–	4	3
Macquarie Office	40	60	–	–	–
Macquarie Leisure	87	12	–	–	1
Stockland Trust Group	95	–	–	–	5
Westfield Group	42	45	9	–	4

Source: Author's compilation.

portfolios (Newell and MacIntosh, 2007). The addition of international property to the LPT portfolio has been shown to give diversification gains, as well as mixed-asset portfolio benefits (Tan, 2004a,b). Importantly, while LPTs have taken on increased levels of international property in recent years, it has been shown that this has not resulted in increased LPT risk levels (Newell, 2006), further reinforcing the effectiveness of the international property risk management strategies adopted by these LPTs. However, recent tighter conditions in global credit markets have raised concerns towards the end of 2007 for those LPTs with significant international property portfolios requiring refinancing of their maturing debt.

Overall, Australian LPTs have been international leaders in including international property in their portfolios at significant levels over the last 10 years, doing so in an effective manner across a wide country profile of USA, Europe and Asia.

Increased levels of debt

Debt levels for LPTs have steadily increased from 10% in 1995 to 35% in 2007. Whilst these debt levels are still low in comparison to US REITs and the overall stockmarket, they are largely attributable to a low interest rate environment and increased international property exposure, with higher gearing used as a natural hedging strategy by LPTs with international property exposure. For example, some 100% international property LPTs have debt levels in excess of 50%, for example, Rubicon America, Reckson NY Property, Macquarie DDR. These increased debt levels further heighten the sensitivity of LPTs to future interest rate changes and tighter global credit markets as has been evident in the latter part of 2007. In structuring this debt profile, LPTs have used a range of sophisticated debt products including CMBS, property trust bonds, hybrids and off-balance sheet financing (Chikolwa, 2007).

Importantly, as LPTs are unable to retain capital, LPTs have been highly successful raising additional capital by new IPOs, rights issues or private placements. This has reflected confidence in the financial markets in the ongoing growth of LPTs, their quality property portfolios and the professional quality of LPT management.

Incorporating property development activities via stapled securities

While the traditional LPT model involved external managers, recent years have seen an increased focus on an internal LPT management structure via stapled securities. This internal management structure has enabled a closer alignment of unit holders and manager interests, no fee leakage and a lower cost of capital, but it has increased LPT exposure to non-property investment risk, in particular, to property development risk. This reduced LPT exposure to rental income has seen this exposure decrease from 96% of income in 2000 to 88% in 2007, with these non-rental income components comprising property development (6.1% of income), funds management (2.8% of income), property management (0.5% of income) and construction (0.4% of income).

Stapled securities now account for over 75% of the LPT market capitalisation, compared to only 29% in 2004. Leading LPTs using this stapled security structure include Westfield, Stockland, GPT, Macquarie Goodman, Mirvac and DB RREEF, with a number of these LPTs engaged in property development (e.g. Stockland, Westfield).

While stapled securities typically take on more risk due to property development risk and higher leverage ratios, stapled securities have been shown to outperform externally managed LPTs on a risk-adjusted basis (Tan, 2004c), with property development being an important value-adding dimension in LPT performance (Tan, 2004d). Importantly, industry surveys have indicated that industry participants consider stapled security returns outweigh the extra risk, and property development being seen as the most effective future growth strategy to optimise returns. Similarly, LPT fund managers do not consider the risk will increase substantially, due to the generally low levels of property development activity undertaken in the overall LPT portfolio. Evidence of strong performance by the stapled securities LPT sector relative to the other LPT sectors over the last 10 years is shown previously in Table 4.5.

This stapled securities structure for LPTs has seen a number of LPTs further develop their fund management activities by establishing significant unlisted wholesale property funds. This has been an effective strategy for accessing the significant growth in pension funds in Australia (over £450 billion in 2007) and the increased appetite for property by these pension funds in their investment portfolios. Examples of these wholesale property funds include the GPT Wholesale Office Fund and Goodman Australia Industrial Property Fund (Newell, 2007a,b).

Whilst LPTs have increasingly adopted this internal management structure in recent years, it has been shown that this has not resulted in increased LPT risk levels in the stapled securities LPT sector (Newell, 2006). This has largely been attributable to managing the extent of the property development activities compared to the lower risk delivered by the stable rental income component from the portfolio of LPT investment properties, with rental income still accounting for 88% of the LPT income stream.

Changing LPT investor profile

LPTs have seen significant changes in their investor profile since 2002. This has reflected increased offshore investor interest from the rapid growth in the global property securities fund sector. In 2007, there were 250 global property securities funds with over US$81 billion in assets under management, including over 51 global REIT funds with assets of over US$21 billion. With the strong previous performance of LPTs and a typical portfolio benchmark weight for LPTs of approximately 13% in these global property securities funds, this has seen these international funds recently take on increased significance in the LPT investor profile. In comparison, other benchmark allocations by these global property securities funds include USA (37%), UK (8%), Hong Kong (12%) and Japan (13%).

In terms of the LPT investor profile, the significant change over recent years has been the increase in the level of LPTs in the offshore funds, having increased from only 5% to 22% over 2002 – 2006. This was also accompanied by a significant increase in allocation by the local property securities funds, having increased from 15% to 25%. The lesser significance of LPTs in general equities funds is also evident, having decreased from 45% to 28%. Given the bottom-up 'stock selection' strategy used by these global property securities funds and their global mandate, the current uncertainty in the LPT market is likely to see many global property securities funds be underweight in their fund's LPT exposure.

Reduced number of LPTs via mergers and acquisitions

Recent years have seen considerable consolidation in the LPT sector via merger and acquisition activity. This strategy has been largely implemented to build funds under management for LPTs and increase their international competitiveness. This has also seen LPTs strategically develop their property portfolios by acquiring existing property portfolios, rather than to incrementally increase their property portfolio via individual property acquisitions. This has seen the LPT sector grow significantly, but the number of LPTs reduces significantly.

Recent examples of this LPT consolidation via mergers and acquisitions include the following.

- DB RREEF, formed from Deutsche Office, Deutsche Industrial and Deutsche Diversified.
- Westfield, formed from Westfield, Westfield America and Westfield Holdings.

This consolidation now sees a significant contribution by a smaller number of large LPTs to the LPT sector market capitalisation, with the top five LPTs (Westfield, Stockland, GPT, Goodman and Mirvac) accounting for 68% of the LPT index (see Table 4.1). Each of these top five LPTs has a market capitalisation in excess of £2.5 billion, with 16 LPTs having a market capitalisation of more than £440 million. With considerable liquidity evident in the LPT sector, the potential impact with this consolidation is for LPTs to behave more like stocks than previously. This consolidation has been offset to some degree by the recent establishment of smaller LPTs, with 16 LPTs now listed on the ASX but not included in the benchmark ASX300.

Emerging property sectors

LPTs traditionally focused on core portfolios of office, retail and industrial properties. However, recent years have seen a movement by LPTs into new property sectors including leisure (e.g. Macquarie Leisure), retirement (e.g. ING Community Living), pubs (e.g. ALE Property Group), self-storage (e.g. Valad), healthcare (e.g. ING Healthcare) and childcare (e.g. Australian Education Trust). Table 4.8 gives details of the emerging property sector LPTs at December 2007, with a number of these emerging property sector LPTs included in the benchmark ASX300 (e.g. Macquarie Leisure, ING Community Living). The structure has normally been achieved as a stand-alone LPT structure, with one LPT (Valad) integrating an emerging sector (self-storage) into its broader LPT portfolio.

This growth in emerging property sector LPTs has reflected the mismatch between available funds and the shortage of core property assets in Australia, and LPTs having considered higher risk value-added property by seeking enhanced returns available from the emerging property sectors. The ageing demographics in Australia has also been a catalyst for the retirement and healthcare sectors being included in these emerging sector LPT portfolios. These emerging sector LPTs have higher risk, but significantly outperformed the traditional LPT sectors on a risk-adjusted basis over 2002–2005, as well as providing portfolio diversification benefits (Newell and Peng, 2006). Table 4.9 gives the performance of selected emerging sector LPTs at September 2007.

Yield compression

2006–2007 has seen increasing bond yields and yield compression in the LPT sector (see Figure 4.2). This yield compression in the property market has seen it become more difficult for LPTs to acquire properties at attractive yields, with LPTs only accounting for 23% of recent commercial

Table 4.8 Emerging property sector LPTs: December 2007.

Leisure/entertanment	
Macquarie Leisure	ALE Property
ING Entertainment	MTM Entertainment
MFS Living & Leisure	Tourism & Leisure
Retirement	
ING Community Living	
Healthcare	
ING Healthcare	
Childcare	
Australian Education Trust	
Agriculture	
Challenger Wine Trust	Coonawarra Australia
Cheviot Kirribilly Vineyard	
Self-storage	
Valad Property Group	

Source: Author's compilation.

Table 4.9   Emerging sector LPT performance: September 2007.

LPT	Average annual returns (%)			
	6M	1Y	3Y	5Y
Macquarie Leisure	14.8	37.1	44.1	52.2
ING Community Living	4.1	23.1	19.5	NA
ALE Property	9.3	33.9	45.9	NA
ING Entertainment	10.0	19.8	14.0	NA
Australian Education Trust	4.9	20.8	NA	NA
Challenger Wine	−5.3	−11.6	2.5	8.0
LPT sector	7.7	20.0	20.7	19.3

property purchases in Australia; compared to unlisted wholesale property funds (41% of recent acquisitions) which have a stronger focus on total returns rather than yield. This has seen the significant growth in the unlisted wholesale property fund sector in Australia, now being over £26 billion in property assets (Newell, 2007a,b).

Private equity investors

As has also been seen for US REITs, 2007 has seen an increasing role by private equity investors acquiring major LPTs in Australia for their quality property portfolios. This has seen Investa (£2.5 billion portfolio of 34 commercial properties) recently acquired by Morgan Stanley and Multiplex (£1.4 billion portfolio of 25 commercial properties) acquired by Brookfield. Increased private equity interest in LPTs is expected, but this may be softened by the recent increased cost of debt and tighter credit market conditions.

Other recent developments

The following are the other recent developments that have impacted on the LPT sector.

• Introduction of performance-based fee structures by most LPTs; in some cases, with significant out-performance of benchmarks, this has presented pressures on net income levels available for distribution to shareholders, with deferred fee structures having to be introduced in some instances.
• Significant international leadership role by LPTs regarding sustainable commercial property (e.g. Investa, Stockland, GPT, Mirvac), with LPTs being included in the various international sustainability performance benchmarks including the FTSE4Good Index, Dow Jones World Sustainability Index, Global 100 Index and Carbon Disclosure Project Climate Leadership Index.
• Introduction of LPT futures as an effective LPT risk management strategy by institutional investors (Newell and Tan, 2004).

Table 4.10 LPT performance: December 2007.

LPT sector	Returns (%)		
	3M	**6M**	**1Y**
LPTs	−13.0	−8.5	−8.4
Office LPTs	−10.5	−11.4	1.1
Retail LPTs	−15.1	−10.0	−12.3
Industrial LPTs	−24.1	−18.4	−23.0
Diversified LPTs	−7.4	−2.5	−1.1
International LPTs	−7.7	−1.2	−2.0
Stapled LPTs	−13.6	−8.8	−8.5
Shares	−2.7	2.9	16.2
Bonds	0.7	2.5	4.0

Source: UBS (2008).

Overall, these recent major developments and structural changes in the LPT sector can have a potential impact on LPT risk levels, and hence their portfolio diversification benefits. Importantly, effective risk management strategies have been adopted by most LPTs and have not reduced the overall attractiveness of LPTs as an asset class.

Changing LPT and property landscape in 2007–2008

Australian LPTs have not been immune to the downturn in major global REIT markets in 2007–2008, which has resulted from property market uncertainty and a tightening of global credit markets. Table 4.10 shows LPT sector/sub-sector performance in 2007 over the last 3 months, 6 months and 12 months. This particularly highlights the significant impact on the LPT sector in the last quarter of 2007 (−13.0% return), with this impact also being evident across all LPT sub-sectors. This has seen LPTs significantly under-perform the overall Australian stockmarket (16.2% return) in 2007, as well as in the first two months of 2008 (LPTs at −18.2% versus overall stockmarket at −11.5%).

This increased cost and reduced availability of credit has had a significant impact on LPTs seeking to refinance maturing debt, particularly these LPTs which were highly geared and with high US property exposure. For example, Centro which is the second largest retail property owner in Australia has recently experienced difficulties in refinancing £1 billion in maturing short-term debt, following a recent extensive US retail acquisition strategy (e.g. £2.5B acquisition of New Plan Excel Realty Trust). This has also seen Centro become a potential acquisition target for both local and international property investors. Given the ~40% level of international property in LPT portfolios, several of which are 100% international with USA or UK/European properties (see Table 4.7), and the typically higher level of gearing in these 100% international LPTs, this has raised concerns over future rental growth, declining property values and future earnings pressure on several LPTs, as well as concerns over their currency risk exposure. This has already seen a number of global property securities funds reduce their allocation to LPTs to be significantly underweight compared to the 13% FTSE EPRA/NAREIT benchmark allocation.

The current situation sees increased concerns regarding LPT risk factors, particularly for LPTs with high levels of US property and high levels of gearing, as well as for LPTs engaged in property development. Whilst these LPT risk factors have been managed effectively previously, risk management strategies by LPTs will take on increased importance to accommodate this current property market uncertainty and the tighter global credit markets.

Conclusion

LPTs in Australia are an important property investment vehicle, offering features such as liquidity, transparency, high yields and access to quality property assets.

Importantly, LPTs in Australia have been seen as a well-performing asset class, with strong defensive characteristics (e.g. low risk) in a portfolio, particularly in a volatile stockmarket environment. Recent structural changes and developments in the LPT sector have also seen increased international investment, increased levels of debt, incorporating property development activities via stapled securities LPTs, a reduced number of LPTs via significant mergers and acquisitions and the inclusion of emerging property sectors in LPT portfolios, as well as a changing investor profile.

The latter half of 2007 and the early months of 2008 have presented concerns and challenges for the LPT sector in Australia, particularly with the re-pricing of risk in global markets and some LPTs experiencing difficulties in effectively accessing the global credit markets for re-financing debt. These features could potentially impact on the future risk profile of LPTs and their strategic contributions to portfolios. Despite these concerns, LPTs have quality property portfolios, quality professional managers and long-term stable returns in the world's most transparent property market, with the future outlook being generally positive. As such, LPTs in Australia are expected to continue to be significant property investment vehicles, both from a local and a global perspective.

References

AME Capital (2008) *Global REIT Research: December 2007*. AME Capital, London.
Chikolwa, B. (2007) The development of commercial mortgage backed securities in Australia. *Pacific Rim Property Research Journal*, 13, 397–422.

Investment Property Databank/Property Council of Australia (2007) *Investment Performance Index: September 2007.* IPD/PCA, Melbourne.

Jones, L.L. (2006) *Real Estate Transparency Index.* JLL, Chicago, IL.

Newell, G. (2006) The changing risk profile of listed property trusts. *Australian Property Journal*, 39, 172–180.

Newell, G. (2007a) The significance of property in industry-based superannuation funds. *Australian and New Zealand Property Journal*, 1, 34–43.

Newell, G. (2007b) The significance of wholesale property funds. *Australian and New Zealand Property Journal*, 1, 216–233.

Newell, G. & MacIntosh, I. (2007) Currency risk management practices by Australian LPTs. *Pacific Rim Property Research Journal*, 13, 214–234.

Newell, G. & Peng, H.W. (2006) The significance of emerging property sectors in property portfolios. *Pacific Rim Property Research Journal*, 12, 177–197.

Newell, G. & Tan, Y.K. (2003a) The significance of property sector and geographic diversification in Australian institutional property portfolios. *Pacific Rim Property Research Journal*, 9, 248–264.

Newell, G. & Tan, Y.K. (2003b) Property trusts enhance their portfolio diversification benefits. PIR Monthly Report, February 4.

Newell, G. & Tan, Y.K. (2004) The development and performance of listed property trust futures. *Pacific Rim Property Research Journal*, 10, 132–145.

Peng, V. (2004) Selectivity, timing and the performance of listed property trusts: implications for investment strategies. *Pacific Rim Property Research Journal*, 10, 235–254.

Property Investment Research (2007a) Property Funds Manager Survey 2007. PIR, Melbourne.

Property Investment Research (2007b) LPT Monthly Review (miscellaneous copies). PIR, Melbourne.

Tan, Y.K. (2004a) Benchmarking international property in Australian LPT portfolios. *Pacific Rim Property Research Journal*, 10, 3–29.

Tan, Y.K. (2004b) The role of international property trusts in Australian mixed-asset portfolios. *Pacific Rim Property Research Journal*, 10, 215–234.

Tan, Y.K. (2004c) Internal management and size the winning factors. *Property Australia*, 19(2), 58–59.

Tan, Y.K. (2004d) Is development good for LPTs? *Property Australia*, 19(3), 50–51.

UBS (2007) *UBS Indices: September 2007.* UBS, Sydney.

UBS (2008) *UBS Indices: December 2007.* UBS, Sydney.

5

Asian REITs: Playing the Yield Game

Joseph T.L. Ooi and Neo Poh Har

REIT markets in Asia

Real estate investment trusts (REITs) emerged in Asia in September 2001 with two REITs launched simultaneously in Japan. This was followed soon after by South Korea and Singapore, which saw their maiden REITs launched in 2002. Since then, the development and growth of REIT markets in Asia has been nothing short of phenomena. Other jurisdictions that have enacted legislation for REITs include Thailand, Taiwan, Malaysia and Hong Kong. Table 5.1 provides a summary status of the different REIT markets across Asia as of April 2007. Within a short period, the aggregate market capitalization of Asian REITs grew to US$ 82.66 billion. In comparison, the REIT market in the USA took 35 years to reach the US$ 50 billion market capitalization. It is estimated that REITs in Asia could reach US$ 200 billion market capitalization over the next decade. There are currently 93 REITs listed in various stock markets across Asia and the number will continue to increase rapidly with new REIT markets, such as Philippines, India and China, expected to emerge in the near future.

Japan currently has 40 REITs listed on the Tokyo Stock Exchange and Osaka Securities Exchange. Their combined market capitalization of US$ 52.29 billion constitutes 63% of the REIT market share in Asia. The next largest REIT market in Asia is Singapore, which has 15 REITs listed on the Singapore Exchange. Hong Kong, despite its late entry into the REIT game, is the third largest REIT market in Asia with a market capitalization of US$ 8.97 billion. Hong Kong Stock Exchange facilitated the largest ever REIT IPO in the world with the successful listing of the US$ 3.253 billion Link REIT in November 2005.

Table 5.1 REIT markets in Asia.

Country	Listing date of maiden REIT	Number of REITs	Market Capitalization* (US$ billion)
Japan	Sep 2001	40	52.29 (63%)
South Korea	Jan 2002	8	0.71 (1%)
Singapore	Jul 2002	15	17.45 (21%)
Thailand	Oct 2003	8	0.63 (1%)
Taiwan	Mar 2005	7	1.81 (2%)
Malaysia	Aug 2005	9	0.80 (1%)
Hong Kong	Nov 2005	6	8.97 (11%)
Total		93	82.66

Source: Datastream (as of April 2007). *Note: Figures in parentheses refer to the size of market capitalization in each country relative to the total market capitalization in Asia.

The pioneering REITs usually start off by focusing on conventional properties such as retail, office and industrial properties. However, as the sector develops, the property asset class being securitized is becoming more diverse. REITs specializing in hospitality, elderly homes and rental housing have emerged in Japan. Moving forward, it is anticipated that more cross-country REITs will be listed in Asia. The Babcock & Brown Japan Property Trust became the first property trust to be listed in Australia for more than 2 years. It is unique because it focuses solely on Japanese real estate (Ooi et al., 2006). Similarly, Guangzhou Investment Co. (GZI REIT) which owns commercial properties in China is listed in Hong Kong. Meanwhile, Fortune REIT and CapitaRetail China Trust, which owns shopping centres in Hong Kong and China, respectively, and first REIT, which owns three hospitals and a hotel in Indonesia, are listed in Singapore. Whilst India has yet to formalize its regulatory framework for REITs, it is reported that Embassy Group, a property developer from India, has filed its prospectus with the Singapore stock exchange to launch a US$ 150 million IPO for a property trust. The trust, which is expected to be listed in mid-2007, will be the first REIT to be based purely on assets in India (*The Business Times*, 25 April 2007).

Riding on the fast growing Islamic wealth management sector, the Malaysian Securities Commission has also issued a set of guidelines for Islamic REITs in November 2005. The guidelines set a 20% cap on the total revenues; an Islamic REIT can derive from tenants engaged in activities not allowed under Shariah law, which prohibits Muslims from investing in properties whose tenants sell alcohol, tobacco, pork or allow gambling and invest in products that charge interests. In addition to the usual appointment of financial and legal advisers, an Islamic REIT also needs to install a panel of internal Shariah advisers. The listing of Al-Aqar

KPJ REIT in August 2006, which owns six hospitals in Malaysia, marks the first Islamic REIT to be publicly traded in the world. The creation of Islamic REITs and private property funds will be attractive to wealthy investors, especially those from the middle-eastern countries, seeking to diversify their asset portfolios.

Table 5.2 shows the REIT regulatory frameworks across different markets in Asia. Singapore, which has the most progressive and responsive REIT regime in the region, granted tax exemptions to both local and foreign individual investors on distribution earned from REITs. S-REITs also enjoy tax exemption on foreign-sourced income. To maintain the REIT status, limits on the trust's asset composition and distribution requirements are commonly imposed. In some jurisdictions, limits on how much debt or development exposure a REIT can take are specified to protect individual investors. However, restrictions on investment and financing activities of REITs have been gradually relaxed to promote further expansion of the REIT markets. For example, in South Korea, the Ministry of Construction and Transportation announced that new amendments to the REITs Act will take effect in July 2007.[1] Similarly, the Malaysian Securities Commission raised the borrowing limit of REITs to 50% of the total value of their assets (up from 35% previously). In another development, Japan's Ministry of Land, Infrastructure and Transport is considering allowing REITs listed in Japan to acquire foreign properties to enhance J-REIT's competitiveness. As the markets compete to become an international hub to attract cross-country REIT listings, it is anticipated that the REIT regimes in Asia will converge to a less restrictive form. At the same time, corporate governance and transparency of REITs in Asia will continue to evolve with likely improvements in the oversight of asset and fund managers, augmentation of interested party transactions and enhancement of disclosure requirements.

Table 5.3 shows the performance of the first three REIT markets in Asia, namely, Japan (J-REIT), Singapore (S-REIT) and South Korea (CR-REIT). Despite a slow start,[2] the REIT markets have grown dramatically: 14.7 times in Japan, 22.5 times in Singapore and 12.3 times in South Korea. Generally, REIT stocks in these countries have outperformed common stocks over the same time period. Since their IPOs, the stock prices of J-REITs, S-REITs and CR-REITs have escalated by an average 10.22%, 38.15% and 23.93% per annum, respectively. On top of that, the REIT stocks generated average annualized dividend yields of 3.84% for J-REITs, 4.79% for S-REITs and 7.25% for CR-REITs.

The decomposition of returns from REITs in these three markets underlines the significance of capital appreciation in the total returns from real estate investment in Asia. This is not surprising since the real estate game in Asia, riding on the strong economic growth in most parts of East Asia until the mid-1990s, had pretty much focused on capital growth.

Table 5.2 Asian REIT legislative comparison.

	USA (REIT)	Australia (LPT)	Japan (J-REIT)	South Korea (CR-REIT)	Singapore (S-REIT)	Thailand (PFPOs)*	Taiwan (T-REIT)	Malaysia (M-REIT)	Hong Kong (HK-REIT)
Enactment of REIT legislation	1960	1971	2000	2001	1999	2002	2003	2005	2003
Listing of maiden REIT	1961	1971	2001	2002	2002	2003	2005	2005	2005
Management	No restrictions	No restrictions	External	External (limited to 5 years)	External	External	No restrictions	No restrictions	No restrictions
Real estate and related assets (minimum ratio)	75%	No restrictions	75%	70%	70%	75%	75%	75%	100%
Ownership of foreign properties	Allowed	Allowed	Prohibited	Allowed	Allowed	Prohibited	With approval	Allowed	Not Allowed
Acquisition of uncompleted development	Allowed	Allowed	Restricted	30% maximum	20% maximum in uncompleted commercial buildings; 10% maximum in single developer	Must be 80% completed	Prohibited	Allowed	Allowed but subject to 10% max limit for non-income producing assets
Development activity (including investing in vacant land to be built upon)	Allowed	Yes, through stapled vehicles	Prohibited	Allowed from July 2007	10% max but REIT must hold the developed property upon completion	Not stated	Not stated	Prohibited	Prohibited

(continued)

Table 5.2 (*continued*)

	USA (REIT)	Australia (LPT)	Japan (J-REIT)	South Korea (CR-REIT)	Singapore (S-REIT)	Thailand (PFPOs)*	Taiwan (T-REIT)	Malaysia (M-REIT)	Hong Kong (HK-REIT)
Other restrictions on asset holding	Nil	Nil	50% of assets must be income producing rental properties and minimum 1-year holding period.	Nil	Minimum 35% must be invested in real estate assets; part ownership of real estate must be held through an SPV	Minimum 1-year holding period	Must be diversified portfolio. Single property not allowed	Must wholly own or able to exercise control of the assets	Minimum 2-year holding period
Gearing Limit (max)	No limit	No limit	No limit	No limit from July 2007	60% if rated	No gearing allowed	35% recommended	50%	45%
Asset valuation frequency	Not stated	Annual	Not stated	Not stated	Annual	Not stated	Every 3 years	Every 3 years	Annual
Minimum payout for tax exemption (percent of taxable income)	90	100	90	90	90	90	100	Nil	90
Tax transparency status	Yes	Yes	Yes	No	Yes	Yes	Yes	Yes for local residents only	No
Other tax incentives	Nil	Nil	Reduction in real property acquisition tax as well as registration and license tax on real estate purchases until 2009	100% waiver on acquisition and registration taxes	Waiver of stamp duty on property purchase by REITs for 5 years to 2010	Withholding tax for non-resident institutional unitholders halved to 10% for 5 years to 2010	Reduced property transfer fees	Need to pay land incremental tax (if any)	6% withholding tax on dividend

Source: Wright (2005) and CBRE Research (December 2006). *Property fund for public offering.

Table 5.3 REIT performance in Japan, Singapore and South Korea.

	J-REITS	S-REITS	CR-REITS
No of REITs	38	13	10
Market capitalization (US$)	31.695 billion	9.453 billion	0.786 billion
Growth (*x*)	14.72	22.50	12.28
Debt ratio (percent of total assets)	38.28	28.62	39.33
Dividend yield (annualized)	3.84%	4.79%	7.25%
Capital gains (annualized)	10.22%	38.15%	23.93%

Source: Datastream (as of 31 August 2006).

Table 5.4 Classification of Asian REITs (by property types).

Sectors	Japan	South Korea	Singapore	Thailand	Taiwan	Malaysia	Hong Kong	Total	Percentage
Diversified	18	1	5	1	5	2	2	34	41
Office	6	6	1	1	1	2	2	19	23
Residential	9	1	0	2	0	0	0	12	15
Retail	2	0	3	1	0	0	0	6	7
Industrial/ logistics	1	0	3	2	0	0	0	6	7
Hospitality	2	0	1	1	0	0	0	4	5
Healthcare	0	0	0	0	0	1	0	1	1
Total	38	8	13	8	6	5	4	82	100

Ong et al. (2000) observe that price appreciation constitutes between 60% and 70% of the total returns from real estate in Asia. Consequently, the growth component will constitute a major part of the total returns of REIT stocks in Asia. Correspondingly, their modest dividend income may not provide the same stabilizing effect it has on REIT returns in the USA and Australia. Gyourko and Siegel (1994), in particular, report that dividend yield comprised 71% of the total returns of US REITs since 1962.

Earnings per share (EPS) and price-earnings (P/E) ratio are commonly adopted by analysts to price common stocks. In the case of REIT stocks, a pricing measure commonly employed is the dividend yield, which is essentially the reverse of the P/E ratio assuming full disbursement of earnings. Table 5.4 compares the pricing of REIT stocks across different markets in Asia as at the end of August 2006. The dividend yield ranges from a low of 2.07% for the average REIT in Taiwan to a high of 7.25% for the average REIT in South Korea. Boosted by strong investor demand, the average dividend yield for REITs in Japan and Singapore has gone down over the years to 3.84% and 4.79%, respectively (from 4.2% to 6.9%, respectively, during their maiden REIT IPO).

The gap between the dividend yield of a REIT and the corresponding yield on newly issued 10-year government bonds is commonly employed to gauge the risk premium of REIT stocks. Institutional investors usually target returns on investment at around 2% over the yield on government bonds. Figure 5.1 shows that the yield spread for the REIT markets in Japan and South Korea have stabilized above the 200-basis point mark. Compared with Singapore's benchmark 10-year government bond yield of 3.4%, the annual dividend yield of the average S-REIT is 4.79%. The current spread of 139 basis points is a huge improvement over the 310 basis points above the corresponding yield for 10-year government bonds offered by CapitaMall Trust, the maiden S-REIT launched in mid-2002. The yield spreads for REITs traded in Hong Kong, Taiwan and Malaysia markets have not yet stabilized with the thin or even negative spread highlighting the speculative nature of REIT stock pricing in these nascent markets.

Ways to enhance distribution yield

To launch a new REIT successfully, it is critical for the sponsor to obtain investor support both domestically and internationally. Whilst local investors are accustomed to the volatile nature of real estate returns in the region, international investors who are used to stable income from real estate in the USA and European markets may find the cash flows associated with real estate in Asia to be less stable. However, as a pass-through vehicle, REIT

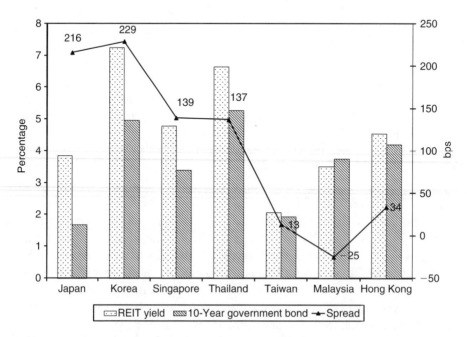

Figure 5.1 Spreads above 10-year government bond yield. *Source*: Datastream (Figures are as of 31 August 2006).

returns cannot differ too much from the cash flows generated by the under-lying properties. Given that the properties in the region tend to be more expensive and have low yields, an initial hurdle faced by REIT sponsors and managers in Asia is how to structure a REIT that can offer the stable and high dividend yield demanded by institutional investors. Drawing on the experi-ence of the REIT markets in Asia, this section examines the various tactics adopted by REIT sponsors and managers to overcome the yield hurdle.

Property valuation

A majority of the REITs in Asia are formed by sponsors who inject their own properties into the REIT, which is seen as an attractive vehicle for the property owners to realize immediate paper gains, boost their bottom line and at the same time, scale down their balance sheet and redeploy the capital locked in the assets into high service content businesses (Ooi et al., 2006). An easy way to increase dividend yield during the IPO stage would be to reduce the price of the assets transferred into the REIT. The popular terminology used to describe this proposition is "taking a hair cut" on the property values. Understandably, many property owners are reluctant to mark down the value of their properties, especially if the same properties could be sold at full value in the open market. The common justification in the marketplace for this practice is that unlike in an outright sale, transfer-ring ownership of the properties to a REIT vehicle would allow the owners to retain control of the properties and create a fee-based income business from managing the trust, as well as the properties sold to the trust. Whilst such a "hair cut" strategy may be necessary for pioneering REITs to gain a wider market acceptance, subsequent sponsors may not need to adopt the strategy in a frenzied IPO market. For example, Mapletree Logistics Trust which was launched in July 2005 in Singapore received an oversubscription of more than 43 times during its public offering (Koh, 2006). Furthermore, it is anticipated that the risk premium required by investors would stabilize as the investors become familiar with REIT stock pricing.

Property selection

Since the primary source of income for a REIT is the rental cash flows from its asset portfolio, it is clear that the type of properties included in the portfolio will dictate the REIT's capacity to pay dividends to share-holders. To replicate the high dividend yields commonly associated with REITs in the USA and listed property trusts (LPTs) in Australia, sponsors of Asian REITs tend to favor properties with high rental yields, particu-larly retail and industrial properties. Although prime grade office buildings may be the preferred choice of asset type for most institutional investors, it is challenging to place them into a REIT because of their low yields.[3]

Table 5.5   Portfolio of diversified REIT.

Sectors	Number	Percentage
Office and retail	9	26
Office, retail and residential	5	15
Office and residential	4	12
Office and hospitality	3	9
Retail and hotel	2	6
Retail and residential	1	3
Retail and carpark	1	3
Office and industrial	1	3
Office and leisure	1	3
Office, retail and logistics	1	3
Office, retail and carpark	1	3
Office, retail and hospitality	1	3
Office, retail, residential and hospitality	1	3
Office, retail, residential and elderly homes	1	3
Office, retail, residential, hospitality and logistics	1	3
Office, retail, residential, hospitality and redevelopment	1	3
Total	34	100

Despite the fact that investors prefer a pure sector exposure, Table 5.4 shows that 41% of the REITs listed in Asia held diversified property port-folios. Whilst risk diversification is often used to justify holding a mixed-property portfolio, it also reflects attempts by REITs to average up the rental yield of prime properties by bundling them together with other properties which produce higher yields. Table 5.5 shows that retail malls, which tend to command high rental yields, are frequently mixed with other property type with the aim of improving the overall cash flow from the asset portfolio owned by REITs.

Acquiring foreign properties, which produce high rental yields relative to local properties, is another route that REIT managers have pursued to increase the distribution yield to their shareholders. Given their huge growth prospects, Chinese properties are prime targets for Asian REITs. GZI REIT, which was established by a Chinese development company and listed on the Hong Kong Stock Exchange in December 2005, is the first property trust to focus solely on properties in China. Its IPO was 74 times oversubscribed by institutional investors and nearly 500 times oversubscribed by the Hong Kong public (Lerner, 2006). This was followed by the successful listing of Singapore-listed CapitaRetail China Trust which owned seven shopping malls worth US$ 690 million located in five Chinese cities.

Financial gearing

REITs also took advantage of the historic low interest rates to gear up their returns by taking on more debt in their capital structure. In a tax-free environment, the effect of borrowings on shareholders' return on equity, r_E, is governed by the following relationship: $r_E = r_A + D/E(r_A - r_D)$, where r_A is the return on the REIT's property assets and D/E is the debt–equity ratio of the REIT. Favorable gearing exists so long as the cost of borrowing, r_D, is lower than r_A. Indeed, this has been the scenario over the past few years as REITs across the world, including those in Asia, were enticed by the positive spread between the low cost of debt and what they can earn on the property.

It should, nevertheless, be pointed out that whilst gearing may magnify the upside returns of REITs, it also amplifies their risks. In other words, the benefits of cheaper debt will be exactly offset by a risk increase to the shareholders. As the REIT's gearing increases, the required rate of return on equity must increase to compensate for the additional risk associated with higher debt ratios. On balance, any gains from using the apparently cheaper debt capital would be offset by the higher cost of equity. This is in line with Modigliani and Miller (1958) proposition that in a world without corporate taxes, both the value of a firm and its overall cost of capital are unaffected by its capital structure.

Moving forward, the scope for REITs to gear up their return on equity will become more restricted. First, most REITs are already employing high levels of debt with the current debt ratios of J-REITs (38.28%) and CR-REITs (39.33%) marginally below to the average debt level of between 40% and 50% employed by REITs in the USA and Australia (Reuters News, 2006a). Although the debt ratios of S-REITs are more conservative (28.1%), they are expected to increase as the debt limit for S-REITs has been raised at the end of 2005 to 60% if they are credit-rated by one of the international rating agencies.[4] Second, interest rates have started to move upwards in recent years. A direct implication of higher interest rates is that it would push up the funding costs for REITs, thus resulting in lower distributions for the shareholders as well as reducing the benefits of positive leverage.

To maintain favorable leverage conditions and reduce their borrowing costs in a rising interest rate environment, a few REITs may decide to issue commercial mortgage backed securities (CMBS) or convertible bonds which carry a very low coupon rate. Hong Kong's Champion REIT, for example, issued HK$ 765 million worth of convertible bonds to fund the acquisition of three floors of Citibank Tower from Kerry Properties. Holders of the 2% coupon convertible bonds can exchange them for REIT units at HK$ 4.6047 before they become due in 2011 (CBRE Research, 2006).

Financial engineering

REIT sponsors have also resorted to other sophisticated and complicated financial structures to artificially create higher distributions for prospective investors. One method that has been employed is to arrange for the purchase price to be paid over several installments. This would artificially inflate the initial yield of the new investment, making the acquisition to appear more attractive than had the entire purchase consideration been paid upfront. Such deferred payment scheme may be employed to disguise yield-dilutive transactions inherently and make them less apparent to the market.[5] Similarly, the sponsors may volunteer to accept new units instead of cash distributions for their retained stake in the new REIT. Whilst these practices may help to align the interests of the managers and sponsors with the shareholders, they also helped to increase the REIT's distribution yield during the initial period.

A few REITs in Hong Kong, such as Champion REIT and Prosperity REIT, have also adopted "step-up interest rate swaps" to enhance their distribution yield. The swap arrangement essentially involves lower cash interest payments in the early years and higher cash interest payments in the later year, usually to match potential increase in rental income (Leung and Smith, 2006). It is doubtful that such artificially inflated yields can be sustained in the long run, especially if the predicted improvement in the property income does not materialize and the REITs are burdened by the higher interest costs in the future.

"Distribution entitlement waiver" is another strategy that has been adopted by Asian REITs. It involves the sponsors agreeing to waive all or part of the distributions due to their units for a limited period of time. The amount waived will then be made available for distribution to other unitholders, thus resulting in them earning higher distributions during the waiver period (Leung and Smith, 2006). Other tactics that have been employed by REIT sponsors and managers to enhance dividend yields to shareholders include paying the fees of the asset and property managers in new units. Again, if there is no corresponding increase in the property revenue, the REIT's EPS will be diluted in the future because the earnings will need to be distributed over a larger base.

An example of a heavily financial engineered REIT is the US$ 348 million Sunlight REIT IPO on the Hong Kong stock exchange in December 2006. It promises an initial annual dividend yield of 8.49%, even though the average yield on the 20 properties owned by the REIT was estimated to be between 2.8% and 3% (Reuters News, 2006b). This implies that around 65% of the promised distribution yield is financially engineered. First, the sponsor transferred the properties into the REIT at more than 20% below their appraised value. The sponsor also provided a rental income guarantee on the properties, which equates to a robust growth rate of 5.9% pa over the next 3 years. In addition, the REIT committed to paying out 100% of its distributable income every year. To preserve cash for distribution to the shareholders, the REIT sponsor who owned 30% of the REIT waived its rights for dividends fully for the first 3 years and partially for the fourth and fifth year. In addition, the REIT manager agreed to receive its fees in the form of units (rather than cash) for the first 5 years. The excessive use of financing engineering to enhance its distribution yield in the short-run was not viewed favorably by the stock market with Sunlight REIT closing at 6.45% below its offer price on the first day of trading. Champion REIT, another Hong Kong REIT that relied heavily on financial engineering to enhance its distribution yields also suffered a similar fate with a first day loss of 15.4%.

Yield-accretive acquisitions

In addition to new IPO listings, the phenomenal growth of REIT markets in Asia is also attributed to the aggressive growth by acquisitions strategy adopted by many of the REITs. Between 2002 and 2006, 281 deals involving some US$ 20.5 billion worth of properties were acquired by REITs listed in Asia (Ooi et al., 2007). Two particularly aggressive REITs in Singapore were Ascendas REIT (A-REIT) and Mapletree Logistics Trusts. Since its IPO in 2002, A-REIT has spent more than US$ 1.28 billion in yield-accretive acquisitions, which expanded the size of its asset portfolio by 12 times from a modest US$ 0.143 billion when it was listed to US$ 1.68 billion in August 2006. Mapletree Logistics Trust, which is the first Asia-focused logistics REIT, was listed in Singapore in July 2005 with an initial portfolio of 15 logistics properties in Singapore. Within 1 year, it acquired property assets in China, Hong Kong and Malaysia with the combined value constituting 43% of its total asset holding (Asia Pacific Equity Research, JP Morgan, September 2006).

Many theories have been advanced to explain why acquisitions take place in a corporate context. Amongst many, these include the differential efficiency theory, which prescribes that more efficient firms will acquire less efficient firms and realize gains by improving their efficiency, the operating synergy theory which postulates that there are economies of scale or of scope that can be achieved through mergers and acquisitions, and the market power theory which holds that merger gains are the results of increased concentration leading to collusion and monopoly effects (Weston et al., 2001). Essentially, the economic benefits of an acquisition come from the belief that either the property is under-priced (or not efficiently managed) or there is potential synergy between the acquired property and the firm's existing asset portfolio.

Nevertheless, one popular justification offered by REITs in Asia is that the acquisitions are yield accretive. To demonstrate the mechanics of a yield-accretive acquisition, let us consider Ascott Residence Trust's (ART) acquisition of the Somerset Olympic Tower in Tianjin, China, for

US$ 47.25 million. In July 2006, ART reported that the proposed acquisition would be yield accretive because the property's 7% annualized yield is much higher than the REIT's portfolio yield of 4.7%. Examination of the price movements of ART stocks shows that the market viewed the yield-accretive announcement favorably as compared to its past average daily return of close to zero since its listing on 3 April 2006. ART's stock price registered a positive 3.7% return on the day after news of its acquisitions on 24 July 2006. The position before and after the acquisition are set out in Table 5.6.

If there are no economic benefits from adding the acquired property to ART's existing portfolio, the market value of the REIT after the acquisition should be equal to the sum of its market value and that of the new property when they are apart. Following the acquisition, ART's market value would increase by US$ 47.25 million to US$ 581.88 million, and its net property income would be similarly enhanced by US$ 3.31 million to US$ 28.44 million. After the acquisition, the weighted average yield of the REIT would increase to 4.88%, which represents an improvement of 18 basis points.

As the asset portfolio of REITs becomes larger, it is doubtful that this strategy can continue in the long-run because any accretive effect from acquisitions is likely to be negligible. Going back to the case example in Table 5.6, the portfolio yield increased by only 18 basis points even though the yield of the acquired property (7.0%) was much higher than the yield of the asset portfolio (4.7%).[6] Furthermore, REITs will find it more difficult to find quality properties that can support the yield-accretive story due to increased competition for a finite supply of institutional-quality properties from new REITs and private property funds entering the market. Already, some REITs have started to venture overseas, undertake development projects or invest in junior bonds,[7] in their attempt to maintain the high distribution income and deliver value to their shareholders. Since t hese ventures expose the shareholders to higher risk, from a theoretical perspective, yield-accretive strategy is a zero sum game that should not have any impact on firm value.

Table 5.6 Impact of a yield-accretive acquisition.

	ART (before acquisition)	Property	ART (after acquisition)
Market value (US$ m)	534.63	47.25	581.88
Property income (US$ m)	25.13	3.31	28.44
Property yield (%)	4.70	7.00	4.88

Source: Ascott Residence Trust (2006).

To appreciate this point, let us revisit the basic valuation model. Based on the principle that the value of an asset stems from the streams of expected cash flows, the price of an asset, P_0, is determined by $P_0 = \Sigma_{t=1}^{H} ((CF_t)/((1+r)^t)) + ((CF_H)/((1+r)^H))$, where CF_t and CF_H are the cash flows during the holding period and reversion, respectively, and r the required rate of return for assets of similar risk class. Applying the valuation framework to stocks, the price of a stock is equivalent to the present value of the cash flows expected by the unit holder: $P_0 = \Sigma_{t=1}^{H}$ $((Div_t)/((1+r)^t)) + ((P_H)/((1+r)^H))$, where DIV_t is the stream of dividend income over the holding period and P_H the estimated price of the stock at the end of the holding period. If the holding period is assumed to be in perpetuity, the pricing model can be simplified to $P_0 = \Sigma_{t=1}^{\infty} ((Div_t)/((1+r)^t))$, which is known as the dividend discount model in the corporate finance literature. This model can be further reduced to $P_0 = (Div_1)/(r)$ if a constant dividend payment is assumed, that is, a zero dividend growth rate; $P_0 = (Div_1)(r-g)$ if dividend is assumed to grow at a constant rate, g.[8]

We can now use the constant dividend growth model to make three simple but important inferences on the pricing of REIT stocks: (a) stock price is directly related to dividend payment and earnings; (b) stock price is inversely related to the discount rate r. For a given dividend and growth rate, a higher required rate of return (discount rate) will result in a lower stock price, and (c) stock price is positively related to growth rate. Conversely, if earnings are expected to decline at a constant rate (i.e., g is negative), the value of $r - g$ in the denominator would be larger, thereby causing the stock price to fall. REIT managers like yield-accretive acquisitions because they get to report higher earnings and pay out more dividends to the shareholders, which is good news for the stock price. Furthermore, by consistently engaging in yield-accretive acquisitions, REIT managers believe that their stocks will be valued as a growth stock since their cash flows and earnings appear to be growing over time. In other words, g is positive, which is again good news for equity valuation. All else being equal, this should result in a higher stock price.

Now consider what would happen if r should rise as a result of an increase in the portfolio risk. Any positive impact from a higher Div_1 and a positive g would be mitigated by a higher discount rate used to determine the stock price. Brealey and Myers (2000; p. 949) call this the "bootstrap effect" because there is actually no real gain created by the acquisition. Whilst the market may be fooled into attributing the increase in EPS to real growth in the short-run, they warned that "in order to keep fooling the investors, you must continue to expand by merger (acquisition) at the same compound rate. Obviously you cannot do this forever; one day expansion must slow down or stop. Then earnings growth will cease, and your house of cards will fall." Thus, even though the dividend income may rise due to yield-accretive acquisitions, the gains would be offset by higher risk exposure and lower future earnings.[9]

Conclusion

The emergence and growth of REIT markets has changed the real estate landscape in Asia. The governing authorities, which were once cautious and suspicious of REITs, are embracing a more welcoming and open attitude towards REITs. They now view REITs as a strategic initiative to revitalize and restructure their local real estate markets as well as to tap into international capital flowing into the regional real estate markets. As an investment vehicle, REIT stocks are popular amongst individual and institutional investors looking for better returns and risk diversification (Ooi, Newell and Sing, 2006). REITs have helped to improve the liquidity and efficiency of real estate markets as well as corporate governance of real estate organizations in Asia. The business model of property organizations has shifted from the traditional asset-heavy real estate ownership model to one that is asset-light focusing on fee income and profits from asset management and property development activities.

The returns composition of regional properties impose constraints on the income potential of REITs in Asia. Focusing on the experience in the Asian markets, this chapter highlights the ways in which the yield game has been played by REIT managers and sponsors. The warning is clear – an overemphasis on achieving high distributions could lead to an unhealthy bias on properties with high yields. By definition, properties with low yield are not necessarily bad; if the properties are priced correctly, a low yield merely indicates that the properties are either endowed with good growth opportunities or have relatively low risk, or both. Conversely, properties offering high current yields are not necessarily good – the attractive returns in the onset may come at the expense of forfeiting future growth, additional risk, or both. Taken to the extreme, a REIT which owns a portfolio of old second grade buildings sitting on short land tenure in non-prime areas may produce high dividend yield in the short term. However, it is doubtful that the rental and capital values of such properties can be sustained over the medium term. Consequently, the REIT is more likely to face falling earnings, rising costs and weak stock price in the future and should this malaise be widespread amongst REITs, the continuing development of the REIT sector in the region may be jeopardized. In conclusion, asset acquisitions should not be undertaken merely on the basis that the acquisitions are accretive on a short-term basis but on the grounds that they are under-valued and have good long-run return potential. This requires an analysis of the competitive environment in order to identify the areas for investment in which the REIT has the greatest potential to generate returns exceeding its true cost of the costs of capital (Bedell, 1997).

Over time, the REIT markets in Asia will evolve to become more disciplined to deliver quality and sustainable total returns, recognizing its true cost of capital and competitive advantage, instead of being driven solely by yield, when making new acquisitions. Moving forward, as investors become more knowledgeable and discerning, we anticipate that there will be a separation of REITs into those which have a strong growth potential and those that are likely to underperform. It is anticipated that with rising interest rates, the gap between good and bad REITs is likely to widen in Asia. In addition to the current focus on dividend yield, more attention will be paid to the management track record, debt ratio and creditworthiness of the individual REITs. To sustain the interest of investors for the longer term, the REIT's ability to consistently deliver quality assets and quality management will be critical. In summary, the surest way to increase shareholder wealth is to improve the rental and capital values of existing properties through active asset management, whilst keeping the risk levels of the REIT at an acceptable level when creating and managing their property portfolio.

Notes

1. Major elements of the revised Act include the reduction of the initial capital requirement from KRW 25 billion to KRW 10 billion, the simplification of regulatory approval procedures by eliminating the requirement for preliminary approval, and the removal of both the restriction on investing in developing projects and the cap on leverage (CBRE Research, 2006).
2. As compared to J-REITs which are currently trading at a premium of up to 50% above their net asset values (NAVs), the two maiden J-REITs were trading at a discount to their offer price during their initial years. Kyobo-Meritz REIT, the first public offer of a CR-REIT in South Korea, received barely enough demand from investors. Around the same period, CapitaLand's first attempt to launch an S-REIT in 2001 failed due to poor demand.
3. CapitaLand, nevertheless, made a breakthrough in May 2004 when it successfully listed the first commercial REIT (Capital Commercial Trust, or CCT) in Singapore. Through a spin-off that does not involve any new equity being raised, shareholders of CapitaLand were given one new share in CCT for every five CapitaLand shares held. 40% of the new REIT would be held by CapitaLand, while 60% will be held by other shareholders. As CCT shares were distributed to CapitaLand shareholders as part of a capital reduction exercise, the company was not subjected to the usual risk of under-subscription or under-pricing associated with a normal IPO process. CapitaLand also did not incur any tax charge or underwriting fees on the CCT spin-off. Keppel Land adopted the same spin-off and capital reduction strategies to launch its office REIT, K-REIT Asia, in April 2006.
4. The maximum debt ratio for an unrated REIT listed in Singapore is 35 % of its total assets.

5. To curb this unhealthy practice, the regulatory framework for S-REITs was amended in October 2005, making it mandatory for REITs to give clear and prominent disclosure of the details of any deferred payment arrangements, including forecasts of distribution yields assuming all deferred payments are settled in full. In addition, the portion of deferred payments would be added to its borrowings when accounting the gearing limit of a REIT.
6. Note that the magnitude of the yield-accretive effect is dictated by the differential yield between the acquired asset and the existing portfolio as well as by the size of the acquisition relative to the size of the existing asset portfolio.
7. Even if a proposed acquisition is not yield accretive, the property could still be injected into the REIT portfolio indirectly through a complicated structure involving asset or mortgage backed securitization. A good illustration is the investment by Singapore's CapitaMall Trust (CMT) on CapitaRetail Singapore (CRS-CMBS), which is a private property fund formed by CapitaLand to hold three suburban shopping malls that it has recently acquired. By investing S$60 million on the junior E-class CRS-CMBS that promises a coupon rate of 8.2%, CMT obtained yield accretion, without having to directly own the three properties which have lower yields than its prevailing distribution yield (J.P Morgan, 2003).
8. Note that any subsequent growth in the assets of the REITs because of reinvested profits will generate growth in future dividends, which will be reflected in current share price. Consequently, the analyst only needs to focus exclusively on forecasting dividends. Any capital gain is simply determined by dividend forecasts at the time the stock is sold.
9. Ooi, Ong and Neo (2007), nevertheless, offer some initial evidence that the stock markets in Asia, particularly in Singapore, like the accretive story and reward acquisitions that lead to higher earnings and dividends for the shareholders.

References

Ascott Residence Trust (2006) Presentation slides on growth strategies, July 24.
Bedell, E.S. (1997) Public lodging companies and the cost of capital. *Real Estate Report.* KPMG Peat Marwick LLP.
Brealey, R.A. & Myers, S.C. (2000) *Principles of Corporate Finance* (sixth ed.). McGraw-Hill, New York.
CBRE Research (2006) Report on REITs Around Asia, December.
Gyourko, J. & Siegel, J. (1994) Long-term return characteristics of income-producing real estate. *Real Estate Finance*, Spring.
J.P. Morgan Securities (2003) Asia Pacific Equity Research Report, 2003. CapitaMall Trust – An Indirect Route to Asset Acquisition, September 10.
Koh, J. (2006) Singapore. In: R.B. Macfarlanes (ed.), *Real Estate Investment Trusts – A Global Analysis.* Globe Law & Business, London.
Lerner, M. (2006) Investor Appetite Grows for Hong Kong REITs, International Forum, Real Estate Portfolio (July/Aug 2006).
Leung, T. $ Smith, P. (2006) Hong Kong. In: R.B. Macfarlanes (ed.), *Real Estate Investment Trusts – A Global Analysis.* Globe Law & Business, London.
Modigliani, F. & Miller, M.H. (1958) The cost of capital, corporation finance, and the theory of investment. *American Economic Review*, 48, 261–297.
Ong, S.E., Ooi, J. & Sing, T.F. (2000) Asset securitization in Singapore: a tale of three vehicles. *Real Estate Finance*, 17(2), 47–56.

Ooi, J.T.L., Newell, G. & Sing, T.F. (2006) The growth of REIT markets in Asia. *Journal of Real Estate Literature*, 14(2), 204–222.

Ooi, J.T.L., Ong, S.E. & Neo, P.H. (2007) The wealth effects of yield-accretive acquisitions: the case of Asian REITs, paper presented at the American Real Estate Society (ARES) Meeting in San Francisco, April 12–14.

Reuters News (2006a) FACTBOX – Debt-to-total asset ratios for REITs in Asia, July 21.

Reuters News (2006b) Sunlight REIT IPO raises $402m, December 14.

The Business Times (2007) India's developer files for Singapore Reit IPO, April 25.

Weston, J.F., Siu, J.A. & Johnson, B.A. (2001) *Takeovers, Restructuring & Corporate Governance* (third ed.). Prentice-Hall, Englewood Cliffs, NJ.

Wright, D. (2005) REITs in Asia: from concept to completion, *Asia Law & Practice*, Hong Kong.

6

European Real Estate Unlisted Vehicles: A Mature Market Now or Is There More to Come?

Karen Sieracki

Introduction

European real estate unlisted vehicles have seen tremendous growth since their inception in the early 1990s. By number of vehicles alone, the increase has been 475% and by value the increase has been 159% since 1993 (these figures also include the German open-ended funds) (INREV, January 2008). There has been a recent spurt in activity since 2001 when funds by number have grown by 92% (2001–2006) and by value 31% (INREV, February 2007). The pace has now slowed (2006–2008) to just under −1% by number and value growth has been negligible at 2.3%, as shown in Figure 6.1 (INREV, January 2008).

The considerations in 2Q 2008 are: Has the growth in performance in the European real estate market run its course for the time being in attracting investor interest? And if that is the case, has the demand for European real estate unlisted vehicles now matured? This chapter will attempt to answer these questions.

Characteristics of European real estate unlisted vehicles

As there are currently 476 European real estate unlisted vehicles with a gross asset value (GAV) of €336bn, the choice is diverse as to style, risk category, location and age. The number of German open-ended funds has remained relatively steady over the past 14 years in both value and number (c. €65–100bn and c. 30–35), whereas the opportunity and value-added funds have seen the largest increase over the same period. Figure 6.2 catalogues the growth in these different styles of funds.

Prior to the early 1990s, the European real estate market outside of the UK, the Netherlands and Germany was less developed in terms of cross-border investment as indeed, in some instances, were the domestic markets themselves. There was a lack of general market information and

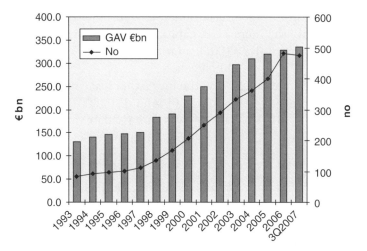

Figure 6.1 European unlisted vehicles. *Source*: INREV.

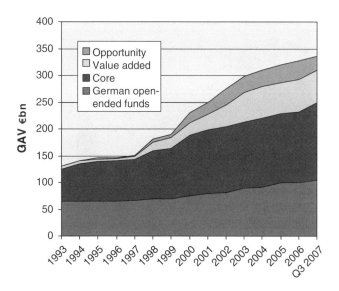

Figure 6.2 Types of European unlisted vehicles. *Source*: INREV.

transparency which inhibited the more risk-averse investors such as the pension funds and insurance companies (wholesale investors) and the German retail investors (man in the street). The French real estate market became more receptive after its loan default crisis in the early 1990s due to the excessive bank lending to real estate. Cross-border capital became more resilient and cognizant of the performance potential for European real estate.

The flow of capital into European real estate has increased with the market benefiting from international as well as cross-border investment. Figure 6.3 shows the increase in capital flows. The year 2007 saw €244.1bn worth of investment (JLL, 2007), an increase of 286% since 2000. This was an increase of 40% from 2005 levels.

Cross-border investment saw the biggest increase of 553% since 2000. In 2007 cross-border investment was €154bn (JLL, 2007), an increase of 54% over 2005. Domestic investment was more sedate at €90bn for 2007 (JLL, 2007), an increase of 27% over 2005, and an increase of 127% since 2000.

The UK, Germany and France were the top three destination points for European direct real estate investment, comprising 62% of the total. Values grew in France by 25% over the year to €29.8bn (JLL, 2007). Germany saw an increase of only 6% over the year to €53.3bn but was able to maintain interest in a more cautious market. The UK's share of investment was down to 30% in 2007 from 49% in 2005 (JLL, 2007). Investment activity fell dramatically in Q3 and Q4 2007. The UK still retained its number one position with activity of €71bn (JLL, 2007). Figure 6.4 shows the diversity of destinations for European real estate investment.

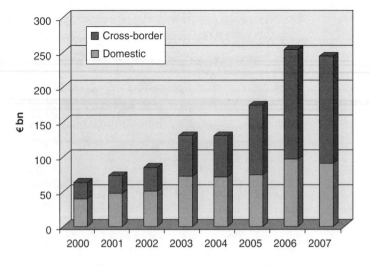

Figure 6.3   European direct real estate volumes. *Source*: JLL.

The capital for investment in European real estate had a widespread of country origin. The UK was the largest source with 26%, followed by others at 27% (mainly the corporates) and global at 15% (JLL, 2007). Global funds continued to be a popular source of capital, and European real estate investment could be said to have finally come of age (Figure 6.5).

In order to gain exposure to the European real estate market, the choices were theoretically more simpler: invest directly and customise the portfolio to one's specific risk return requirements, invest in listed real estate securities (which is limited on a European basis) or invest in third-party vehicles to gain the breadth and depth of a second-hand portfolio.

As the previous figures show, many investors chose the indirect route to gain exposure and benefit from the management skills contained within these vehicles. These investors did not necessarily have large sums of capital for investment or the management resource or skills set. Therefore

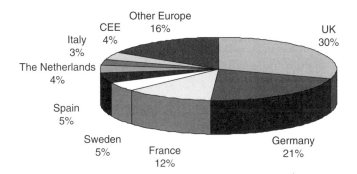

Figure 6.4 Destination of European direct real estate investment 2007. *Source*: JLL.

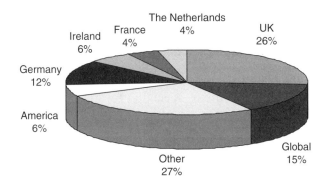

Figure 6.5 Source of capital invested in European real estate 2007. *Source*: JLL.

it would have been difficult to achieve the desired portfolio mix in terms of risk and return. Also, some investors were not permitted to use leverage, whereas the indirect vehicles could do so. For the investors with larger sums of capital, investment in indirect European real estate vehicles provided an additional avenue to reach those sectors and/or locations for risk diversification and performance returns. The next four subsections will discuss in more detail the main features of European real estate unlisted vehicles.

Investment style

There are three main unlisted vehicles styles: core, value added and opportunistic. Each one is distinguished by its risk return profile. Core vehicles are the least risky and usually invest in prime properties that are expected to provide a constant and stable return. Gearing levels are low at around 35% (INREV, January 2008) and expected returns range between 5% and 7% p.a. The portfolio style aims to be diversified usually across all sectors and low-risk locations, or across particular sectors and/or locations. The expected return does change over time much in accordance with the prospects for the real estate market itself.

Value-added vehicles embody rather more risk than core, and the optimum assets are those where the value can be enhanced through active management (e.g. regearing of leases, letting vacant space, refurbishment, limited development). This can take the form of improving secondary property, strengthening prime property or being the second mover into a new location or sector. The portfolio is usually diversified but there could be a disproportionate weighting to certain properties and locations to achieve above average returns. The average level of gearing is 50% (INREV, January 2008), and expected returns in the region of 8–12% p.a.

The opportunistic vehicles are at the far end of the risk return spectrum where portfolio diversification is not the critical issue, and each opportunity is judged on its own merits to secure the desired higher return. 'Anything, anywhere' would be the theme of the opportunistic vehicle. Such vehicles are usually the first movers into locations and sectors. They are positioned high up the risk curve. The average level of gearing is 70% (INREV, January 2008), with expected returns in the region of 12% + p.a.

Core and value-added vehicles can be further subdivided into specialist or multi-based. In this context, specialist means investment within a single country or sector. Therefore, the vehicle focuses on either sector or location (which usually means country). Multi-based means various sectors and countries and therefore the vehicles are not focused on any particular sector or country.

Table 6.1 shows a brief summary of investment vehicles styles when looking at the risk profile and expected return.

Table 6.1 Vehicle style summary.

Vehicle style	Main investment stock	Average level of gearing (%)	Expected return (% p.a.)
Core	Prime, good quality stock	35	5–7
Value added	Asset management the key, make the property better by realising the gaps	30	8–12
Opportunistic	Anything goes, anytime, any place	70	12+

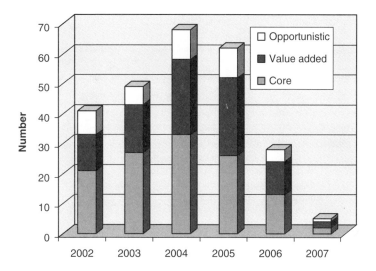

Figure 6.6 New vehicle launches by fund style. *Source*: INREV.

New vehicles

In looking at new vehicle launches over the past 6 years (2002–2007), the year 2004 was the peak year with a total of 68 new vehicles by number (INREV, January 2008). The majority were core vehicles at just under 50% of the total by number, which has been the norm over this time period. The launch of new opportunity vehicles has been more changeable by absolute number, but the average for this time period has been around 14% of total new vehicle launches. Figure 6.6 shows new vehicle launches by fund style for 2002–2006.

As achieving target returns became more challenging, the vehicle-launches across all fund styles reduced in 2006 and 2007. The year 2007 saw only a total of five new vehicles launched as property markets became more uncertain as the year progressed. Table 6.2 shows some of the latest entrants covering August 2007 to October 2007 (INREV, January 2008).

Table 6.2   New vehicles coming to the market August 2007–October 2007.

Vehicle manager	Vehicle	Target GAV (€m)	Strategy
Aberdeen Property Investors	Aberdeen Property Fund, Russia	1500	Closed fund, Russia, target IRR 14–18%
Accent Real Estate Investment Managers	Accent Russia Opportunity Fund, GP LP	1850	Closed opportunity fund, Russia target IRR 24.5%
Anderson Real Estate Investment Management	AREIM Fund I	745	Closed value-added funds, Sweden
Beacon Capital Partners	Beacon Capital Strategic Partners V	10 000	Global office fund, USA and Europe, target IRR 18–20%
Catella Real Estate KAG	Focus Nordic Cities Fund	n/a	Open fund, Scandinavian and Baltics
Cordea Savills	UK Property Ventures No 1 Fund	730	Nontraditional areas of UK market, target IRR 20%
Cordea Savills	Cordea Savills Nordic Retail Fund	500	Closed fund, retail sector in Sweden, Finland, Norway and Denmark as well as Baltics
Cushman Wakefield Investors/KGAL	Paris Office Growth Fund	400	Closed, value added, office sector in Paris
Delta Lloyd	Delta Lloyd Dutch Property Fund	500	Closed core fund, Netherlands, target IRR 8.2%
Grosvenor Fund Management	Grosvenor Italian Retail Investments	250	Closed, core fund, Italian retail, target IRR 10%+
Heitman International	Heitman Russia and Ukraine Property Partners	n/a	Developing, acquiring and owning property in Russia and Ukraine
Prologis	Prologis European Property Fund II	7500	Open, equity €3bn, target leverage 50–60%
Aberdeen Property Investors	AIPP Asia Select	400	Closed fund of funds, Asia, target IRR 13–17%
Aberdeen Property Investors	AIPP II	600	Closed fund of funds Europe, target IRR 10–14%
Franklin Templeton Real Estate Advisors	Franklin Templeton Asian Real Estate Fund	200–350	Closed value added, Asia, target IRR 17–19%
Franklin Templeton Real Estate Advisors	Franklin Templeton European Real Estate Fund of Funds 2	300	Closed, value added, Europe, target IRR 15%
Valartis Asset Management	Valartis Global Real Estate Select – Emerging Markets	250	Open opportunity fund of funds, Europe, Asia and Latin America, target IRR 13–16%
Valartis Asset Management	Valartis Global Real Estate Select – Asia/Pacific	350	Open value-added fund of funds, Asia and Australia, target IRR 11–13%

Source: INREV.

Seven of the potential vehicles are concentrating on Russia and Asia Pacific. Six of the potential vehicles are fund of funds structures. This vehicle type has grown over the past few years as clients look for mixed exposure over a range of funds in terms of style as well as specialist and multi-based styles. The aim is to offer diversification in European real estate markets across the unlisted sector. However, two levels of fees are incurred – one by the manager of the fund of funds vehicle as well as those fees paid indirectly to the manager of the underlying vehicles. This double fee element does have an impact on performance, hopefully to be offset by the risk adjusted return.

Capital raised

Looking from the investor side, in 2006 institutions put €10.2bn into 63 European unlisted real estate vehicles (INREV, January 2007). It was estimated that this constituted 27% of funds that have raised capital in 2006. Pension funds were the most active investor group, at just under 50% of the capital invested, followed by insurance companies. The fund of funds investor groups, who were the newest and currently the most active ones, committed 10% of the equity. Figure 6.7 illustrates this increased share.

The US investors were the most active investors in the European unlisted real estate market with just under €2bn (i.e. 20%) (INREV, January 2007). The UK followed with €1.8bn, and then the Germans with €1.25bn and the Netherlands at €1.05bn (INREV, January 2007).

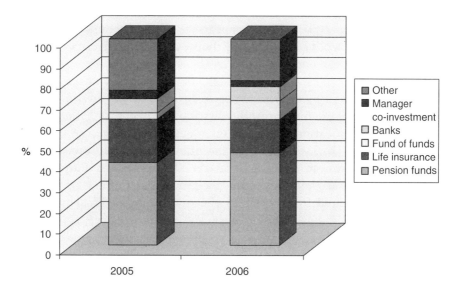

Figure 6.7 Source of equity capital by investor group. *Source*: INREV.

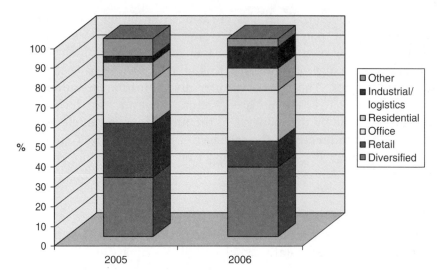

Figure 6.8   Equity by target sector. *Source*: INREV.

The destination of investor capital can be subdivided by investment style and sector/location. The majority of capital favoured the core style (52%), followed by opportunity vehicles (27%) and value added (21%) (INREV, January 2007).

The value-added vehicles have been more successful in finding stock by requesting 51% of capital commitments, followed by the core vehicles calling in 42% (INREV, January 2007). The opportunity vehicles have been less successful and have demanded only 10% of capital commitments (INREV, January 2007). There appears to be a disconnection between where investors would like to place their capital and what can be actually achieved, taking the opportunity vehicles as an example.

Diversified vehicles were the most popular vehicle target by 33% of investors, followed by the office sector by 21% of the investors (INREV, January 2007). Figure 6.8 shows the distribution of equity by target sector.

In looking at location, single country continued to be the favourite by 49% of the investors, followed by the more diversified Europe region for 18% of the investors (INREV, January 2007). Western Europe (France, Germany, UK, the Netherlands and Belgium) was the least popular location, being favoured by just 2% of the investors (INREV, January 2007). Figure 6.9 shows the desirability of the various locations.

Open or closed structure

Another important characteristic is whether the European real estate unlisted vehicles are open or closed. Of the 476 vehicles in the INREV

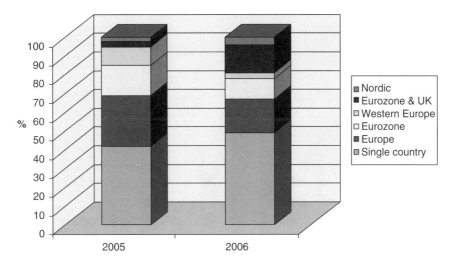

Figure 6.9 Equity capital by target regions. *Source*: INREV.

database as at April 2008, 305 vehicles had a finite life (INREV, April 2008). Of the remaining 171 vehicles, 30 were German open-ended funds. The German open-ended funds are regulated by specific German legislation as to the methods of valuation, investment location and liquidity.

In August 2006 INREV completed a study on the termination of vehicles with a finite life. The INREV data estimated that the total number of funds scheduled to terminate in the next 5 years was 123 vehicles with a then current total value of €71.5bn. Forty-five percent of these were core vehicles, with value added at 23% and opportunistic at 33%. Figure 6.10 illustrates the timeline.

There were four main identified options for finite life vehicles.

1 Liquidation of the portfolio either as a single entity or progressively by the gradual disposal of individual properties.
2 Extension of the vehicle's life by an additional 1–2 years.
3 While retaining the existing investors, transferring the assets into a new vehicle as a preliminary one to restructuring into a new format.
4 Initial public offering which would see the unlisted vehicle becomes a quoted one.

The exact route chosen would most likely depend upon the following.

1 The state of the real estate market at the time.
2 The wishes of the investors.
3 How this termination would fit the investors' respective strategies?

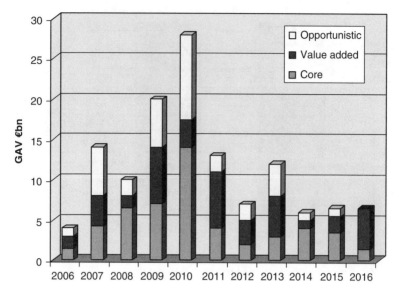

Figure 6.10   Finite vehicle end year by style. *Source*: INREV.

4 What is in the prospectus?
5 Any change to the written course of action could depend upon the unanimous decision of the investors or the Board.

To terminate a vehicle takes time, and the larger ones would be more likely to start the process earlier. As terminations are due to peak within the next 2–3 years, it will be interesting to see what happens.

Performance of European real estate unlisted vehicles

Performance will be the key issue for the investor, validating the reason for investing in the first place. However, not all vehicles are in the IPD INREV Index. There are 206 funds in this index compared to a total of 490 as at the end of December 2006. For some vehicles, performance becomes really important only if the vehicle's life is finite and the profits distributed. This is usually the preferred route for opportunity vehicles, which take high-risk positions in the expectation of quick and substantial growth, to be returned to investors in the form of high capital gains.

Depending upon the vehicle style and whether it is specialist or diversified, performance is benchmarked in various ways. IPD is most commonly used for core and value-added vehicles where there are relevant country IPD indices. However, IPD coverage can be light in certain sectors and locations and accordingly attention must be paid to the biases of the various country and European IPD indices. Opportunity and some value-added vehicles use an absolute return or a hurdle rate as the performance benchmark. The IPD INREV is available but again there are issues of breadth and depth in the various vehicle type segments.

The headline total return figure in 2006 for the IPD INREV Index was 12.5% p.a. and 10.1% p.a. in 2005 (IPD, 2007). The 3-year annualised total return was 10.9% p.a. and the 5-year figure was 8.9% p.a. (all total return figures are in euros) (IPD, 2007). The index consisted of 208 funds with a GAV of €153bn. All European vehicles ex-retail investors once saw a return of 20.9% pa for 2006, less than that seen in 2005 at 22% p.a. The 3-year total return was 9.1% p.a. and the 5-year figure was 13.6% p.a. (IPD, 2007). Table 6.3 summarises the headline figures.

These average figures can hide wide variations by country and sector. On the country level, France saw the best return in 2006 at 26.3% p.a., followed closely by Norway at 26.2% p.a. The multi-country vehicles for institutional investors saw a return of 24.1% p.a. in 2006, but the retail investor vehicles saw only 4.9% pa. Table 6.4 shows the performance summary of vehicles by country in euros.

Sector performance in multi-country vehicles in local currencies shows a relatively wide range from 6.3% p.a. in 2006 for diversified sectors to 20.4% p.a. for retail in 2006. Table 6.5 illustrates the diversity.

The above performance figures illustrate the range and diversity of investment styles, sector and location that underpin the European real estate unlisted vehicles. From the investor standpoint, the manager, strategy, style and timing are the determining factors.

Looking ahead, the performance for European real estate is expected to be weaker across the various countries and sectors. Yield compression has occurred and, as interest rates rise, there is now a cross over where swap rates are higher than some property yields. Debt is becoming more expensive, which narrows the investor demand for real estate investment.

Over the next 5 years (2007–2011) real estate total returns across Europe (mainly North, South and Central Europe) are expected to be single digit. Table 6.6 provides an indication of forecast returns.

Rental growth is forecast to slow, with capital growth turning negative as investor demand wanes for European real estate and economic growth slows.

Management fees

Another influence on performance is the level of management fees. These will vary according to the vehicle style and whether the vehicle is specialist or diversified. According to the INREV study (INREV, November 2007),

Table 6.3   Summary of headline performance figures in Euros by general vehicle.

Vehicle type	Total return 2005 (% p.a.)	Total return 2006 (% p.a.)	Total return 3 years (% p.a.)	Total return 5 years (% p.a.)	Number of vehicles 2006	NAV (€bn) 2006
Europe–domestic ex-retail investor	21.1	20.3	19	13.6	116	69.6
Europe–all vehicles ex-retail investor	22	20.9	19.1	13.6	173	82.8
Europe domestic	18.4	18.1	16.7	11.9	128	78.5
Europe all vehicles	10.1	12.5	10	8.9	206	152.8

Source: IPD INREV.

Table 6.4   Summary of headline performance figures in Euros by country vehicle.

Vehicle type	Total return 2005 (% p.a.)	Total return 2006 (% p.a.)	Total return 3 years (% p.a.)	Total return 5 years (% p.a.)	Number of vehicles 2006	NAV (€bn) 2006
France	29.6	26.3	–	–	7	0.96
Germany	–	5.2	–	–	6	2.2
German institutional	–	25.1	–	–	5	0.64
Italy	6.8	10.1	8.3	8	19	5.16
The Netherlands	12.6	14.4	12	11.9	17	8.83
Norway	–	26.2	–	–	3	1.27
Portugal	6	3.4	5.6	7.7	9	1.49
Switzerland	4.9	3.9	5	3.9	10	8.78
Switzerland retail investor	4.7	4.5	5.2	4	9	7.1
UK	24.8	23.7	22.3	14.7	57	49.77
Multi-country	5.1	7.6	5.7	6.8	7	74.37
Multi-country institutional	26.6	24.1	19.9	13.8	57	13.21
Multi-country retail investor	2.5	4.9	3.7	5.8	21	61.15

Source: IPD INREV.

GAV was the most common basis for management fees. The average annual fee for core vehicles was 0.61% of GAV. Value-added vehicle management fees were also 0.61% of GAV and for opportunistic ones it was 0.59%.

The study also found that fees were usually lower for those vehicles investing in one country as compared to those investing in several. The same applied to single sector and multi-sector vehicles, with the single-sector vehicle management fees generally lower. For the single-country

Table 6.5 Summary of headline performance figures in local currency by multi-country vehicles.

Vehicle type	Total return 2005 (% p.a.)	Total return 2006 (% p.a.)	Total return 3 years (% p.a.)	Total return 5 years (% p.a.)	Number of vehicles 2006	Aggregate NAV (€bn) 2006
Diversified	2.9	6.3	4.5	6.2	53	64.00
Industrial/ logistics	30.1	24.9	–	–	7	1.60
Office	21.0	15.7	9.6	–	9	4.37
Residential	–	–	–	–	–	–
Retail	27.2	20.4	23.7	–	9	3.98

Source: IPD INREV.

Table 6.6 European real estate total returns 2007–2011.

Country/ city	Sector	Total return 2007–2011 (% p.a.)	Country/ city	Sector	Total return 2007–2011 (% p.a.)	Country/ city	Sector	Total return 2007–2011 (% p.a.)
Central London	Office	3.0	Ireland	Retail	5.1	Berlin	Logistics	6.4
Frankfurt	Office	2.5	Spain	Retail	11.7	Hamburg	Logistics	5.7
Berlin	Office	1.6	Sweden	Retail	10.3	Lisbon	Logistics	4.1
Amsterdam	Office	1.6	Italy	Retail	8.4	London	Logistics	2.7
Sweden	Office	8.1	France	Retail	9.2	Madrid	Logistics	2.7
Ireland	Office	1.6	Portugal	Retail	9.5	Milan	Logistics	4.0
Paris	Office	6.0	Netherlands	Retail	9.5	Paris	Logistics	5.7
Italy	Office	3.2	Germany	Retail	8.5	Prague	Logistics	3.3
Spain	Office	4.3	UK	Retail	2.8	Stockholm	Logistics	5.8

Source: PMA.

vehicles, the UK and Dutch had lower management fees than in those vehicles that invested in other European countries. The INREV study involved 160 European vehicles targeted at institutional investors and covered 26% of the GAV of the INREV universe (i.e. GAV of €336bn). Table 6.7 illustrates the different level of fees for the various vehicle types.

However, annual management fees can be increased by the inclusion of performance fees. Seventy-nine percent of the sample used some form of performance fee structure (INREV, November 2007). For core vehicles, 35% did not apply any performance fees, while all opportunity vehicles used some form of performance fee. Figure 6.11 shows the performance fee structure by vehicle style.

Periodic performance fees or a combination was the most popular basis for the value-added and opportunistic vehicles. Opportunistic vehicles had the highest usage of periodic fee type (42%), using an absolute IRR or total return measure (INREV, November 2007). Other bases for periodic

Table 6.7   Summary of annual management fees by style.

Fee basis	Core average (%)	Value-added average (%)	Opportunistic average (%)
Drawn commitment	–	1.33	1.79
GAV	0.61	0.61	0.59
NAV	0.92	0.99	–
Rents	–	–	–
UK vehicles	0.54	0.52	–
Other single country	0.58	0.58	–
Multi-country	0.67	0.68	–
Single sector	0.61	0.54	–
Multi-sector	0.61	0.71	–

Source: INREV.

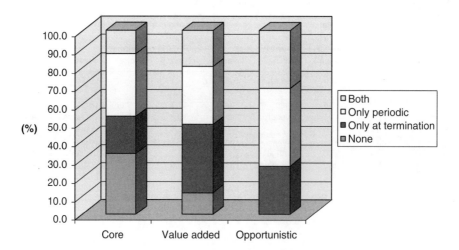

Figure 6.11   Performance fee structure by style and number of funds. *Source*: INREV.

performance fees were IRR/benchmark, capital gain or income return. Table 6.8 shows the distribution of periodic performance fees by style.

There is a trade-off between the relative risk of the vehicle and the level of fees; the higher the risk, the greater the total fee which most likely includes performance fees. Core vehicles, on the whole, have lower management fees, but the risk profile was the least. Specialist vehicles in terms of sector and/or country had lower management fees than the diversified ones. Expected returns are the important consideration for vehicle choice but management fees do have an impact, particularly if the vehicles are underperforming.

Table 6.8 Bases for periodic performance fees by style.

Basis	Core (%)	Value added (%)	Opportunistic (%)
Absolute IRR/Total return	14	25	68
IRR/benchmark	24	24	5
Capital gain	–	–	–
Income return	4	2	–
Other	6	2	–
No periodic performance fee	52	47	26

Source: INREV.

Discussion and conclusion

As the European real estate market is slowing down, liquidity can become critical. The capital flow figures into European real estate indicated that many investors had already invested on the assumption of sustained favourable performance. Usually when investor demand wanes, property yields move out and capital growth becomes sluggish to negative. This has already happened in the UK in the second half of 2007.

For those already invested in European real estate unlisted vehicles, it could be extremely difficult to exit the finite life funds before their termination dates. Secondary trading in these funds is minimal due to the different frameworks and prospectuses. There have been attempts at ensuring investment platforms are similar with regards to definitions, prospectuses, fees and exit, but with only minimal success. TPlus, the secondary trading platform, began in January 2006 but was suspended in May 2007. It was organised to boost liquidity in the unlisted vehicles market and had a life of just 18 months. Investors are faced with being locked into underperforming vehicles or those that no longer suit their strategy.

Where investors would have to wait for the end of the unlisted vehicle's life, the monies raised from the sale of the properties will be dependent upon market conditions at the time. As REITs or similar structures become more accessible in Europe (UK, France, Germany, Belgium, the Netherlands and soon Italy), the unlisted vehicle could emerge as one of these. After 15 months in the UK, there are currently 19 REITs with a market capitalisation of £25.6bn (April 2008). In Germany, there is only one REIT which is a very disappointing response.

This involves cost considerations as well as satisfying the various legal requirements. This route could be favoured by single-country vehicles. However, it would not be suitable for multi-country vehicles whether they are specialist sector or diversified. This is because different European legal jurisdictions would be involved, significantly complicating matters, thus proving difficult to achieve. This is why there are currently no cross-European REITs.

Another exit route could be listing on the alternative investment market (AIM) but again pricing would be very much dependent upon the prevailing European real estate market conditions and investor demand.

For the open-ended vehicles, investor exit is through redemptions whose timing and amount is generally governed by the terms of the prospectus. The issue here is the degree of protection afforded to the remaining investors so they will not be disadvantaged. Sometimes this can take the route of a downward price change in the units which would affect those investors who exercised their redemption right. The vehicle managers could also close the fund. Usually the first ones to redeem are in a more beneficial position.

There is also the issue of uninvested capital. This affects those vehicles that have recently launched. INREV recently completed a study on the uninvested capital ratio (UCR) (INREV, February 2007). Of the 286 finite life funds, 126 were included in this study. Both the specialist (either single country or sector) value-added and opportunistic vehicles comprised the largest segment of uninvested capital.

These vehicles' current GAV was €49.2bn with a target GAV of €85.8bn, leaving a net €36.6bn to be invested (INREV, February 2007). The average UCR was 41.6% (i.e. 41.6% of the vehicle's capital was uninvested), but could be as high as 88.5% for newly launched vehicles. There has been tough competition for European real estate stock which has made it difficult to find investments at acceptable price levels. However, as the market changes, this capital can be useful in securing real estate at lower prices if investors are prepared to wait. The other alternative is to have the capital returned.

European real estate unlisted vehicles are arguably now at a crossroads. They have provided an investment route into European real estate through their diversity of investment style and country/sector focus. They have provided choice for the investor. However, this provision of choice does carry risk in that some vehicles have, and will, perform much better than others. Also, there is the issue of exit and lack of secondary trading which come to the fore as investors become disillusioned with the vehicles or have a change in strategy. As real estate derivatives throughout Europe become more widespread, their use by European real estate unlisted vehicles is likely to increase on both a speculative and/or a hedging basis.

As European real estate unlisted vehicles becomes more mature, standardisation across the various structures should be possible. This would facilitate secondary trading as well as offer other exit routes for investors.

As of April 2008, the European real estate market has begun to slow, taking its cue from the UK. Those vehicles that can play on the differential rates of decline across sectors and locations with unused capital will be in a better position to retain investor interest and money. However, the fear is that there could be more disappointment from existing vehicles unless the managers adopt defensive strategies and display more realism in advising their investors as to future prospects.

References

Richard Ellis, C.B. (2007) European Investment Year End 2006.
Richard Ellis, C.B. (2008) European Investment Year End 2007.
EuroProperty (2007) European Property Fund Management. EuroProperty INREV Survey.
INREV (2005) Management Fees, September.
INREV (2006) Guidelines for a Secondary Market, February.
INREV (2006) Management Fees and Terms Study, April.
INREV (2006) Quarterly Report, August.
INREV (2006) Core Definitions, December.
INREV (2007) Investment Intentions Survey, January.
INREV (2007) Quarterly Report, February.
INREV (2007) Reporting Guidelines, March.
INREV (2007) Capital Raising Survey, April.
INREV (2007) Management Fees and Terms Study, November.
INREV (2008) Quarterly Report, January.
INREV (2008) www.inrev.org, April
IPD (2007) IPD INREV Index 2006.
JLL (2007) European Capital Markets Bulletin 2006.
JLL (2008) European Capital Markets Bulletin 2007 and Views of 2008.
PMA (2007) European Sector Forecasts, Spring.
PMA (2008) European Sector Forecasts, Spring.

7

Constructing a Global Real Estate Investment Index

Ian Cullen

Introduction

Investment property databank (IPD) has been building indices of real estate investment returns in individual national markets for more than 20 years. Today we are publishing 14 indices for European national markets and a further six in markets elsewhere in the world. It was not until 2004 that we embarked upon the major project of publishing cross-border indices and so combining individual national market results into larger composites. The consultation release for a pan-European index was made available in that year and full pan-European indices have been produced and reported in each of the last 4 years.

In 2006 IPD embarked upon the much larger project of extending its pan-European initiative to a global arena. In November 2006 the first consultation release of a global index was published in which the returns to 17 IPD market indices and two produced by partnering organisations were combined in a cautious first step towards building a truly global real estate index.

This chapter reports the aims, methods and results of this major development project. Our plan was to collate feedback upon a single consultation release and commence publication of a fully branded global index series in July 2007. In the event the task proved much larger than a 1-year project, and the full index was launched for the first time – simultaneously in London, Paris and Tokyo – in June 2008. This first IPD global property index covers returns from the most mature real estate investment markets around the world – 22 national markets in total. The five largest markets contributing to the index are the USA, the UK, Germany, France and Japan. The index tracks global performance over the 7 years from 2001 to date.

The purpose of the index is to provide a global measure of the performance of property as an asset class, in line with those already available for equities and bonds. As such it reflects the coming of age of property as a global investment medium and the increasing transparency which is being created in the sector by IPD and others.

Top down or bottom up?

A great deal of effort and research has been invested in the two major cross-border index projects that IPD has undertaken over the past few years. An obvious first question therefore is 'why bother?' In the mid 1990s a company called Global Property Research (GPR) was formed in the Netherlands and very soon after commenced its programme of global index publication. At the end of the 1990s the European Public Real Estate Association (EPRA) was born as an international trade association dedicated to maintaining standards and providing information for listed property funds, initially across Europe but subsequently further afield. EPRA started publishing European real estate indices soon thereafter and very quickly formed an alliance with the US National Association of Real Estate Investment Trusts for the purpose of publishing a global index. In February 2005 this initiative was taken over for computation purposes by FTSE. Since then the FTSE, EPRA and NAREIT global index has undoubtedly become the international standard for reporting the global share price returns to listed real estate funds of one sort or another.

Against this backcloth of initiatives elsewhere, it is reasonable to ask 'why bother?' to produce direct real estate indices when global reporting appears to be cost effectively possible by drawing upon the returns reported to real estate companies on most of the world's major stock exchanges. This top-down approach has the joint merits, not just of ease of data capture, but also of frequency of reporting. The approach is reasonably described as top down in that the aggregated results encompass the bottom line equity returns for the largest corporations who share a specialism in the development and management of real estate assets. It is thus many financial layers removed from the returns to the individual assets that these companies hold.

IPD's main mission over the past 20 years has been to assemble and maintain consistent and comprehensive financial and descriptive records of the real estate assets themselves, which are held in property companies and other investment funds across the mature investment markets of the world. This has enabled us to report the true underlying property returns on a fair and strictly comparable basis, stripping away the financial overlays which combine to varying, but often very significant, extents to impact upon the share price returns of listed companies.

Perhaps the most important reason however for focusing upon the underlying real estate assets – despite the labour intensity of this task – is that this is the only way of revealing on a transparent and strictly comparable basis the returns that the asset class of real estate is actually delivering. It is not just that the financial overlays of tax, fees, debt and cash may and often do distort and/or exaggerate the performance of the underlying real estate. The perennial problem with indices which simply report the share price returns of listed property companies, is that they, at least in the short term, much more commonly reflect the sentiment in their trading environment rather than the performance of the assets themselves. Thus, when a dot.com bubble bursts, it really does not matter whether the listed company is investing in real estate or selling groceries, the share price in both cases will come tumbling down along with the market in which those shares are traded.

IPD's bottom-up approach has the merit not just of stripping away both the financial overlays and the impact of stock exchange sentiment, but also that of extending the net to a far wider range of investment interests in real estate. In all national markets, listed property companies and real estate investment trusts are included (where present), but the assets held in less liquid and less accessible funds are every bit as much part of the underlying real estate investment market. So the segregated accounts of pension funds and insurance company life funds are included along with both the listed and increasingly important unlisted pooled funds now available to end investors in most markets. These include property unit trusts in the UK, 'SCPIs' and now 'OPCIs' in France, and the extremely important open-ended funds in Germany.

Indeed the starting point for a definition of the universe of real estate investments from which a global index may be drawn focuses primarily upon the nature of the financial interest in the asset itself. So long as this asset is held for investment purposes and is either let to a tenant under a lease, or targeted for such use, then it is in principle eligible for inclusion in any of IPD's national market and cross-border indices. In practice, the universe definition has to be circumscribed further, largely because of the very long tails of private investment interests in all markets which are very unlikely to yield the information streams required for investment return indices. The rules of inclusion therefore remain essentially bottom up, but focus upon those assets which are structured into portfolios which are themselves professionally managed and thus capable of yielding the information streams required for the purpose.

Rolling out national market indices

IPD has been focussing upon the bottom-up construction of national market indices since the project was initiated in the UK in the mid 1980s.

The exercise has been directed towards the dual purposes of establishing asset class return measures which are strictly comparable in their construction and computation, with those for the other directly held asset classes of equities and bonds, whilst at the same time enabling precise comparability within the real estate sector across national markets. This has meant identifying and tracking each of the individual assets held in real estate portfolios of the sorts enumerated above, and applying very strict rules to the definition of the various financial elements that combine to generate those asset returns. This rule book has been built and continuously refined over the past 20 years and now forms the basis of a single data process and database from which all of the IPD Indices are derived.

Table 7.1 lists each of the markets in which such indices are currently being produced (in some cases still on a consultation basis and in other cases – Finland and the USA – from non-IPD sources), and some of the key parameters of those market indices which affect their credibility within national markets and the way in which they have to be combined in cross-border indices. IPD has always strived to achieve as close to universe

Table 7.1 Databank profiles and estimated market sizes – end-2007.

	Number of funds	IPD databank number of properties	IPD databank capital value (€bn)	IPD databank capital value ($bn)	Total market size estimate (€bn)	Total market size estimate ($bn)	IPD coverage, end-2007 (%)
Austria	18	932	8.2	12.0	17.7	25.8	46
Belgium	24	292	6.0	8.8	37.0	53.9	16
Denmark	21	1036	13.6	19.8	28.3	41.2	48
Finland (KTI)	35	2697	19.1	27.8	28.8	42.0	66
France	57	6929	108.3	158.0	203.3	296.6	53
Germany	51	3901	44.5	64.9	277.6	405.0	16
Ireland	12	324	5.9	8.6	7.6	11.1	78
Italy	45	1225	17.0	24.8	65.2	95.1	26
The Netherlands	43	5020	44.9	65.5	86.4	126.0	52
New Zealand	12	316	3.7	5.3	10.3	15.1	35
Norway	14	542	14.2	20.7	32.1	46.8	44
Portugal	26	671	9.2	13.4	13.8	20.1	67
South Africa	21	2183	13.4	19.6	20.1	29.3	67
Spain	24	553	16.5	24.1	34.3	50.1	48
Sweden	15	1113	24.6	35.9	84.4	123.1	29
Switzerland	27	3466	30.3	44.2	97.2	141.7	31
UK	287	12 234	250.2	364.7	411.3	599.9	61
Australia	20	751	56.0	81.7	171.6	250.3	33
Canada	29	2266	60.3	88.0	113.5	165.6	53
Japan	42	897	33.3	48.5	201.2	293.5	17
Korea	9	89	3.7	5.4	14.8	21.5	25
USA (NCREIF)	–	5711	212.0	309.3	1287.2	1877.9	16
All IPD Eurozone	335	22 544	279.6	408.0	771.7	1125.8	36
All IPD Europe	699	40 935	612.4	893.3	1424.8	2078.6	43
IPD Global	832	53 148	994.9	1451.2	3243.5	4731.7	31

coverage as is possible in each national market, but this clearly remains a theoretically impossible task, and the table indicates the variation in coverage ratios achieved. In the next section we will discuss how those coverage ratios are computed and their importance for the purpose of constructing pan-European or global indices. For the moment it is sufficient just to note the variation and thus the varying levels of caution which should be attached to the utilisation of national market index results. We should be far more confident of returns reported in Ireland or the Netherlands than those for instance published for Japan or Germany.

In order to progress beyond return reporting market by market, it is clearly essential that the data should be consistently defined in each national market so that aggregation is both transparent and seamless. It is also necessary that data meets the requirements for return computation on a standardised basis. The standards for asset class return computation are typically set outside the real estate arena. Ever since April 1999 a Global Investment Performance Standard (GIPS) has existed which defines the way in which returns shall be computed and reported by investment managers if they wish to conform to that standard. It was not until March 2006 that the second edition of that standard was published and the standard now explicitly extends to the more specialist asset classes of real estate and venture capital.

The standards require a consistent time-weighted basis for return computation. In fact IPD, in advance of the publication of the new GIPS yardsticks, shifted the return computation for all of its national services to a single monthly time-weighted basis by January of 2005. A monthly regime was chosen not because it is mandated by the standard (although for all other asset classes no less than a monthly refreshment frequency is acceptable), but also because there are already property services in some national markets which require this frequency of reporting. Ever since the late 1980s a monthly index has been published in the UK, encompassing something in the region of 25% of the investment universe which attracts a full monthly revaluation. More recently a monthly indicator service has been launched in Japan to capitalise on the monthly rolling pattern of information flows in that market.

The project to roll out consistent and high-standard indices across all mature national markets continues to progress. The Austrian index was launched for the first time in the autumn of 2006, and a Belgian consultation release was added to the European mix in 2007. Currently we are also progressing index development systematically across the Central and Eastern European region, with a view to carving out component national indices as viability is demonstrated.

Elsewhere our work in Japan progresses on both annual and monthly timeframes, and a consultation release has now been published in Korea. Meanwhile exploratory studies are looking at least at the possibility of work in both Singapore and Hong Kong. Finally, we have now completed our takeover of both the Australian and the New Zealand Indices from their respective Property Councils.

The first IPD multi-market index – the pan-European

It was not until 2004 that IPD embarked upon the major project of attempting to combine the market returns reported in each of these national indices by compiling and publishing a fully consistent cross-border index for the mature Western European property markets. A consultation version of our first pan-European index was released in July 2004, and full pan-European Indices have been produced and reported in each of the last 4 years.

The challenges were twofold: to design and implement a method for accurately rebalancing the varying levels of IPD's national market coverage so that the resulting composite index fairly reflected the component real estate markets, neither under- nor overstating the contribution of any one constituent; and to report this market rebalanced composite in all major investor currencies and in sufficient detail to permit the full exploitation of the product.

The importance of rebalancing the markets which are to be included in the index has already been alluded to above. Whilst IPD's overall strategy of maximising coverage in each international market and taking care not to publish national market data based upon samples which are too thin has been fine as a guiding principle for establishing the authority of those indices, it is clearly an inadequate basis upon which to start combining these markets. The levels of coverage detailed in Table 7.1 vary significantly even within Europe – between just under 20% in Belgium and Germany to between 60% and 80% in Finland, the Netherlands and Ireland. Simply to combine the asset level data available to us in each of the 14 markets identified without any attempt at rebalancing would thus seriously overstate the importance of the latter three investment markets and understate the importance of the former two.

For this reason, market rebalancing becomes an essential part of the index compilation process. It is thus incumbent upon us to develop robust market size estimates and the requisite market definitions as well as developing a clear methodology for aggregating and rebalancing the included national markets.

The definitional questions have fairly clear and probably unarguable answers, given the approach to direct property market measurements through the development of national indices outlined above. There is no question of attempting to identify the total investible market including assets which are currently owner-occupied, nor would it be feasible to attempt to capture those long tails of very small private interest in real estate which are all technically parts of each national investment market. The market size we are, therefore, aiming to capture is that of assets already held in professionally managed investment portfolios, some of which are not (yet) included in IPD Indices. These ratio estimates are kept constantly under review and have been adjusted (albeit marginally) in each of the last 3 years of this project. There is no definitive source in any national market for the total size of its real estate investment component and so this *ad-hoc*, bottom-up approach – using a multitude of different sources – is the only one source available to us, and its opportunism means that as new information emerges so ratios have to be adjusted on an annual basis.

Figure 7.1 indicates the impacts of applying these ratios – as of December 2007 – to the raw IPD index size figures drawn directly from each national service.

The tabulated coverage ratios demonstrate the importance of the exercise because they show how seriously the German market would be understated without adjustment and how some other markets, including the Netherlands and Ireland, would be accorded a disproportionately large contribution to the pan-European composite. Western Europe is however a relatively mature and homogeneous market and so there are no huge adjustments required on the basis of very radically varying percentage coverage ratios.

It should be noted that whilst the rebalancing is a relatively straightforward arithmetic exercise, it does involve currency conversion as at each calendar year end so that the various national indices, produced and calculated in various local currencies, can be properly rebalanced using a consistent numeraire. Since this is a spot year-end exercise it does not impact upon the investor

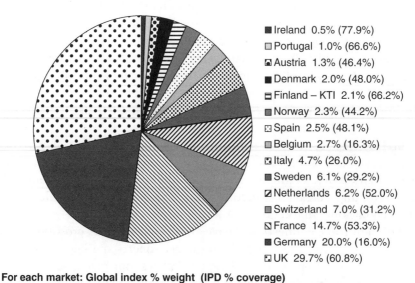

- Ireland 0.5% (77.9%)
- Portugal 1.0% (66.6%)
- Austria 1.3% (46.4%)
- Denmark 2.0% (48.0%)
- Finland – KTI 2.1% (66.2%)
- Norway 2.3% (44.2%)
- Spain 2.5% (48.1%)
- Belgium 2.7% (16.3%)
- Italy 4.7% (26.0%)
- Sweden 6.1% (29.2%)
- Netherlands 6.2% (52.0%)
- Switzerland 7.0% (31.2%)
- France 14.7% (53.3%)
- Germany 20.0% (16.0%)
- UK 29.7% (60.8%)

For each market: Global index % weight (IPD % coverage)

Figure 7.1 IPD and partner databases re-weighted to European market coverage: December 2007.

currency performance series, whose calculation involves month-on-month cross-rate adjustments to the locally based performance series.

Introducing this monthly currency adjustment has been the second major challenge of the pan-European and global index projects, as noted above. It was decided at an early stage that, as with all pan-European and Global Indices for other asset classes, the outputs would only have widespread general utility if they were reported not only in local currencies but also in end investor currencies. For the pan-European exercise it was decided that the main publication should report performance not just in Euros but also in Pounds Sterling, Yen and US Dollars – these currency choices reflecting the importance of the USA, Japanese and UK/Eurozone markets as capital sources in current economic circumstances.

Thus, once the money values of the monthly components of total return – the start and end month capital valuations, capital expenditure and income receivable – have been derived for each national market and these single market aggregates have then been rebalanced to reflect the different coverage ratios in IPD national indices, then these re-weighted monthly totals are systematically converted into common end investor currencies as at each month end. Currency conversion has an impact on local market returns as recorded changes in values and cash flows from 1 month to the next are partly the result of underlying local property market and asset movements, and partly due to fluctuations in currency cross-rates.

Figure 7.2 indicates plainly how important these relative currency movements can be. The pan-European index runs from December 2000 to December 2007 and the chart indicates not only the Dollar-, Yen-, Sterling- and Euro-based end investor returns, but also the local currency returns (i.e. market rebalanced returns combined to take no account of month-on-month currency movements). Whilst the latter are in a sense hypothetical, since they assume that a cross-border portfolio is fully hedged against currency risk outside the structure of the investment vehicle itself (and so that vehicle bears none of the costs nor risks associated with the end investor currency conversion), nonetheless it can be an interesting benchmark against which to compare single currency end investor returns. This 'local currency' composite, as the chart demonstrates, produced around a 7% p.a. return for the first 3 years of the 7-year period, and thereafter accelerated modestly up to peak at 12.4% by the end of 2006 before dropping back to its lowest recorded level in 2007.

In contrast the US Dollar returns have shown a very different path over that same period. The weakness of the Dollar in the calendar years 2002–2004 had as its silver lining a hugely beneficial impact upon European property market returns taken in the USA – delivering between 18% and 24% per annum in each of those years. In 2005 the Dollar, at least for a short period, strengthened relative to a basket of European currencies, and this had the serious negative impact upon returns that the

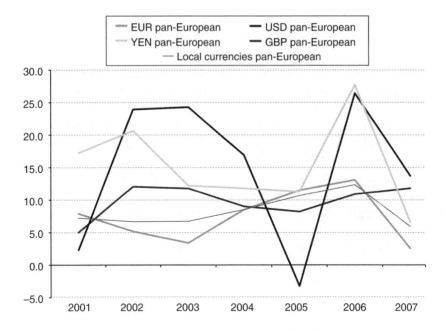

Figure 7.2   Pan-European total returns in investor currencies, % p.a., 2001–2007.

chart demonstrates, resulting in a 3% negative return for the full calendar year. European real estate returns taken in Sterling demonstrated a sort of 'mid-Atlantic' position, tracking but significantly diluting the Dollar trend, whilst crossing and loosely tracking throughout the period the path of the Euro denominated property returns.

...and finally the world – IPD's first global index

Most of the rules and procedures designed for the pan-European index were applicable to the Global project. The major new challenge was that of integrating an index for the largest single component national market – the United States – within a compilation and computation framework designed around the IPD standard. Whilst one partner index has been used now for 5 years in the European project – that of the Finnish market produced and published by KTI – that index has for the whole of the relevant period used an identical time-weighted method to IPD's, and IPD has been accorded asset level data access for re-computing and re-aggregating Finnish results (Figure 7.3).

Between the initial global index consultation in 2006 and the eventual publication in June 2008 of the first full index, a further three markets were added – Belgium, Korea and New Zealand. The above chart is included here not in an attempt to clearly differentiate the return paths of

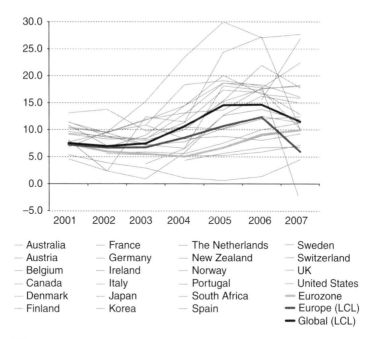

— Australia	— France	— The Netherlands	— Sweden
— Austria	— Germany	— New Zealand	— Switzerland
— Belgium	— Ireland	— Norway	— UK
— Canada	— Italy	— Portugal	— United States
— Denmark	— Japan	— South Africa	— Eurozone
— Finland	— Korea	— Spain	— Europe (LCL)
			— Global (LCL)

Figure 7.3   IPD, partner and composite index returns, % p.a., 2000–2007.

all 22 separate national markets over the last 7 years. The point is rather to demonstrate the scale of the challenge in combining the 15 European markets already included in our pan-European exercise, with the remaining seven relevant and (partially) available non-European indices for the purpose of supporting a global index.

Whilst some of the decisions on the boundaries of the pan-European index may have been questionable, there were fairly obvious and unavoidable reasons for restricting that product to the mature, Western European markets capable of producing the required level of property market information. For a global index these questions become far more challenging.

One strategy would certainly have been to take just the major European markets – maybe the UK, France and Germany – and aggregate those with some of the major economies outside Europe – the USA, Russia, Japan and perhaps even China. Since at least two of these economies, however large, remain immature as investment markets and thus incapable of providing the requisite data, such a strategy was clearly not viable.

In the end the European index design policy was rolled out on a global scale, without there being much scope for choice and selection. In other words, an attempt was made to identify all of the mature investment markets worldwide and to combine them into a single index. Real estate market maturity – by which we mean the relatively transparent organisation of investment interests into professional managed portfolios – is only very weakly correlated with the size of the host economy. China and Russia are undoubtedly large economies but have only very recently attracted portfolio-based interest in their real estate investments. For some years to come therefore it is almost certain that they will be excluded from the IPD global index.

The final market selection indicated in Table 7.1 in this chapter represents the only realistic list of indices which may be included in such a project, and this list is determined as much by indigenous investment market maturity as it is by market size. Thus no small European or non-European markets have been excluded simply on the basis of their size. So long as reasonable percentage coverage of each of these markets has been achieved then they are included in the ultimate composite though obviously with a very small impact on its bottom line.

Even given this limitation upon index design, Figure 7.4 demonstrates clearly how much more significance there is in the market rebalancing at a global as opposed to European scale. The market coverage ratios which were employed for the pan-European index, with just two exceptions were all well over 25%. The range is stretched painfully farther at the bottom end when it comes to rebalancing the global index. This is because several of the key markets included – specifically Germany, Japan and the USA – are markets in which the industry standard indices represent significantly smaller coverage ratios.

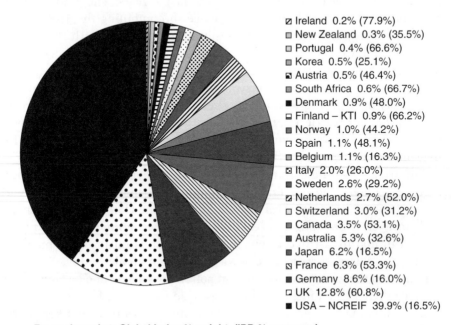

Ireland 0.2% (77.9%)
New Zealand 0.3% (35.5%)
Portugal 0.4% (66.6%)
Korea 0.5% (25.1%)
Austria 0.5% (46.4%)
South Africa 0.6% (66.7%)
Denmark 0.9% (48.0%)
Finland – KTI 0.9% (66.2%)
Norway 1.0% (44.2%)
Spain 1.1% (48.1%)
Belgium 1.1% (16.3%)
Italy 2.0% (26.0%)
Sweden 2.6% (29.2%)
Netherlands 2.7% (52.0%)
Switzerland 3.0% (31.2%)
Canada 3.5% (53.1%)
Australia 5.3% (32.6%)
Japan 6.2% (16.5%)
France 6.3% (53.3%)
Germany 8.6% (16.0%)
UK 12.8% (60.8%)
USA – NCREIF 39.9% (16.5%)

For each market: Global index % weight (IPD % coverage)

Figure 7.4 IPD and partner databases re-weighted to global market coverage: December 2007.

The IPD Japanese index is still proving difficult to compile in a timely and authoritative manner. This largely reflects the fact that the usable investment market data drawn from JREITs and other semi-transparent portfolio structures still represent no more than 16.5% of the total estimated market size. The rolling valuation regime also injects very significant delays in information assembly. However historical tests have demonstrated that mid-June estimates, drawn exclusively from JREIT data, have proved sufficiently robust at the all property and main sector levels.

Though the NCREIF index of the direct real estate market performance in the USA is much larger and has a far longer track record than the IPD index in Japan, the market coverage ratio – given the huge size of the US market – is no greater, at only just over 16% of the professionally managed portfolio structured US real estate investment market. It suffers also from a restriction to unlisted tax-exempt property funds.

Overall, the European markets are relatively well and homogeneously covered compared with those outside Europe, with the important exception of Germany – as noted above – for which we also achieved no better than 16% cover in 2007. As a result, the application of necessarily large adjustment ratios for both Japan and the USA has huge impacts in determining the shape of the global index. The US weighting factor takes the raw NCREIF contribution of just over 20% up to almost 40% after rebalancing. Inevitably there is a mirror image impact upon the combined European contributions, taking it down from an unadjusted fraction of over 50% to an adjusted contribution of well below 40%.

The totality of the global market covered – after all grossing up adjustments – is just short of €3.25 trillion as at the end of 2007. This reflects huge contributions, each in the region of just over €1.2 trillion from the USA and European markets and significantly smaller contributions from Japan/Korea, Australia/New Zealand, Canada and South Africa.

Before these rebalanced contributions to the global index can be reported as an internally consistent composite performance series in end investor currencies, a further challenge (noted above) is that of integrating the US NCREIF index where the national computation methodology differs in subtle but important detail from that applied by IPD in all other markets. This issue was partially addressed in the case of the Finnish market within the pan-European index, but with the benefit of a long and well-established collaboration arrangement, IPD was able to produce a Finnish contribution to both that and the global index from raw asset level data processed through an identical monthly time-weighted methodology.

NCREIF nonetheless participated whole-heartedly in support of this project and within the limits of the confidentiality agreements made with their contributors provided us with all the necessary aggregated data components, quarter by quarter, over the relevant 7-year period. The quarterly

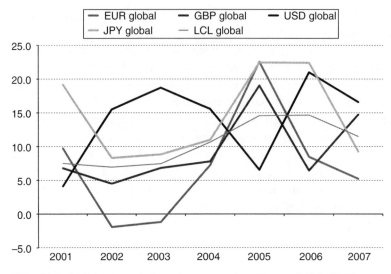

Figure 7.5   Global total returns in investor currencies, % p.a., 2001–2007.

data structure reflects the adopted time-weighted calculation and reporting period in the USA. At IPD we developed systems to interpolate these inputs into a monthly data structure for the purpose of strictly comparable re-aggregation into the global index. One of our future aims is to see if we cannot improve upon this reconciliation methodology – perhaps by using masked asset level data – and thus upgrade the approach to integrating the all important US data within the IPD global index project.

Though there is undoubtedly scope for improvement in this and many other ways in taking the project forward – it is still very much a development product – the bottom line results are nonetheless fascinating. Figure 7.5 shows the 7-year performance of this 22 market global composite in each of the end investor currencies reported for the pan-European index (Euros, Dollars, Yen and Sterling) and for comparability and completeness reports a local currency total return series because of the continued interest in this as a baseline measure (Figure 7.6).

Some of these results reflect the currency impacts already noted with regard to the pan-European index, for instance, the relatively high rate of global investment success delivered to US investors by the weakness of the Dollar in all years apart from 2001 and 2005. The inclusion of the USA as the world's largest investment market (40% of the total), however, generates some very interesting market dynamic features to the results when the canvas is stretched to this global scale.

Perhaps the most interesting of these is the way in which all but Dollar-based investors saw very significant acceleration in their performance in 2005, due to a coincidence of both property market and currency impacts.

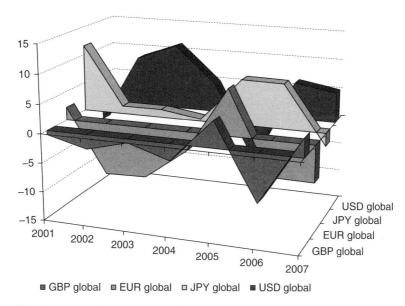

Figure 7.6 Impacts of cross-rate shifts on local currency returns (horizontal zero line).

The short-term weakening of the Euro, Sterling and Japanese Yen relative to the Dollar over that period gave an initial exchange rate boost to investment returns. However, the most important factor was that these returns were being driven by very strong and more or less perfectly synchronised performance acceleration from the two largest markets – the USA and the UK – in the index. Thus end investors were receiving the returns from a strong global economy dominated by two very strong and very large property investment markets mediated through a benign phase of currency realignment.

This all fell apart over the next 2 years, as first the Dollar and then Sterling faded against the Euro, and to confuse investors even further, the USA/UK 'dream team' fell apart with the collapse of the 3-year UK property market boom into seriously negative territory in 2007.

As this project progresses over the next couple of years, so we hope to introduce refinements to both our input data and methodology. This will mean that the fascinating results revealed in this first full publication can be built upon with confidence, rendered robust in terms of their data and methodological infrastructure, and turned into a central and definitive feature of the transparency of the world's property investment markets for many years to come.

8

Property Derivatives: The Story So Far

Gary McNamara

Introduction

This chapter takes us through the history of the UK property derivatives market and to where the market is up to Q1 2008. This journey includes the rise and fall of the London Futures and Options Exchange (FOX) and the sporadic activity in property income certificates (PICs), and takes a look at where the traded commercial and residential property swap market is today both in the UK and globally.

Growth in the property derivatives market can be attributed to a number of factors including increased education, pricing history and established trading operations. These factors have brought the market to a stage where derivative pricing is used as a guide in the marketplace and also forming part of the finance curriculum. The volume of trading has continued to grow each year since 2005 and is forecast to continue doing so.

Since 2005 and the first major year of trading we have seen the peak of the UK commercial property market and rapid correction which was somewhat advanced by the credit crunch that is currently being experienced in 2008.

The history and innovation behind the property derivatives market

As the property derivatives market grows each year, the number of funds and institutions organising new mandates that enable them to consider property derivatives as part of their investment strategy both in the UK and in Europe is increasing. More recently, real estate capital markets have seen a surge in a range of new structured products offering alternative conduits of managing property market exposure with the property derivatives market being the underlying driver.

The main types of property derivative instruments currently available in the market are total return swaps (TRSs), structured products and secondary trading of both of them. Some background of each in the order they have evolved to the current over the counter (OTC) market is given below.

FOX exchange

In May 1991, FOX launched four index-based futures contracts in an attempt to launch the first property derivatives market in the UK. The aim of FOX was to develop UK hedging, arbitrage and price discovery facilities in the commercial and residential markets. Trading in the FOX contracts was withdrawn in October 1991 due to insufficient liquidity, which led to an uneconomically viable trading volume. There were also allegations of false trading which created the impression of higher activity in the market.

Whilst the concept of property derivatives was an effective method of portfolio management, the markets' experience of the FOX exchange cast a shadow over its use. Following the downfall of FOX, the market ceased trading for a number of years until the evolution of PICs.

Property income certificates

PICs are structured as Eurobonds, listed on an exchange with coupon payments linked to the Investment Property Databank (IPD) index. PICs are a specific structured product in which the returns of PICs are split into two components, namely, an income return (the all property income return) and a capital return (the all property capital return).

The income return is linked to the IPD all property income return and is paid each year for the certificate. The capital return is linked to the IPD all property capital return and is paid upon expiry of the certificate.

BZW (now Barclays Capital) arranged the first PIC issue in 1994. Following this, further issues were made in 1995, 1996, 1999, 2005 and 2006. The latest issue in 2006 was for £90 million of 4 1/2-year PICs targeted at private banking and wealth management clients. There are currently over £600m of Barclays PICS in issue with expiries up to 2011.

Barclays Capital also issued property index forwards (PIFs) between 1996 and 1998 in a number of private placements. PIFs are structured in a similar way to 'a contract for difference' with returns linked to the IPD all property index.

With Barclays PICs being listed on an exchange, they have the ability to be sold or traded in the market.

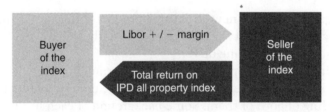

Figure 8.1   Initial TRS process.

Figure 8.2   Current TRS process.

Total return swaps: Libor and spread

A TRS is a contract between a buyer of total return on the IPD index and an IPD total return seller. Initially TRSs were structured where the total return seller pays the total return of the IPD index and receives a floating rate payment from the total return buyer. This floating payment was priced as Libor plus or minus a margin that a party would pay in order to receive IPD total return.

Figure 8.1 shows the initial TRS process.

As of 15 January 2008 TRSs are priced as a fixed percentage return in order to receive IPD total return. The Libor rate or margin is now accounted for in the market prices that are quoted.

Figure 8.2 shows the current TRS process.

Structured products

As the market has evolved, a number of products (Barclays as discussed below) have been introduced which provide alternative methods of gaining synthetic property market exposure. Structured products are used to repackage swaps into recognisable fixed-income instruments for institutional investors or for private placements. They are fully funded upfront and they take many different forms and cover a range of income return and capital return profiles in order to suit many different types of investors.

The primary advantage of these is that they can be tailored to suit the end-user investment strategy as they can be structured to provide capital or income protection, gearing or pan-European. Such a structure would work in the manner shown in Figure 8.3.

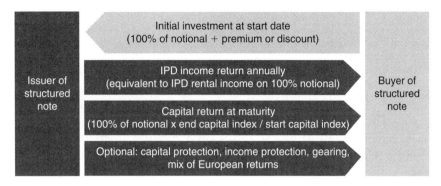

Figure 8.3 Operation of structured products.

The drivers for change

There are a number of reasons why the property derivatives market has been slow to develop. These have been analysed and addressed by market leaders in the field. Many critics now believe that the property derivatives market is here to stay.

Professor Paul McNamara, OBE of Prudential, is one of the main instigators in driving the property derivatives market. Professor McNamara has stated four main factors which have hindered the development of property derivatives in the past. These are as follows:[1]

1 admissibility issues for life funds;
2 taxation uncertainties;
3 timing in the market;
4 education.

These issues have now mostly been resolved. Admissibility issues for life funds were tackled in November 2002, following a paper to the FSA and extensive discussions, which were led by the Property Derivatives User Group (PUDG now called PDIG). These discussions gave rise to a letter from the Financial Services Authority (FSA) in November 2002 that appeared to approve simple derivatives based on IPD indices as an admissible asset for life funds in solvency ratio calculations. The FSA stated that life funds must be content that admissibility guidelines have been met.

Following this the FSA released a consultation paper (CP185) in May 2003, that set out proposed changes to the rules contained in the Collective Investment Schemes sourcebook (COLL). In March 2004 the FSA released a policy statement (PS04/07) that contained the new COLL sourcebook for UK authorised and collective funds. This stated that derivatives based on property indices are permissible assets thus providing far greater flexibility in the creation of property-related investment vehicles.

The taxation uncertainties were eased following the pre-budget announcement by the Chancellor of the Exchequer in December 2003, which stated that equity and real estate derivatives were the subject of a simplified taxation regime to encourage the development of a UK market. This was followed by the 2004 Finance Act, which allowed investors to offset capital gains and losses on derivative products against direct property. Any losses made on property derivatives can be carried back for a maximum of 2 years.

It seems that the timing has never been more fortuitous for a property derivatives market to develop. The recent appetite for property market exposure has put heavy upward pressure on capital values and has driven initial yields to historic lows. As a result the UK market has peaked and is at a stage where property returns are falling. This has stimulated property investors into investigating other potential modes for managing property exposure such as property derivatives.

Education of property investors has been critical to the development of the property derivatives market. At the start of 2006, relatively few property specialists had a full appreciation of property swaps and even fewer had mandates to use them. The increase in awareness has mostly been achieved by the promotion of the derivatives market by the IPF, PDIG, brokers and banks. This has sparked a growing interest from the media, which has helped improve information transparency and build confidence in the market. There is also a new range of conferences and initiatives to help end-users gain the necessary experience of how to use derivatives.

User groups
As discussed above, the legislative changes introduced have reduced yet another barrier to the use of property derivatives. The growing interest and knowledge in the market place is the result of the hard work of a number of people. Such people include Paul McNamara, Ian Reid, Ian Cullen and Ed Stacey amongst a number of others. Awareness of the market was aided by the formation of the Property Derivatives Users Association (PDUA), led by Paul McNamara in 2000. This led to a further push in terms of time and research spent on property derivatives. In September 2005 the PDUA evolved into the Property Derivatives Interest Group (PDIG) and became a special interest group within the Investment Property Forum (IPF). The stated aim of the PDIG is to improve awareness of the market and encourage best practice. The PDIG offers industry support by providing training, a point of contact, news- and information-relating property derivatives. In new markets industry groups are very important as sources of professional awareness, education and development.

The PDIG is helping to provide the market with transparency and liquidity, as these are the main areas which need to be developed further to open up the market. To address liquidity the market requires more property end-users to enter the market and follow the lead of the investment banks. The quarterly trading volume released by IPD provides transparency with respect to the volume of trading in the market.

Hermes trading forum

From October 2005 to May 2006, Hermes Real Estate Investment Management set up a property derivatives trading forum under the auspices of the IPF that gave potential participants in the market an opportunity to trade on a virtual basis upon paying the registration fee. The forum met four times and each session conducted over £7 billion of business by the 60 teams of investment bankers, fund managers, swaps traders and property company executives. The forum gave potential property derivative users a practical insight into how to trade property derivatives and the opportunity to debate on how to establish prices for specific trades.

PDIG quarterly breakfast meeting

Following the Hermes Trading Forum the property derivatives market now meets in various locations on a quarterly basis organised by the IPF PDIG committee. At this meeting the most recent market trading volumes are released by IPD and a discussion with market participants is held.

IPD index background

The UK swap market is underpinned by the IPD index. IPD has UK commercial property return records from 1971. The robustness of the underlying index is a key for parties entering into derivative contracts. For commercial property derivatives the benchmark used in the UK is the IPD Annual Index, which covers over 12 000 directly-held UK property investments. The portfolio was revalued in December 2007 at over £184 billion. It is estimated that this coverage represents over 45% of the total combined value of the property assets held by UK institutions, trusts, partnerships and listed property companies. This is just under 50% of the total professionally managed UK property investment market. IPD produces a monthly estimate of the annual index which is used as a guide to the current performance to date during the year along with a quarterly index.

Banks

At present there are 22 banks with licenses to trade property derivatives on the IPD index and these are shown in Table 8.1. This activity by investment banks in creating two-way pricing over a range of maturities has proven a key role and has paved the way in moving the market forward. It has helped the

Table 8.1   Banks with licenses to trade property derivatives on the IPD index.

Abbey National	Deutsche	Merrill Lynch
ABN AMRO	EuroHypo	Morgan Stanley
Bank of America	Goldman Sachs	National Bank of Canada
Barclays Capital	HSBC	Royal Bank of Scotland
BNP Paribas	HSH Nordbank	Toronto Dominion
Calyon	Hypo Vereinsbank	UBS
Commerzbank AG	JP Morgan	
CSFB	Lehman Brothers	

Source: IPD to 28/02/08.

creation of an all property curve that shows actual buying and selling interests across different maturities from 1 to 10 years. This has led to the IPD annual all property index being the core index for the main bulk of trading.

The creation of the sector curve that includes Offices, Retail and Industry is gradually being developed. As providers of liquidity, credit enhancers and possible speculators, banks are vital players in helping to expand liquidity but property end-users are required to enhance this. As well as using the IPD annual index, banks are also willing to price and use the IPD quarterly index to execute trades and also other national indices. Having the banks interested in the middle does mean there is no need to match a trade, and this adds to liquidity of the market.

As will be discussed below a number of the banks' names mentioned earlier also have licenses to use the FTSEpx index run by MSS.

Brokers
Brokers have been instrumental in helping the market to develop. This was initiated in the mid-2005 with derivative brokers linking up with property advisors including CBRE & GFI and DTZ & Tullett Prebon. They have played a particularly important role in terms of educating real estate end-users about derivatives and also improving the banks' understanding of real estate. By providing daily market prices brokers give the market confidence in terms of liquidity. An indication of such prices can be seen on various pricing screens including Bloomberg, Reuters and www.propex.co.uk.

Brokers provide a platform for best pricing in the market where marking to market is necessary and a location where market participants and banks can go to get best available independent pricing. Brokers also help documentation management, trade execution and post-trade confirmations. Their role will become increasingly important as the number of market participants grows.

The brokerage charged varies per transaction and is considerably less than the usual 1% for physical property. The *'IPF Pricing Property Derivatives: An Initial Review'* suggests that initially typical brokerage fees may be 10–20 bps depending on maturity although this is likely to reduce over time.

Pricing and underlying index activity

Property derivatives are priced as a fixed percentage total return. This percentage total return is the price which a counterparty is willing to buy or sell future property total return risk at today. The derivatives curve can be then used to imply where IPD property total return risk is being priced in the future. It is not an exact forecast but it shows where future property total return risk is priced today taking account of everyday economic indicators and sentiment.

If the market price for a Dec07–Dec08 contract is −11% and your expectation for 2008 IPD total return is −7%, then you should buy the contract. Alternatively if you expected IPD total return to be −15%, then you should sell the contract.

With the current low pricing being experienced in 2008, it is possible for property investors to guarantee out performance of the IPD index using a property swap.

Figure 8.4 shows historical pricing of different contracts and how they have moved over time. Of particular note is the drop off in the expected future total return from July 2007 pre and post the start of the credit crunch.

Figure 8.4 shows the mid market price per annum over the life of the contract. So a Dec09 contract price will have the Dec08 performance priced in to it as a Dec10 contract would have Dec08 and Dec09 performance priced in to it.

Figure 8.5 shows how short-term total return expectation has fallen with slight recovery into 2009 and 2010. In particular the Dec08 contract price movement has been immediately affected by major banking issues including Societe Generales losses and the collapse of Bear Sterns.

Figure 8.5 shows the current market priscing of the UK IPD all property curve as at 1 April 2008 and the implied total return.

From this figure the high total returns from the UK IPD all property from 2004 to 2006 is to be noted along with the large drop in total return in 2007. The performance on this figure is the implied total return from the property derivatives market. This shows a further fall in 2008 total return to approximately −11.5% for 2008 with slight recovery into 2009.

Underlying indices and UK trading activity to Q1 2008

Further to the development of IPD swaps in 2005, the years 2006 and 2007 saw the introduction of a number of new indices, trackers and structured products in order to manage property market exposure without buying or selling the physical product.

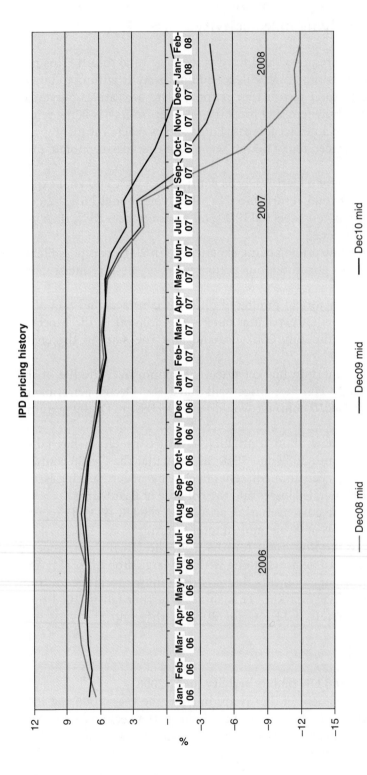

Figure 8.4 IPD pricing history. *Source*: IPD and Tullett Prebon.

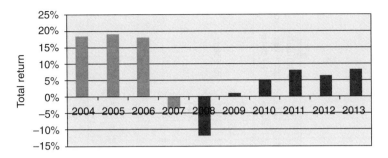

Figure 8.5   Current market pricing of the UK IPD all property curve.

At the time of writing this chapter, trading has been recorded only until Q1 2008. Trading has occurred in waves throughout the year with more trading being carried out in Q1 or close to the release date of the relevant index number. Also more trading is noted when estimates of the index or other influential research publications are released. To date, the main bulk of trading has been through the major investment banks with a number of them disclosing transaction volumes over £600m in both commercial and residential markets. From a property end-user point of view, Morley Fund Management stated that they have traded around £500m up to June 2007 and expected to trade a similar amount to the year end.[2]

In the UK, the IPD all property TRSs are mostly liquid and prices are available in contracts ending from December 2007 to December 2016. This means that there is a price that shows the levels at which counterparties are willing to receive or pay for the IPD all property total return.

Table 8.2 shows the trading activity on the UK IPD commercial property index up to Q1 2008.

This table shows a noticeable increase in Q1 trading in each year. Also to note is the large quarterly variance in the outstanding average deal size executed each quarter (£m).

The market has evolved with initial trading occurring on the IPD all property index soon followed by the first sector trade on the all retail index in Q3 2005. This was then proceeded by further sector swaps including trades on the all office index. In August 2006 the first sub-sector trade was carried out on the IPD shopping centre index. This has paved the way in showing the market that such opportunities are available and possible to be done.

Quarter 1 2007 saw a large increase in trading volume due to various reasons. These reasons include the continued desire to manage property exposure, greater understanding of the subject, increased participants and also less uncertainty as to the performance until the end of year.

There is continued growth in the number of enquiries regarding the sub-sectors including City & West End offices and retail warehouses.

Table 8.2 Trading activity on the UK IPD commercial property index up to Q1 2008.

	Q1–Q4 2004	Q1 2005	Q2 2005	Q3 2005	Q4 2005	Q1 2006	Q2 2006	Q3 2006	Q4 2006	Q1 2007	Q2 2007	Q3 2007	Q4 2007	Q1 2008	Cumulative totals executed to date
Total outstanding notional (£m)	260	485	806	927	1100	1963	2466	4124	6686	6769	7266	7916	9032	9069	
Total notional of trades executed each quarter (£m)	260	225	321	121	183	853	513	1658	864	2927	970	1660	1662	3441	15 656
Total outstanding number of trades	10	14	42	56	80	139	189	279	415	428	473	543	703	750	
Total number of trades executed each quarter	10	4	28	14	24	59	54	90	87	153	90	96	214	257	1180
Average outstanding deal size (£m)	26	35	19	17	14	14	13	15	16	16	15	15	13	12	
Average deal size executed each quarter (£m)	26	56	11	9	8	15	10	18	10	19	11	17	8	13	

Source: IPD.

This interest is reflective of the sentiment in the underlying physical market. At this sub-sector level the market can then offer increased control over property market exposure. Although possible, sub-sector trading is not common as counterparties can be very difficult to find.

Parties have entered into swap transactions for various reasons, one of these reasons being the ability to lock in returns. Alternatively some property companies have used derivatives to get quick access to property-based returns or to reflect their view of the market. Investment banks have been taking a number of long and short positions in order to satisfy client interest, or alternatively to take further property risk onto their own books. IPD property derivatives provide the opportunity of a hedge for property portfolio owners and also offer the opportunity speculatively gain exposure to the market in order to reflect a view. They also enable a holder of property to re-weight their portfolio without selling the underlying asset by reducing exposure to the sector via an IPD derivative.

TRS trades in the UK to date have been structured on the following indices:

- IPD all property index;
- IPD all retail index;
- IPD all office;
- IPD all industrial;
- IPD Central London offices;
- IPD UK shopping centres.

European trading activity to Q1 2008
In Europe to date trades have been carried out in France, Germany, Switzerland and Italy.

In France, the French IPD all office TRS is mostly liquid and in Germany the IPD all property mostly traded.

Table 8.3 shows the trading activity on the French all office IPD index up to Q1 2008.

Table 8.4 shows the trading activity on the German all property IPD index up to Q1 2008.

Again note the larger Q1 volumes which in each year was following the path of capital looking to get into the market at this time.

Global event timeline
In December 2006 Merrill Lynch and AXA REIM carried out the first French property derivatives swap trade linked to the IPD France Offices annual index.

In January 2007 it was reported that Goldman Sachs had sold the first option on the IPD/DIX German all property index.

Table 8.3   Trading activity on the French All Office IPD index up to Q1 2008.

French IPD derivative volume	Q1 2007	Q2 2007	Q3 2007	Q4 2007	Q1 2008	Cumulative totals executed to date
Total outstanding notional (£m)	400	586	613	670	904	
Total notional of trades executed each quarter (£m)	400	186	108	93	116	904
Total outstanding number of trades	11	28	34	45	69	
Total number of trades executed each quarter	11	17	19	16	6	69
Average outstanding deal size (£m)	36	21	18	15	13	
Average deal size starting each quarter (£m)	36	11	6	6	19	

Table 8.4   Trading activity on the German All Property IPD index up to Q1 2008.

German IPD derivative volume	Q2 2007	Q3 2007	Q4 2007	Q1 2008	Cumulative totals executed to date
Total outstanding notional (£m)	181	260	273	391	
Total notional of trades executed each quarter (£m)	158	109	16	119	394
Total outstanding number of trades	21	35	38	61	
Total number of trades executed each quarter	20	20	4	20	64
Average outstanding deal size (£m)	9	7	7	6	
Average deal size starting each quarter (£m)	8	5	4	6	

In February 2007 Sun Hung Kai Financial and ABN AMRO jointly executed the market's first ever Asian property derivative-based trading, the University of Hong Kong's Hong Kong Island Residential Price Index (HKU-HRPI).

In May 2007 BNP Paribas structured a pan-European basket swap for a Scandinavian retail bank Den Norske. The medium-term payout profile reflected average returns on the UK IPD all property, French IPD all office and German IPD all property.

Also in May 2007 ABN AMRO carried out the first Australian property derivative with Grosvenor. This was a $A10m 2-year test trade based on the Australian PCA/IPD all property total return index.

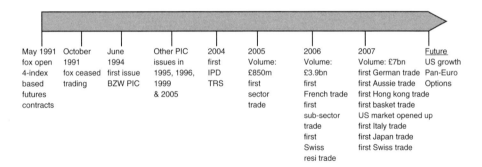

Figure 8.6   Global events timeline.

In July 2007 Grosvenor & RBS transacted the first Japanese property derivative trade using the IPD Japan Monthly Indicator property index.

In September 2007 ABN AMRO and Zurcher Kantonalbank (ZKB) carried out the first Swiss commercial property derivative based on the Swiss IPD property index.

In October 2007 BNP Paribas carried out the first Italian property derivative transaction with Grosvenor again as a 2-year test trade.

As the market develops, further alternative hedging opportunities will emerge. Real estate companies can hedge property portfolios in terms of both capital value and rental income. On a European level, this will lead to the possibility of, a European property fund that is overweight to say Dublin offices and underweight to Stockholm offices, to sell a swap relating to the performance of Dublin offices and purchase a swap on Stockholm offices (Figure 8.6).

Alternative indices and products being traded

HBOS house price index background and trading activity

For residential property derivatives the HBOS house price index (HPI) non-seasonally adjusted index is used. The HBOS HPI was formerly called the Halifax HPI and is the UK's longest running monthly house price series with data covering the whole country going back to January 1983. This UK Index is typically based on the mortgage data of around 15 000 house purchases per month and covers the whole calendar month. It is also a capital-based index, not a total return-based index and is not directly comparable to the IPD total return index.[3]

The years 2006 and 2007 have seen healthy growth in the residential derivatives market or HPI market. Traditionally UK institutions have not held residential assets although it is more common in continental Europe. HPI forwards make it possible for counterparties to gain or reduce property exposure to the residential market using a forward or a fully funded structured product. Trading in residential derivatives has been taking place since about 2001. The market has been somewhat hidden due to a lack of major banks in the market and with limited institutional investment into this sector. Furthermore, there is a lack of forecasting and research capabilities available in the residential market, in comparison to the commercial market.

The residential derivatives market has seen significant growth in 2006 and 2007, and as a result, they have become a more frequently traded product. HPI forwards are structured as contracts for difference (CFD) meaning there are no cashflows to look after until maturity. To date no specific details have been released on the volume of trading that has taken place in HPI forwards.

Since approximately 2001, Abbey Financial Services (now Santander) has been most active in this market and have executed over £1bn of HPI-related transactions with various counterparties. They are also behind the many HPI-related products that have been issued by its institutional clients. Such products can be structured with a maturity of 30 years, and there is potential to include high levels of gearing which proves an attractive option in the long term.[4]

In November 2006 Barclays issued a number of capital guaranteed property-related products for retail customers with a minimum investment of £10 000. One of these was the 'Guaranteed UK HPI Tracker Bond Issue 2'. This is a limited issue offshore savings product that offers a combination of high interest and growth potential without the risk of losing your original capital. It offered an interest rate of 8% gross/AER on one-third of your capital and returns determined by the performance of the UK housing market.[5] The Guaranteed UK HPI Tracker Bond Issue 2 is effectively three accounts in one product.

- 33.33% of capital is placed in a 1-year cash deposit account.
- 33.33% of capital is placed in a 3-year index-linked deposit account offering growth potential linked to the UK housing market performance.
- 33.33% of capital is placed in a 5-year index-linked deposit account offering growth potential linked to the UK housing market performance.
- All with the added peace of mind that your capital is safe.

In August 2007 Morgan Stanley completed the UK's first residential property derivative trade with an embedded exotic option based on the Halifax HPI. Under terms of the deal, the counterparty gains if the index rises, subject to a maximum payout but his capital is protected unless the index falls beyond an initially specified point. This type of exotic contract includes a 'knock-in put' option and Morgan Stanley said this is the first property derivative trade to include the component.[6]

MSS FTSEpx fund

In June 2006 FTSE saw a new set of indices for the UK property market called the FTSE UK commercial property index series launched. MSS has the exclusive licence, from FTSE, to develop and provide the property fund performance data that drives the daily FTSE indices. The index series is driven by the performance of the FTSEpx fund, a dedicated property unit trust. Net asset values and accrued income figures that make up each index calculation are provided from the fund which is invested in a diverse portfolio of property assets. The underlying assets are a representative and diversified portfolio of UK-based real estate assets. The fund has exposure to more than £15 billion of prime, institutional retail, office and industrial properties and was launched in April 2006.

Both Abbey Financial Markets and Royal Bank of Scotland provide pricing and have issued property-linked structured products using the FTSEpx index.

Goldman Sachs tracker index

In August 2006, Goldman Sachs launched a London-listed structured product, tracking the UK's direct commercial property market aimed at retail and institutional investors. The tracker follows the performance of the UK IPD annual total all property index in the UK. The tracker is structured as a securitised derivative with a 5-year timeframe from its launch, meaning that investors will get their money back in March 2011 after publication of the 2010 IPD index. The product has a minimum investment of £10 and maximum of £100 000. The group was seeking £25 m from the issue.

Investors are not bound by the term and can buy or sell shares when they wish, allowing them to make calls on whether the market will rise or fall by the end of the 5-year period. The stock exchange listing gives real-time liquidity and price transparency. As a share, there is no adviser commission available although there is a 2.8% per annum fixed annual index adjustment payable.

Hedge funds

In April 2006, Morley Fund Management acquired a 56% stake in hedge fund management company ORN Capital. In January 2007, ORN Capital launched the first property derivatives hedge fund to capitalise on the growth in the property derivatives market. In September 2007, the ORN Capital property derivative hedge fund became a casualty of the credit crunch and ceased trading with ORN focusing on its core funds.

The year 2007 then saw the introduction of a number of property-related hedge funds with the capacity to use property derivatives to outperform the market.

In May 2007, CBRE and derivatives specialist Reech AiM launched the first of a series of hedge funds tailored to the global property market. The Iceberg alternative real estate fund will invest in property-related financial instruments such as property derivatives, unlisted real estate vehicles and listed securities.

Also in May, Sir Ronald Cohen and Lord Rothschild launched Portland Capital hedge fund to invest in global property stocks and derivatives.

In July 2007, Alpha Beta Fund Management LLP launched a UK Residential Index Fund specialising in residential property derivatives products.

In October 2007, New Star set up a property hedge fund with the aim to profit from volatility in listed real estate shares. The fund will take both long and short positions in listed pan-European property shares and has the ability to use property derivatives.

In November 2007, Thames River Capital launched a long/short real hedge fund called the Thames River Longstone fund investing in real estate stocks and derivatives.

Each of the above indices and trackers has their own relative merits and issues. The entry, exit and holding costs potentially hinder investment into some of the retail products issued. The low minimum investment levels, easy management and the diversification are attractive to retail investors. From an institutional point of view, property derivatives are a method of managing property exposure that can support fund performance.

IPD all property swaps provide exposure to over £184 billion worth of property in the UK as per the December 2007 value from IPD. It is a robust index with a long track record. The FTSEpx fund run by MSS comprises £15 billion of property exposure in the UK, but also the ability of purchasing the underlying assets in the MSS fund. Managing market exposure via a property derivative can be carried out on both the IPD and FTSEpx index, but the decision of the choice of index is down to the investor profile. For instance if the investor was a fund benchmarked against IPD, then it is unlikely that he/she would use the FTSEpx index to manage exposure unless he/she was sure of a specific correlation or opportunity. In reply to this, if the investor owned units in the MSS fund, then he/she could perfectly hedge or increase exposure via a derivative using the FTSEpx index.

Has the market achieved the results expected of it?

The market has gained further momentum each year since 2005 with the volume of transactions increasing in the UK. In Q1 2006, the over the counter (OTC) market in commercial derivatives was greater than the entire trading volume witnessed in 2005. Up to Q2 2007, derivative trading volume was greater than that of the whole year in 2006.

The market is a fast-attracting interest from new entrants to the property market that has an appetite for quick alternative exposure and returns linked to this desirable asset class. There has been a concerted effort by those active in the market to increase the availability of property index-related products such as the Goldman Sachs property index tracker and a variety of tailored product issued by banks. There has also been willingness by property investors to consider property derivatives as part of their overall investment strategy. Many institutions have appointed dedicated personnel within their organisations to concentrate on this market. The growth of the HPI market is a further indication of sustainable growth of the property derivatives market.

Standardisation

The wave of new entrants into the market and the increased availability of pricing has led to a requirement for the standardisation of documentation regarding dates, times and terms. Standardisation is a key driver in aiding smoother transactions and continued growth. Unification by market participants was shown on 15 January 2008 when all active parties agreed to change the pricing and structure of contracts to make more comprehendible to the wider market. This changed pricing from using Libor plus or minus a margin, starting on the most recently published monthly estimate of the IPD annual index to quoting a fixed percent return starting from the most recently published IPD annual index with a December year end.

Derivatives markets are recognised by the International Swap Dealer's Association (ISDA), which represents participants in the privately negotiated derivatives industry and is the largest global financial trade association. ISDA is the body that produces standard documentation and among its most notable accomplishments are developing the ISDA Master Agreement; publishing a wide range of related documentation materials and instruments covering a variety of transaction types ISDA also aims to advance the understanding and treatment of derivatives and risk management from public policy and regulatory capital perspectives.

In May 2007, ISDA released property derivative definitions to be recognised and used for property derivative transactions. One specific difference with the documentation for property derivatives in comparison to other derivative documentation relates to index substitution and failure to publish the index.

Both commercial and residential derivatives globally follow ISDA documentation.

Leaders in the market

The current leaders in the market are the main investment banks that are quoting two-way prices along the all property curve for various swap maturities. Investment banks have been trading on behalf of end-users in the market including institutions, property companies and hedge funds. ABN AMRO was the first bank to establish a dedicated property derivatives desk in 2005. It conducted the first sector-specific swap (UK retail) with Merrill Lynch in November 2005, and the first UK office sector swap in January 2006 with Lehman Brothers.

Merrill Lynch are also involved in a number of the pioneering deals including the first sector-specific swap (UK retail) and the first sub-sector trade on UK shopping centres with ABN AMRO. In December 2006 Merrill Lynch was also involved in the first French property derivatives swap trade linked to the IPD France Offices annual index.

Merrill Lynch reported trades over £600m to July 2006, and other banks such as Royal Bank of Scotland, Goldman Sachs, Lehman Brothers and ABN AMRO are each reputed to have on several hundred million pounds of trades, according to derivatives experts.

The market has evolved to a level that regular marking to market is possible by the banks trading. If there is pricing attractive this position can then be sold on in the market as a secondary trade installing further liquidity.[7]

From a property end-user point of view, the major UK institutions have been involved in the market at including Standard Life, Morley, Quintain, AXA, Grosvenor, British Land, Prudential, Threadneedle. There are also a number of hedge funds that are active in both commercial and residential property derivatives and current pricing and volatility make this an interesting space for their skill set.

User profiles

To keep the market moving at a steady pace there needs to be increased activity from those with direct property exposure including property companies, funds and institutions. This will provide further depth to the market. This increased activity will help the market move forward and expand into Europe and beyond.

The profiles of a number of parties that have been either transacting or enquiring about the property derivatives market are shown below.

- Pension fund manager
  A fund manager might consider buying the all property index as a means to diversifying the asset allocation within the portfolio.
- Property asset manager
  An asset manager looking to reallocate funds could buy or sell IPD sector indices rather than disposing of assets within their portfolios. For instance, a fund wanting to reduce its retail exposure could sell the IPD all retail index for the IPD all property index.
- Hedge fund manager
  The low costs associated with entering into a swap and the speed with which a party can gain or reduce exposure to the property market appeals to this class of investor.
- Real estate companies/long-term property holders
  Investors anticipating a downturn of returns in the market or indeed any particular sector to which they have exposure could sell the relevant IPD index.

- Private customers/retail customers
  Investors diversifying their portfolio with property exposure using structured products issued by banks. The potential of principal guaranteed
  exposure is desirable to this class of investor.

Global evolution

The UK model for a property derivative market has followed an open and
clear path that has been well-supported by the IPF and many leading figures in the UK property market. This has driven education, transparency
and liquidity as the main areas of development to further stimulate the
market.

Interest in European and International property derivative markets has
continued to grow. At present the countries that have seen most interest are those which are seen to have a credible and robust property index,
underpinned by historical data and appetite from property investors. The
credibility and robustness of the index is crucial as trades can last a significant period of time. The historical data is integral to analysing past market performance with the aim of modelling potential future performance,
whilst taking into account current market factors. Table 8.5 names countries that benefit from both investor interest and a robust IPD index:

The composition of the indices in each country varies. The UK IPD
index comprises retail, office, industrial and other, whilst the Dutch,
French and German indices also include varying proportions of residential.

The launch of IPD's pan-European index gives rise to the future potential of gaining pan-European property market exposure. The pan-European
index is based on the IPD indices for Denmark, France, Germany, Ireland,
Italy, the Netherlands, Norway, Portugal, Spain, Sweden, Switzerland, UK
and the KTI index for Finland. The index comprises over 40 000 properties worth just over €625 billion as of end December 2006. This equates to
approximately 46% market coverage.

Table 8.5 Countries that benefit from both investor interest and a robust IPD index.

Country	All property total return 2006	All property total return 2007	Estimated market coverage	Index start date
France (%)	21.7	17.8	59	1986
Germany (%)	1.3	4.5	21	1996
Ireland (%)	27.2	9.9	83	1984
The Netherlands (%)	12.5	11.3	60	1995
Sweden (%)	16.2	14.9	34	1984
United Kingdom (%)	18.1	−3.4	49	1971

Source: IPD.

The University of Hong Kong real estate indices

In Hong Kong, a residential property index based on repeat sales has been created to support the property derivates market in this region. This index was created and will be maintained by the University of Hong Kong's Department of Real Estate and Construction. The index series is called 'The University of Hong Kong Real Estate Index Series' (HKU-REIS). This series uses residential transaction information and will provide four indices, covering all of Hong Kong, Hong Kong Island, Kowloon and New Territories.

European Public Real Estate Association indices

The European Public Real Estate Association (EPRA) is a common interest group, established as a not-for-profit body under Dutch law in October 1999. The EPRA/NAREIT global real estate index series are designed to track the performance of listed real estate companies and REITS worldwide. The FTSE EPRA/NAREIT global real estate index series is broken down into eight index families and 141 indices in Asia Pacific, Europe and North America. These include 18 real-time indices covering the world's largest investment markets in various currencies. The EPRA series acts as a performance measure of the overall market, and it is possible to use it as the basis for derivatives and exchange traded funds (ETFs).

American evolution

NCREIF

In the USA, the model for property derivatives has changed. The original model comprised an exclusivity agreement with Credit Suisse and the National Council of Real Estate Investment Fiduciaries (NCREIF), the provider of the main US index. In October 2006, Credit Suisse waived its exclusive rights held by it for 2 years to the use of the NCREIF property index (NPI) as the benchmark for writing private real estate market derivatives. The license with Credit Suisse is still in effect with Goldman Sachs, Lehman Brothers, Morgan Stanley Bank of America & Deutsche Bank joining them.

Other US indices

During the period of the exclusivity agreement between Credit Suisse and NCREIF there was a handful of trades done. During this period a number of index providers developed indices to take advantage of the new market potential. This has led to a position where at least five alternative property indexes have emerged as contenders to structure 'TRS'. The five main indices that can be traded in the USA, all have differing markets, methodologies and coverage. Going forward it is likely that one or two indices will prove more successful than others although at the moment, there is no clear favourite in the USA.

The NCREIF property index is seen by some players as the frontrunner because it is familiar to institutional investors and is widely used as a benchmark return index. The NCREIF index is based on appraised property values in both commercial and residential properties.

The other five indexes are produced by Standard & Poor's/global real analytics (GRA), real capital analytics (RCA), REXX and Radar Logic.

- S&P/GRA indices are based on average sale price per square foot on commercial property.
- S&P CME Housing Futures and Options index is a partnership between Chicago Mercantile Exchange, Fiserv Case Shiller Weiss and Standard & Poor. These derivatives will enable investors to take a position on the direction of the housing market, either for the nation as a whole or for 10 major cities including New York, Los Angeles and Chicago.
- Real estate analytics (REAL) indices are derived from repeat sales (same property realised price changes) of properties in the RCA transaction database on commercial property.
- REXX indices are based on metropolitan area rents as well as capital value changes on commercial property. The office index will produce, on a quarterly basis, total return and sub-indices for 15 individual office markets.
- Radar logic residential price index tracks 25 metropolitan statistical areas (MSAs) around the country. Individual index numbers are available for each, as well as a US composite number for the whole country that is derived from the MSA's.

How have derivatives changed the market place?

Perhaps one of the most important opportunities to date with property derivatives is that it is now possible for investors to enhance investment strategy by managing their property exposure using derivatives. The market has also led to the release of new investment products that are linked to property returns.

The development of pricing screens on Bloomberg, Reuters and www. propex.co.uk has been a major step forward. While there is basis risk between a specific property and the relevant IPD index, the advantage of the property derivative pricing curve is that it should reflect real-time information including interest rate expectations, retail sales numbers, property transactions and market sentiment. As a result this should at least provide some insight into the market direction and valuers may one day be required to integrate this information into their working practice. At this moment in time, the market is not liquid enough to consider this approach, but may become more relevant as the market matures.

Promotion of the market

Since June 2005, activity with large property agencies and city broking houses coming together to participate in this market was seen. This activity offers market participants combined property and derivative expertise.

The increased press coverage the market is receiving is positive, as transparency and education are essential in helping it to evolve. There have also been an increased number of lectures, seminars and full conferences exploring the property derivatives market globally. There have been more requests by university students for information about the market as the subject is forming part of the curriculum. At universities the subject usually forms part of an investment module and as yet is not a stand-alone topic, but perhaps in the future derivatives may become a module in its own right. Such skills to be enhanced include modelling correlations of historical data along with interpreting property research as a guide to future performance in relation to other asset classes. Also the understanding of financial products such as derivatives and structured products and their relationship to real estate is important.

Along with the evolution in property derivatives, global markets in 2006 has also seen new funds and products linked to property returns. In 2006 IPD launched its UK quarterly index and its pan-European IPD index. The MSS hedge fund launched the FTSE UK commercial property index series and Goldman Sachs has launched a UK IPD tracker product that has a low minimum investment attractive to retail investors. Further to this Abbey have also released a number of structured products in commercial and residential markets.

Both commercial and residential derivatives enable efficient management of real estate exposure, which has allowed banks and institutions to create retail products.

Future expectations, unintended consequences and lessons learned

Future expectations are positive with regard to liquidity and transparency as awareness and activity are increasing. As liquidity in the sector and sub-sector markets increases, property derivatives will potentially be of more interest to end-users.

Diversification

Property derivatives allow property companies, life funds, pension funds and business owner-occupiers to manage property risk cheaply and efficiently in the same way that they manage their foreign exchange or interest rate exposure with swaps. In the future it will be possible to hedge out market rental risk for a fixed return. A developing European property derivatives market gives rise to an excellent opportunity to gain from the advantages of these derivatives. Such advantages include speed of exposure, reducing round-trip transaction costs, hedging the value of physical assets in a falling market, reflect a view on one property sector relative to another, managing compliance restrictions, managing risk through diversification, cross-border exposure, property exposure while waiting to find the right property and speculative property investment.

Relationship with indirect and other vehicles

The excitement surrounding the advent of UK Real Estate Investment Trusts (REITs) in January 2007 has not accelerated the development of the derivative market. If the REIT market grows rapidly, for example, the cashflow-driven share prices could potentially start to put pressure valuations in the underlying market, inducing volatility and hence increasing the value of derivatives both as a hedging tool and as an investment asset.

In the chancellor's pre-budget report on 6 December 2006, he announced changes to the regime which aim to facilitate the floatation of new REITs and this relates to the use of derivatives in the following two ways.[8]

1 The computation of tax-exempt profits currently includes only taxable movements on derivatives hedging an asset of the property rental business. This will be extended so that it also includes hedges of rent and expenses relating to the asset. It is to be hoped that expenses in this case will include interest paid on debt of the tax-exempt business. This amendment is removing an anomaly.
2 There will be a revision to the exclusion from profits for the purposes of the 75% test to exclude fair value movements on derivatives. This removes an anomaly created by accounting treatment.

In other words, the government has given the go-ahead for REITs to invest in property derivatives. Provided the derivative is used to hedge either interest rate risk on loans or existing investment in property, it will be included within the 75% tax-exempt part of the business. Straight investments in derivatives (synthetic property) will not be tax-exempt.

Property derivatives can also be used as a method of hedging or gaining further exposure with indirect property vehicles. The main key here is the relationship between the vehicle's performance and the index to which it is being referenced and this will become more apparent over time.

Conclusions

Since 1991 the UK property derivatives market has been on a long journey in reaching its current status. The year 2007 was the year when property derivatives went global and experienced a large increase in volumes and users. This is mainly due to the investment banks' participation and an increasing number of end-users exploring the market. A number of the main funds, institutions and property companies are also taking a more serious approach to the property derivatives market and a number of them have dedicated people working specifically on derivatives. The increase from end-users follows on from the number of mandates that are now in place to enable such companies to trade.

Most derivative markets, such as the interest rate, credit and ABS swaps market, have trillions of pounds worth of transactions although growth in each market is specific to the actual market being looked at. Property is now another asset class joining them.

In the investment world, property has traditionally been kept very detached from other asset classes. Over the past 2 years, this gap has been reduced with property evolving in the capital markets family. This can be directly seen with the growth of capital markets teams in the normally traditional property consultancies with the aim of linking property solutions in further with other financial markets including stock market and bond market. Property is now joining the rest of the investment universe, and consequently direct property, indirect property and derivatives are all going to be part of this. The differing investor viewpoints, the variety of derivative products and the range of buyers and sellers will facilitate effective pricing. The derivatives market is fast attracting interest from people that are outside the property world who are eager to gain quick exposure to returns linked to this desirable asset class.

A vision of the future could entail property derivatives being an integral part global property strategy with exposure being managed with the effective use of sector-specific derivatives. With this ability the focus of investors would lead to growth in the size of property portfolios with the aim of outperforming the market through active management. In doing so they can use derivatives to lock in returns on their portfolio or alternatively if they are nervous about the market and their relative performance hedge their risk and the potential to maintain a position in a rising and falling market.

Notes

1. Property Forecast – Property Derivatives – An Essential Guide 2005.
2. Reuters UK, 27 June 2007.
3. HBOS Plc Housing Research.
4. Terrapinn Property Derivatives Conference 2006.
5. Barclays Structured Deposits at www.barclays.com.
6. Reuters 30 August 2007.
7. Estates Gazette Interactive (Egi) 15 July 2006 and 12 August 2006.
8. KPMG Update on Pre Budget Report December 2006.

9

Property Markets in Central and Eastern Europe

Stanley McGreal, Jim Berry and Alastair Adair

Introduction

The emergence of free markets combined with financial liberalisation, privatisation, globalisation, tax and legal reforms and infrastructure development has combined to increase the availability and attractiveness of markets in central and eastern Europe to international investors. A key catalyst has been the accession of several countries in the region into the European Union which has focussed attention on the region's ability to encourage investment. Progress in these countries is reflected in reports such as the 2004 JLL Global Real Estate Index, which indicated that, although the Czech Republic, Hungary and Poland were predictably further down the league table than their west European counterparts, these countries have all improved their scoring relating to market transparency. However, despite significant progress, a number of fundamental risks remain with regards to property investment in central and eastern Europe. The region's economic infrastructure is less well developed than in the west, legal and tax systems are subject to frequent change, regulatory frameworks are often contradictory or unclear, land legislation in parts is still generally poorly developed while more recently political uncertainty fuelling significant currency fluctuations has highlighted the risks of foreign investment.

Central and eastern European countries have experienced considerable turmoil in embracing the realities of a market economy, though the extent of the transformation has been significant. This has been instrumental in the establishment of real estate markets particularly in the three leading countries in the region: the Czech Republic, Hungary and Poland.

The level of foreign direct investment (FDI) into the region has been significant (Adair et al., 2006) and is arguably one of the principal driving forces behind economic performance providing a barometer of investor sentiment regarding a country and its prospects for future growth.

This chapter briefly reviews the literature on the development of real estate markets in central and eastern European countries. However, the main focus of the chapter is upon two key factors concerning the operation of markets, namely, accessibility of data on the real estate markets and the role of bank lending and lending policies to investors and developers in the real estate market. This chapter concludes that there is a certain mismatch between the levels of market information and the willingness of banks to lend on real estate in the region.

Development of real estate markets

One of the most definitive accounts of the evolution and development of real estate markets in central and eastern Europe has been that by Keivani et al. (2002) based on the market maturity paradigm developed by Keogh and D'Arcy (1994). Keivani et al. (2002) focussed specifically on the capital cities of Budapest, Prague and Warsaw and concluded that with respect to flexible market adjustment all three cities exhibit a dynamic development sector which is capable of response to long-term market change. However, they observed that information sources were considered to be poor in all three cities with transparency, lack of market transactions and the absence of reliable statistical data placing constraints on the property market. Basic information was often lacking and there was frequently an absence of objectivity in relation to data collection and interpretation with major questions regarding reliability. Perversely, the discrepancy in data at an official level was seen by some actors notably in Warsaw as promoting a level of competition. Although adding to the risk dimension, the inadequacy of data was interpreted as not necessarily being a negative influence in an emerging market. In this respect market inefficiencies offer opportunities for investment in under-priced/under-valued sectors of the market. Sectoral openness was largely dependent on the general development of the financial and investment base, permitting the substitution between property and non-property sectors.

Keivani et al. (2002) highlighted the role of international banks, particularly German and Austrian, in providing development finance through local subsidiaries. The importance of external sources of finance was seen as a key consideration with major developments funded by foreign capital as local financing instruments were not sufficiently sophisticated. Keivani et al. (2002) concluded that the underdevelopment of local financial capacity was a major factor that could limit the future development of the real estate markets and their attractiveness to international capital. This is particularly evident in the more domestic-oriented sectors of the market such as housing and smaller commercial, retail and industrial development activities where there was limited scope for profitable involvement by international finance capital. On the basis of the market maturity paradigm, Keivani et al. (2002) concluded that all three city markets have a weak form of integration into the global finance system but were starting to develop characteristics of a mature property market.

In considering impact of international demand and supply, Keivani et al. (2002) identified three phases of development activity; firstly, initial rehabilitation and refurbishment in the central city areas to satisfy the sudden and large-scale demand from international firms; secondly, consolidation of rehabilitation and refurbishment and new development in the city centre areas to meet the continuing demand, and saturation of central areas, particularly in Budapest and Prague; and thirdly, expansion to fringe and out-of-town locations, particularly with respect to retail development. The first and second refurbishment phases were seen to be facilitated by the restitution programmes and spurred on by the rent and functional gap as a result of under-utilisation of space in central areas due to the low administrative value or rent set for such areas during the communist period and high demand for space particularly by international agents. According to Keivani et al. (2002) in spite of substantial amounts of FDI in the three case studies, particularly in commercial and retail property development, all three cities have lacked city wide co-ordination for either attracting or directing international development activity. They observed that at the city level there is a tremendous degree of confusion and lack of direction. Planning and development decisions in all three cities were prone to political influences, cronyism and corrupt practices, thus making most rules and regulations less effective in terms of development control and planned urban growth. The need for organic and informal relationship was acknowledged by private as well as public actors in all three cities and signifies that in spite of much regulation urban development was essentially international private property led. This has promoted peripheral expansion of the urban areas with the pattern of development having more of an organic than planned nature.

In determining the fundamental balance between potential and risk, Cushman and Wakefield Healey and Baker (2003) undertook a detailed comparative analysis of emerging European economies, examining nearly 50 variables including economics, politics, corruption, property market structures and occupier and investor demand. Data was scored and weighted to determine an overall ranking for growth and stability/risk, as illustrated in Table 9.1. This analysis demonstrated that the differences in

Table 9.1 Growth and stability/risk ranking of emerging European markets.

Percentage of maximum score		Ranking for: growth	Stability/risk	Overall
83	Hungary	1	1	1
80	Czech Republic	2	3	2
74	Poland	3	4	3
67	Estonia	4	2	4
64	Slovakia	5	6	5
61	Slovenia	6	5	6
59	Lithuania	8	7	7
58	Russia	7	11	8
52	Latvia	9	8	9
49	Bulgaria	10	9	10
47	Turkey	12	10	11
47	Romania	11	13	12
43	Croatia	13	12	13

Source: Cushman and Wakefield Healey and Baker (2003).

opportunity that exist across central and eastern Europe was a function of risk and growth potential. The grouping of countries placed Hungary, the Czech Republic and Poland as the top three countries on a risk-adjusted basis, but with Estonia challenging strongly despite the limitations of its relative size. Estonia is ranked second for stability behind Hungary whilst Poland slips to fourth place.

Watkins and Merrill (2003) note four distinct phases in the emergence of real estate markets in central and eastern Europe. First, inactivity, with 45 years of state ownership of property, plant and equipment and rigid control of the resource allocation system, leading them to suggest that it was not surprising that both local and international developers and investors waited, or were forced to wait, for the markets to solidify before proceeding. Constraints included uncertain property rights, restrictions regarding foreign ownership in property, and currency risk. Second, cautious beginnings, where international corporations saw the re-opening of the markets of the former Soviet Union as a potential bonanza while developers gradually became aware of the opportunity to provide modern space to the market. Concurrent with removing financial and legislative barriers, developers began to see that the expected returns were so favourable that they could afford to bear substantial risk. Third, a period when market rents well in excess of construction costs provided the context for the spike in construction activity during the hypergrowth phase and many newly constructed properties, particularly those that were delivered early in the cycle, attracted tenants and proved profitable for the developer. As more space came on line, however, tenants began to differentiate and properties that were poorly designed, constructed or located met with little demand, forcing owners to reduce rents. Thus, the hypergrowth phase is characterised by significant construction activity and declining rental levels. Fourth, seeking equilibrium, development activity declined and only those properties with the strongest international developers or favourable location or efficient designs attracted pre-leasing commitments and construction financing. The result was a development market based on a closer alignment with the demand for space.

According to Watkins and Merrill (2003), one of the key characteristics in moving from one stage of the cycle to the next is the perception of risk; it is widely accepted that investors' aggregate perception of risk indicates that real property cashflows in central and eastern Europe embody greater uncertainty than those in more developed and mature markets. Adair et al. (2006) identified that data issues and data transparency were fundamental concerns. Parsa et al. (2000) considered that information sources were poor with lack of market transactions and the absence of reliable statistical data placing considerable constraints on the property markets. A survey of investor opinion by Parsa et al. (2000) concluded that the accuracy of data was perceived as the second most significant risk in central and eastern European markets (Table 9.2).

McGreal et al. (2002) stated that the paucity of information was considered to have inhibited the development of property markets, with fragmented information available only from the early to mid-1990s, and often only reported on Western-style buildings, rather than for the total office stock. Problems also arose as a result of the varied sources of data, with stock figures compiled from a mixture of sources including local authority,

Table 9.2   Sources of property investment risk in central and eastern Europe.

Risk factor	Mean score
Asset pricing	3.67
Valuation of property	3.87
Measurement of yields	3.67
Lease structures/ownership	4.13
Thin markets	4.29
Taxation	3.73
Currency	3.96
Accuracy of data sources	4.16
Market transparency	4.13
Availability of finance	2.52
Political factors	3.91
Economic conditions	4.15
Lack of demand	3.69
Planning and development policy	3.96
Bureaucracy/officialdom	4.02
Corruption	4.04
Repatriation of profits	4.11

Source: Parsa et al. (2000). Results of survey of international investors.

developer, investor and consultants' forecasts, and even if a relatively reliable estimate of current stock was established, tracking the data back to create a time series of stock, and new completions proved problematic due to inadequate local authority records.

Property markets, data availability and economic competitiveness

The availability of accurate and up-to-date market data is one of the distinguishing characteristics of mature land and property markets (Jones Lang LaSalle, 2006). The degree of data transparency, availability of market information, level of real estate service provision and volume of property transactions have been identified as key contributory factors to economic competitiveness and attraction of inward investment flows (D'Arcy and Keogh, 1998; Keogh and D'Arcy, 1999). Significant additional inflows of foreign capital spurred the creation of reliable office market data sets by the Research Forums in the major cities of central and eastern Europe. Normally being an expensive and time-consuming process, data capture took advantage of modern electronic information processing to reduce costs. Countries and increasingly cities, that possess comprehensive property data, demonstrate a competitive advantage and are more likely to attract international investment flows. As the number of principal international agencies has expanded their operations across central and eastern Europe, so the availability of market information has also increased. Each of the principal commercial property agencies with offices in the region publishes reports for the key property markets thereby opening up domestic offerings to an international audience. The majority of agents also produce statistics for the smaller markets and consequently the level of research coverage is increasing. Reports covering the markets in second-wave countries such as Romania and Bulgaria are relatively easy to source, although the level of information is understandably less comprehensive than for first-wave countries such as the Czech Republic, Hungary and Poland. To the east of the region, data coverage for the Baltic States and markets along the border with Russia is less significant as markets are not as well developed.

Agents' reports for the central and eastern European region generally follow the standard structure utilised for Western property markets, covering analysis of macroeconomic market drivers, office, retail and industrial market demand, supply and rental levels, yields and brief details relating to activity in the leasing markets including key deals. The time series of published property data typically extends to 5 years. While in many cases this is likely to encompass the total extent of data being held by the agents, it is not significantly less than the amount of information published for many developed markets. Research undertaken by the University of Ulster for the RICS Foundation examined the impact of data availability on the development of land and property markets in central and eastern Europe (Adair et al., 2006). The study, based on structured discussions with senior professionals operating within and outside the central and eastern European region, examined the relationship between the availability of market data and the development of properly functioning markets – the attributes that have encouraged the growth of market information and the impact of data availability on patterns of property market development across the region.

The findings of this study reinforced the view concerning the lack of both public and privately held commercial property market data in central and eastern Europe prior to 1989. The arrival of international agents in the early 1990s was seen as one of the two principal drivers in the development of information for the central and eastern European region. The second driver was the latent demand from institutional investors. One of the principal mechanisms behind these drivers were Research Forums established in Budapest, Prague and Warsaw in the late 1990s comprising representatives from the principal international agencies with the goal of agreeing the market position on key variables including office stock, take-up and vacancy data and to minimise the degree of variation, principally attributable to the use of different boundaries and definitions. Such developments in property market information standardisation, particularly in the office sector, are well in advance of many western European countries. This led to the situation where the collection and use of data was initially very opaque to one where there is much more trust and co-operation in which reaching a consensus through the Research Forums is in everyone's interest. In addition, it was noted that property developers in central and eastern Europe frequently instruct advisors on a joint agency basis, notably in the office sector. As a result there were multiple companies working on the same projects, so there was not the same degree of privacy with regards to leasing data. Sharing of information in the office sector has become common in the Budapest, Prague and Warsaw markets aided by the establishment of Research Forums in these cities.

It was the view of international real estate service providers that over the medium 5-year term, the quality of the occupational data in the principal markets of Budapest, Prague and Warsaw could be the envy of Western Europe. This is widely attributable to the fact that stock characteristics and absorption in a very compact market can be measured, tracked and interpreted reasonably accurately. Furthermore, data collection and analysis has started from a strong skills base due to the market penetration by London-based real estate firms and through recruitment of professional research analysts.

In terms of sector coverage, although the availability of office market data has increased significantly over the last decade, the supply of data for retail property remains poor. The contrasting situation is largely attributable to the dominance of one or two international agencies in each city and reluctance on behalf of both agent and retailer for occupational data to be widely distributed, thereby contrasting with the office sector. The level of available data for the warehouse sector is poor due to the limited base of modern stock across the region, much of which has only been developed since 2000. However, the warehouse and distribution sector is forecast to experience an increase in demand in the short to medium term as a result of EU accession, with the region forming the eastern boundary of the EU and offering significant benefits regarding low-land values, labour and construction costs.

The other principal driver regarding the development of quality data in central and eastern Europe is the latent demand from international investors. While risk-averse opportunists and speculators dominated the development markets and enjoyed spectacular returns in the early 1990s, the investment market was slower to evolve due to a lack of product. In addition, institutional investors exercised a greater degree of caution, which was arguably attributable to the lack of market transparency and property data. A number of respondents shared the opinion that the availability of data, while only for a very short time series, triggered the start of investment markets in the late 1990s in the capital cities of Budapest, Prague and Warsaw: markets that have grown significantly since 2002. There is also evidence of investors starting to look beyond these cities to the Baltic States, and in particular Estonia, where the retail sector is particularly well developed.

Evidence from the study highlighted a lack of standard valuation practices. While appraisal practice in mature markets is strictly regulated by means of both professional liability case law and guidance from the main professional organisations, the absence of private property markets in central and eastern Europe during the communist era meant that there was no requirement for market-based valuations. As such, a market has evolved where professionals carry out valuations according to either RICS or TEGOVA standards. A number of respondents agreed that the lending institutions are the principal determinants of the valuation techniques utilised though there is evidence that local surveyors are increasingly using RICS standards as all of the international agencies have London-based headquarters, and the RICS is starting to be accepted as the industry norm. There is also evidence of German and Austrian banks, which are key players in the region, requiring valuers to be RICS qualified.

The drivers that encourage growth in property investment, thereby stimulating a need for performance measurement, have been witnessed across the central and eastern European region, specifically: the internationalisation of economic activity, bargain hunting by international investors, deregulation, leasehold reform, property being released onto the market in attractive locations and at attractive yields, growth expectations offsetting transaction costs, more efficient market operation and lower transaction costs including fees and taxes. The main downside, notably within Poland, is security of title with registration of ownership a lengthy process. While Adair et al. (2006) acknowledge that data quality has improved considerably in central and eastern Europe, for the future development of these markets, the next step needs to be the development of an investment performance index. In this respect the Research Forums are well placed to play a more proactive role in agreeing investment market definitions and in ensuring that both international and regional property measurement standards are adopted to meet the needs of a maturing market and to facilitate the requirements of institutional investors.

Bank lending on property in central and eastern Europe

As a consequence of the high risk associated with the emerging markets, there has been cautious involvement by the banks and financial institutions in lending on property investment and development transactions in central and eastern European countries. This section considers the second core theme of this chapter namely the criteria necessary to provide confidence for banks to finance property development and investment transactions in central and eastern Europe. To address this issue, a series of structured discussions were held with a selected number of senior personnel from the leading banks in the UK and Ireland, and Europe. The discussions were structured to address the lending criteria such as property type, property data, lease structure, borrower characteristics, terms of loan and any other perceived financial/lending conditions, for example, the Basel II effects associated with the risk-reduction aspects of lending across property markets.

Interviews undertaken with representatives from Irish-based banks indicate that lending in central and eastern European countries is structured on similar criteria to that applying in the more local mature economies. The key lending criteria comprise borrower characteristics, terms and amount of loan, property type, investment/financial data on the property, lease structure and other perceived financial and lending constraints. The lending decision is based on all of these attributes. Lending practice to investors in these markets is client driven. In central and eastern Europe outside of Poland, the banks would normally lend only to the larger, more experienced developer/investor due to the higher risks.

In the case of development finance, the rate of loan is base rate plus 150 bps up to 300–400 bps depending on the stage in the development/ construction cycle and the associated risk. The investment loan depends on the type, size and location of the investment property/project. Cross-collateralisation may occur depending on the gearing. The loan to value (LTV) is normally 70–80% but will be determined by the risk factors (currency, country, legal). The level of risk is reflected in the debt coverage ratio which is 150 bps for central and eastern Europe whereas more mature markets such as the USA are in the range of 110–130 bps The debt coverage ratio will depend on the property characteristics of location, type and performance of project. In addition the more favourable position in the UK concerning upward only rent reviews compared to the shorter and more uncertain lease arrangements in central and eastern Europe influences the debt coverage ratio.

Non-recourse financing is a dimension of the property market culture and applies more to the bigger players and to the larger developments. Moving down the scale to the smaller players and to medium-sized developments, non-recourse financing is more restricted. Pre-payment penalties are not used given that most developers are in and out within a relatively short time period. The normal length of loan is 15–20 years for investment and 2–5 years for development. The maximum permissible loan rates are set under the confidential risk guidelines by the banks. Funding in the central and eastern European markets is dependent on presenting a detailed business case including knowledge of country and property market risk. The location, security of title and the shorter lease structure in these markets are seen as the determining criteria that will influence lending. The other related issues include the need for greater transparency on comparable property data transactions, the difficulties posed by a cumbersome legal system, and the importance of reliable local knowledge on property market dynamics. On the returns side property investment performance can be variable due to erratic nature of local markets.

Lending is across sectors including retail, office, logistics, and industrial with the focus on the Czech Republic, Hungary and Poland; and more selective deals in Romania, the Baltic States and Russia. Turkey (Istanbul) is the latest country of interest alongside a watching brief regarding the emerging opportunities in Slovakia, Croatia and Romania. The use of research and market knowledge of each country is perceived to be essential. Lending policy entails the carrying out of in-depth research and building linkages with local expertise. Significant emphasis is placed upon in-house research (other research helps to develop a base). The cost for undertaking research specific to the needs of the investor is normally covered within the fee structure. Where the investor decides to play in the emerging markets, the client becomes the driver to research new opportunities across the different market sectors. Increasingly the evidence points to more clients willing to invest cross-border in the prospect of better return commensurate with the risk in those countries. This can be explained by the availability of cheaper European debt and the wider gap between initial yields and the cost of borrowing. However there is a concern that yields are falling in eastern European markets signified by almost 100 bps yield shift in 2005.

The role of the London office of the bank is normally client introduction with local offices being the main source of research and local expertise including feasibility studies on locations and schemes and market analysis for projects. The importance of due diligence is key to any lending decision especially for banks providing both investment and development finance. Lending criteria were seen to differ little from western Europe. Lending was in euros (possibly US dollars in the case of Poland). Both fixed and variable rate products are available with loan to value ratio (LTVR) in the range from 70% to 75% senior debt (the bank's main focus) and 85% if junior debt, though client driven. A debt coverage ratio of 120% and term of 5 years appears standard. Loan limit is not a significant issue, the market/scheme being more important. The upper limit was not revealed though potentially could be up to several hundred million euros, but one is unlikely to find such product in central and eastern Europe.

For central and eastern Europe, borrower credentials are gauged on the basis of international players with an established track record. Cross-collateralisation is welcomed in that it widens geographical distribution and brings diversification. Shorter lease structures of 3–5 years introduce a re-leasing risk that should be priced into the downside risk. Knowledge of where the market will be in 5 years is therefore important, with the situation of Warsaw with rents only 50% of post-transition period providing a realism of what these markets can do. Data availability is weak on historical and time-series trends, but current data is considered to be relatively good. Use of joint ventures is perceived to be unnecessary for central Europe, though may be required for the Romanian market. The setting-up of SPVs to hold property directly is considered to be the preferable alternative in most central and eastern European markets.

Interview evidence suggests that the second-level risk is of greater importance in that it is a largely untested market due to the low number of sales transactions. A senior debt provider works on tight margins of 100 bps return and with the higher risk in central and eastern Europe relative to the more mature economies of western Europe, there is a perception that this presents the main barrier for entry to these markets. It is also highlighted that shorter lease structures are priced into the investment market and will depend on a number of factors including the weight of money, indexation and rental growth. The compression of yields is possibly making the market less attractive with a perception of too many investors chasing limited markets. The development market is considered to be the most active in the area, and this is where working with local operators with local knowledge of the property and land markets is important. With development operating through SPVs, cross-collateralisation is difficult. Terms are driven by the nature of investors with 3–5 years often being the norm. Interest rate can be fixed or variable depending on the LTVR and whether the borrower's strategy is based on long-term holding or trading and use of hedging.

In terms of risk tolerance, perspectives differ across the countries. Poland, the Czech Republic, Hungary and Slovakia are classed in a similar manner. The Baltic States are seen as very small markets whereas Romania, Croatia and Russia are classed in a different scenario with limited developer–investor activity. Romania is viewed as over-priced with yields in Bucharest not standing up to analytical scrutiny. Both the information and the product are limited. The main risks are the relatively small market and high volatility. Croatia also attracts concern with Slovakia viewed as a small market. The higher growth economies of central Europe are better placed, but there is perceived to be a wall of money chasing little product. In this respect a lot of investors are too late, with early deals in 1998–1999 achieving yields of 11–11.5% compared to 7–8% in 2005–2006.

Interview evidence from European-based banks confirmed that the 'core' markets of the region having lost their special status are now increasingly recognised as mainstream European countries. Hence, a fund building a pan-European portfolio is as likely to include central European assets as those in any other western European country. In terms of countries, a distinction is made between the first-wave countries (Hungary, Poland, Czech Republic) and second-wave countries (Romania, Bulgaria, Croatia). Markets within the region are seen to be part of an evolutionary process with the second-wave countries lagging by 6–8 years in terms of risk and transparency of the markets. Lending policy is based on sustainability involving a range of products such as issue mortgage bonds, commercial mortgage-backed securities, longer-term lending and the re-financing of larger projects. The banks will lend on both development and investment activity. The current split is normally 30% development and 70% investment lending. On the investment side, the bank will seek to fix the loan rate for as long as possible whereas for development this is normally on a floating rate basis for up to 2 years which can then be converted into long-term investment financing (hedged through a fixed rate cap or an interest rate swap).

Loan to value ratios can be up to 100% but varies by country and property type. For logistic centres, LTV is lower and repayment more rapid due to the shorter life-time of projects. LTVs for offices can be as high as 90%, more usually 80%, depending on location. Hotels are seen as presenting greater challenges (managed properties requiring specialised knowledge). For debt coverage ratio, 120% appears standard and rarely will fall below 115%. The term of loan can secure a maximum term of 10 years which would apply in countries such as Slovakia, possibly less so for Romania, though differences depend more on the property and the client than the country. Market size therefore matters in terms of the capacity of cities to absorb stock. For example, Budapest has 23–25 shopping malls, Bucharest has four (only two modern), and Sofia and Bratislava has two each. In this context Budapest is over-provided, Sofia and Bratislava lack critical mass for further major development, but Bucharest may require 10–12 shopping centres.

Cross-collateralisation is seen to work within a country but can be extremely difficult for cross-border portfolios. In this context the key issues include which law is enforced and which should take priority. Banks favour the use of ring-fenced special purpose vehicles with no third party and no recourse to other creditors. In this type of structure the bank would have first call. Lease structure is dependent on the property market, the type of property and the number of tenants. There is a desire on the part of the bank for long lease terms, for example, in shopping centres where 10–20 years may be secured. In some countries, for example, Poland, there is an automatic right to cancel after 10 years whereas the second-wave countries are not likely to fix long lease terms. Transparency is again a major concern for the European-based banks, with historical property information often missing. The legal environment in many countries is frequently not sufficiently supportive and land registry information is often incomplete. Restitution claims are still an issue in Romania, the Czech Republic and Slovakia, in contrast to the situation in Hungary where the issue was dealt with early on in the transformation process. Differentiation is therefore apparent between the first- and second-wave countries in terms of market data sources.

It was recognised that higher yields were still possible in other countries: Romania, Croatia, the Baltic States and Russia. These countries constitute the 'second group' of markets beyond the 'core' countries and would have appeal to the opportunistic investor. They were seen to represent a continuation of the trend with a 2–3 year time lag in matters pertaining to market liquidity and pricing. While the Baltic States and Slovenia are in the forefront of the transformation of the region, they did not attract the same level of recognition. As smaller markets, they do not have the same scale of product or market liquidity.

The issue of yield compression can be viewed as part of the 'success' story with the purchasing power of Prague quoted as an example. Despite yield compression there was not any evidence of a 'cooling-off' of investment interest in the first half of 2006. This is seen to be part of the same story across the whole of the European market, not just simply the central European region. There is a view that the weight of money is heavier than the economic rationale would suggest. However, with the moving up of interest rates in the euro-zone, the gap between yields and funding costs are approaching the stage where markets can be too expensive suggesting that yields may have fallen too much.

Yield compression for property has characterised the central and eastern European markets over the past year. There are two main factors which have contributed to this yield compression, firstly the favourable influence of the capital markets and secondly improving property fundamentals that have raised expectations of rental growth. This has contributed to the growing weight of money into the sector where the demand for property as an investment medium remains high. In 2005 southern Europe experienced for the first time lower average property yield levels than northern Europe. The rate of compression slowed for both northern and southern Europe, but accelerated for central Europe (Figure 9.1). Central and eastern Europe traditionally had higher property yields due to the smaller and more opaque nature of these markets, the risk premium was higher which took into account the lack of transparency, the limited nature of investment flow and deals as well as political and economic uncertainty. This is illustrated in Figures 9.1 and 9.2 showing prime office and retail warehouse yields across the European landscape for the past few years.

Conclusions

Property market data transparency across central and eastern Europe has improved markedly in recent years. The key drivers that affect property market development in the region include increasing levels of FDI, demand by institutional investors and the establishment of local offices by international chartered surveying practices. Clearly the degree of interplay between the international and local players is important in providing the main source of research and expertise in undertaking feasibility studies on locations, property market sectors, use types and viability of development and investment-led projects. There has been significant change and progress, most notably through the formation of Research Forums, which has greatly enhanced the quality of office sector occupational data through more accurate measurement and the promotion of agreed definitions. Although data quality has improved considerably, there is nevertheless a requirement for better levels of time series data in order to enable the markets to be accurately measured, tracked and interpreted. Investment in central and eastern European property markets is perceived as high risk, though investors who employ risk-averse strategies may feel that the level

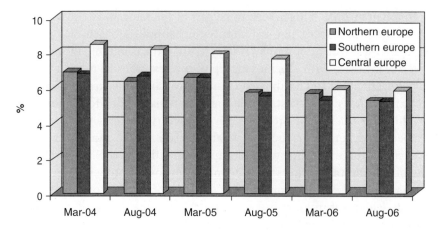

Figure 9.1   Prime office yields. *Source:* KASPAR, EuroProperty.

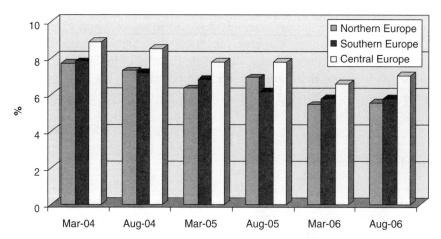

Figure 9.2   Prime retail warehouse yields. *Source*: KASPAR, EuroProperty.

of return adequately compensates for the added uncertainty. However, this depends on the size and strength of the portfolio and whether the investor can offset the risk in other geographical areas or sectors. Accessibility to investment data in the private sector is restricted due to the relative immaturity of the investment market, a lack of supply of suitable product and a limited number of transactions. There is a perception that the quality of public sector records has improved greatly as a result of EU accession. Research indicates that the lending institutions are promoting the adoption of internationally recognised valuation standards. Markets in the region are continuing to mature but require an element of self-regulation through a local code of practice and above all the need for the benchmarking of property investment performance if the development of these markets is to be taken to the next level of transparency.

The countries of central and eastern Europe (Poland, Czech Republic and Hungary) are increasingly being recognised as mainstream European property markets. Second-wave countries such as Romania, Bulgaria, Croatia, Russia and Turkey are perceived to lag the prime central and eastern European markets by 6–8 years in terms of risk and transparency. In central and eastern Europe a higher risk premium is applied due to the lack of transparency, the limited nature of investment transactions as well as political and economic uncertainties. The upward movement of interest rates in the euro-zone during 2006 has widened the gap between yields and funding costs to the point where markets are considered to be too expensive for borrowing by international investors. There is the likelihood of higher returns on the development rather than the investment side due to yield compression on the latter. Property development is increasingly perceived as the principal opportunity for value creation.

On the investment side, banks will fix the loan rate for as long as possible whereas for development a floating rate basis will apply for up to 2 years with the option to convert to long-term investment financing. Bank lending and funding strategies in central and eastern Europe relate primarily to the perceived maturing of the first wave of central and eastern European markets in terms of investment opportunities, returns and risks, and the ability of the second-wave countries to create institutional structures and market conditions that are attractive to inward investment. Evidence drawn from the London-based international banks indicates a concerted policy towards doing business in central and eastern Europe and a willingness to increase exposure in new markets although client needs and relationships still remain paramount in terms of lending criteria. The continuing appetite for prime assets is reflected in yield compression in investment markets and the realisation that development offers greater opportunities for value creation.

References

Adair, A., Allen, S., Berry, J. & McGreal, S. (2006) Central and Eastern European property investment markets: issues of data and transparency. *Journal of Property Investment and Finance*, 24 (3), 211–220.
Cushman and Wakefield Healey and Baker (2004) *Emerging Europe Summary 2003.* Cushman & Wakefield Healey & Baker, London.
D'Arcy, E. & Keogh, G. (1998) Territorial competition and property market process: an exploratory analysis. *Urban Studies*, 35 (8), 1215–1230.
Jones Lang LaSalle (2006) *Real Estate Transparency Index.* Jones Lang LaSalle, London.
Keivani, R., Parsa, A. &McGreal, W.S. (2002) Institutions and urban change in a globalising world. *Cities*, 19 (3), 183–193.

Keogh, G. & D'Arcy, E. (1994) Market maturity and property market behaviour: a European comparison of mature and emergent markets. *Journal of Property Research*, *11*, 215–235

Keogh, G. & D'Arcy, E. (1999) Property market efficiency: an institutional economic perspective. *Urban Studies, 36* (13), 2401–2414.

McGreal, W.S., Parsa, A. & Keivani, R. (2002) Evolution of property investment markets in Central Europe: opportunities and constraints. *Journal of Property Research, 19* (3), 213–230.

Parsa, A., McGreal, W.S. & Keivani, R. (2000) Globalisation of real estate markets and urban development in Central Europe, end of award report to the Economic and Social Research Council UK, Swindon.

Watkins, D. & Merrill, C. (2003) *Central Europe: A Brief Introduction to Participating in Reemerging Real Estate Markets.* Heitman Real Estate Investment Management, Chicago, IL.

10

Islamic Finance and Shariah-Compliant Real Estate Investment

A.R. Ghanbari Parsa and Mohammad Ali Muwlazadeh

Introduction

Over the past three decades there has been much development in the political, social and economic aspects of the Islamic world. The reassertion of Islamic ideology and political will in different parts of the Middle East, Africa and Asia has been partly a reaction to the encroachment of its traditional and ideological values by western cultural influence exerted by increased military and economic actions. Moreover, the substantial increase in oil revenues in recent years has contributed to growing financial influence of a number of countries in the Islamic world. Subsequently, this has been manifested in calls by Muslims to develop a socio-economic system, based on the principles of the Islamic law. To practice what they preach, Muslims have decided to put the system into effect. The establishment of Islamic social and economic institutions such as Islamic banking and Shariah-compliant[1] finance are major landmarks in this movement (Aggarwal & Yousef, 2000; Abdul Hamid & Norization, 2001). The purpose of this chapter is to provide an insight into the methods of Islamic finance and criteria for compliance with principles of Shariah law. Therefore, it is not the intention of the chapter to investigate how the system works, nor how the Islamic socio-economic system fares as compared to other socio-economic models in detail. But it is important to find out to what extent the Islamic finance system, namely Shariah-compliant funds, is applied to real estate investment.

Different Islamic schools of thought

The main basis of all Islamic ideology is the 'Shariah' (Islamic law) which is historically derived from the Quran (the Holy Book) and the Sunnah (tradition). The Quran, as the pivot of Islamic ideology, is the main source of the 'Shariah'. The principles of the law in the Quran are interpreted and amplified in the Hadith (sayings of the prophet), which together constitute the second basic source of the Shariah. The literature of the Ahadith (plural of Hadith) is extensive, the more important and reliable elements of which are known as Sehah-al-Set, the six reliable sources. Among these, the Bukhari by Mohammad Ismail al-Bukhari holds the first place. The interpretation of the Quran and the Hadith by different Islamic scholars has resulted in the creation of five distinct schools of thought. They are: The Hanafi; Maliki; Ash-shafii; Hanbaly and Jafari (Shiia). Each of these schools tends to predominate in a different region of the Muslim world. However, not all sources of the above-mentioned schools are accepted by the Shiia sect. Rather, they have eight reliable sources, of which the Osul-al-Kafi by Kollaini is the most important.

Concept and basis of Islamic economy

The Islamic economy in general is deemed by Muslim economists as being founded on ethical values. In their view, ethical values are not treated as exogenous, as they are treated in conventional economics (Naqavi, 1981). Quranic verses that deal with economic issues are intermingled with those that deal with ethics and morals. So are the Traditions. Ethics and Islamic norms are a set of axioms upon which the philosophy of Islamic economics is established, leaving no question as to what comes first or what dominates what – ethics or economics (Al-Ashkar, 1987). Naqavi (1981) argues that Islamic ethical principles not only determine individual choice and collective choice, but also provide a principle of integrating the two. The primary function of Islam is to guide human development on correct lines and in the right direction. It deals with all aspects of economic development and never in a form divorced from this perspective (Kahf, 1978, 1989). This is why the focus, even in the economic sector, is on human development with the result that economic development is considered an integrated and indivisible element of the moral and socio-economic development of human society.

Universal principles found in Ahadith (the sayings of the prophet) include the maxim that there is no legal validity in any action that brings injury to oneself or others, which does not protect a person from injury and does not prohibit him from causing damage to his neighbour, to society or to creation as a whole (Abdul Rahman, 2004). This is an intrinsic part of the religion, since it claims to improve the system of life as a whole, boost the spiritual development of individuals and rectify the socio-economic structure of society by promoting social justice. It could be said that Islam has carried the seeds of the spirit of capitalism since its early days (Al-Ashkar, 1987).

The recognition of profit, the encouragement of the creation of wealth, the respect for free enterprise, the organization of legal and financial matters and the high regard given to private ownership are some major characteristics accepted in the Quran and the Traditions, (Ahmad, 1980). Almubarak (1974) and Ahmad (2007) view production and profit (in an Islamic system) not as ends but means to achieve goals. The moving force of current systems is profit, but in the Islamic system it is human welfare (Al-Mubarak, 1974). Islam thus has a set of goals and values encompassing all aspects of human life including the social, economic and political. Since all aspects of life are interdependent and the Islamic way of life is a whole, its goals and values in one field determine the goals and values in the other fields as well. This is a holistic view of society, economy and government.

It is something unique and different and exclusive to Islam. How unique and how different is essentially the key issue. Hasanuz Zaman (2007) offers the following definition: 'Islamic economics is the knowledge and application of injunctions and rules of the Shariah (Islamic Jurisprudence) that prevent injustice in the acquisition and disposal of material resources in order to provide satisfaction to human beings and enable them to perform their obligations to Allah (God) and society'. Akram Khan considered that 'Islamic economics aims at the study of human falah (Salvation) achieved by organizing the resources of earth on the basis of cooperation and participation. The role of the Shariah (Islamic Jurisprudence), the notion of (justice) and falah (salvation), cooperation and sharing are central to Islamic economic philosophy of the total system of Islam' (Akram Khan, 2007).

Market structure in Islam

Free competition is a fundamental feature of the Islamic market structure. Various sayings from the Traditions emphasize that the prices of goods and commodities should be determined by market forces, demand and supply. All forms of monopolistic power, hoarding of wealth and mobile assets are condemned (Al-Sadr, 1968; Yusoff, 1992). The essence of the Islamic state interference is based on the notion that 'all sovereignty belongs to Allah'. The state is one of the means that brings human beings closer to Him. Consequently, we find a Muslim scholar like Al-Mawardi defining the objective of the Islamic state as to continue the function of prophethood in safeguarding religion and managing the worldly affairs (Kahf, 1994). Having explained some of the Islamic economic principles, it is desirable to discuss the concept of resource allocation in Islam. This is a prerequisite to the understanding of Shariah-compliant investment (SCI) which is the primary aim of this chapter.

Mannan (1999) argues that the efficient allocation of resources in an interest-free economy is possible providing the Islamic concept of 'accounting price' for capital is considered as one of the decision criteria.

The accounting price of capital is an Islamic value-loaded term that, depending upon the national plan requirement and overall priorities, might be different for different sectors of the economy (Ibid, 1999). Based on Islamic value systems, the link-up of material considerations with economic ethics is a must. Therefore, the criteria upon which the allocation of resources in an Islamic economic system depends are both objective and subjective. The 'accounting price' of capital will present the objective criteria that must be based upon the Islamic opportunity cost, while the subjective criteria, based upon the injunctions of the Holy Quran and Sunnah, will be represented by the economic ethics. So, the scope of allocation of resources is both wide and narrow at the same time. When the allocation of resources must take place within the restrictions put forward, by the Holy Quran and Sunnah, it is classified as narrow. It is considered wide when the allocation of resources must take the market and non-market forces such as externalities, secular and religious factors including moral, social and economic values of Islam into consideration (Ibid, 1999).

Allocation of resources in Islamic economic system

The Islamic allocation of resources is quite distinct from that in a capitalist or socialist system in which the interest rate plays a vital role. This might be due to the fact that the capitalist system is based upon consumer's sovereignty, while the socialist radical paradigm is based upon producer's sovereignty. Therefore, the allocation of investment resources under producer's sovereignty is quite different from marginal productivity criterion under consumer's sovereignty (Ibid, 1999). Rosser and Rosser (2004) are of the view that 'Muslims present their view not just as a change in personal moral codes, but as a total system of economic and political organization of the society, a possible third way between capitalism and socialism' (Rosser & Rosser , 2004). In his book *The Making of the Islamic Economic*, Mannan (1999) summarizes the following differences among the three economic systems of capitalist, socialist and Islam.

'(i)　In a capitalist system interest is considered as an element of cost of production while Islamic economic system rejects interest as an element of the cost of production. Unlike capitalist system that considers wage, rent, interest and profit as distributive shares, the distributive shares in Islamic system are three: rent, wage and profits. There is no place for interest in the Islamic economic set up since it is not included in the cost of production in the Islamic economic system.

(ii)　According to Marx, the welfare function for influencing investment decision is created from the source within the society and it represents the will of the Communist Party in power. The welfare function in

Islam is created from the source outside the society and it represents the will of God explained by the principles of Shariah. This does not mean that there is no scope for new thinking or argument in Islam. The real allocation of resources in Islam mainly depends upon subjective factors that may be expressed in terms of Islamic welfare criteria'.

Unlike the Marxian economic function which disregards non-material values, Islam has focused on social and moral objectives in addition to its economic objective. However, it does not mean that the Marxian social system is value neutral.

In Islam, there is no exploitation by producers, consumers or anyone else. Rather they cooperate with each other for the well-being of the society. Mannan (1999) asserts that the 'accounting price' of capital in Islam must consider factors such as the preferences of the consumer, and the private and public sectors, in addition to the displaced alternatives in terms of scarcity and profitability at home and abroad (Mannan, 1984). He also suggests that the concept of 'accounting price' may be applied in the following cases of resource allocation.

(i)   Resource allocation in the pure public sector: There is a need for supplying social good in this sector and externalities exist in this sector. In this case, market system does not work. The national importance of this sector is very high.

(ii) Resource allocation in the pure private sector: In this sector, smaller investment is needed for producing consumer goods. It is assumed that goods producers and the consumer do not feel the need of borrowing.

(iii) Public sector–induced investment with private sector: Projects in which risk exists and the private initiative is not encouraged in investment; the participatory investment on the basis of profit and loss sharing is welcomed.

(iv) Externally induced investment: The investment on the basis of profit and loss sharing may be made in those sectors where there is a scope for technology transfer from one country to the other. Market mechanism in Islam generates the demand and supply forces in a manner that must be consistent with the value system derived from faith in Allah. It means, if a project is chosen on the basis of objective consideration led by market forces, it should also be acceptable from welfare view points (Mannan, 1984).

Muslims' belief in the life before and after death has two effects as far as allocation of resources by the consumer is concerned. This means that a choice of action has both immediate effect in this life and effect in the life to come. They believe that virtue from using one's income in interest-free loans (Qard-al-Hasana), and donations (sa daqah) to the poor and the needy will be gained by them in the life hereafter. The accepted concept of goods and commodities in Islam, therefore, is based on their moral outcomes. In other words, the useful, beneficial consumable materials whose utilization does not bring about the material, moral and spiritual betterment for the consumer are not accepted. These are things which are prohibited in Islam and not regarded goods in the Islamic sense. The concept of goods in Islam are those which are exchangeable and morally useful (Choudhury, 1991).

The principles of resource allocation in Islam

Shariah experts specify at least four principles and 12 criteria of welfare to allocate resources in Islam. The four principles are: permissibility, consistency, balancing and desirability. The welfare criteria are: ideological promotion, efficiency in resource allocation, equity in distribution of resources, collective good, priority to the immediate need, stability, certainty, continuity, productivity, human consideration, universality, ethics and morality (Mannan, 1999).

(a) Permissibility: The allocation of resources for investment should be allowed by Shariah (Halal).
(b) Consistency: The concept of consistency is very dynamic. It means that the consistency of a particular investment with the Shriah principles should already be decided by the Ijtihad and Qiyas.
(c) Balancing: In Islam, the balance between subjective and objective factors of life is desired, that is, to maintain an honest living with the appropriate and balanced use of human intellect and God's bounties. Therefore, if the principle of balancing is violated, then it may give rise to a problem of inconsistent use of resources.
(d) Desirability: To be in line with this principle, projects should be desirable and beneficial in order to satisfy the basic elements of Maslahah and secure the well-being of the society as a whole. Welfare criteria will be used as a yardstick for choosing among different investment projects to allocate resources on the basis of Islamic Shariah. Most of these criteria are mutually overlapping, but they are just indicative and not exhaustive.
(e) Ethics and morality: In order to obey and to serve the cause of God both in the world here and hereafter, the allocation of resources should be made in such a way that it meets the noble objectives of ethics and morality (Choudhury, 1991).

Defining SCI

Shariah-compliant investment represents a type of ethical investment organized in compliance with Islamic law. The range of investment opportunities complying with Muslim economic systems has historically been restricted. Shariah-compliant funds have been established to offer a new way of self-invested personal pensions, or a small self-administered scheme for interested investors (Jobst Andreas, 2007). This does not allow non-Islamic transactions, including options trading and interest-based transactions such as margin trading and short selling. Shariah property funds are also ethical funds organized around the main principles of Shariah law. For instance, Shariah property investment funds will not rent properties to organizations involved in trades such as alcohol, armaments, tobacco, pork products or gambling.

Shariah investment criteria

Overall, Shariah investment must be in compliance with the fundamental Islamic principles. An Islamic financial institution is guided and supervised by a Shariah board (a committee of Islamic scholars) in the development of Shariah-compliant products. The most fundamental aspect is their compliance to Quranic principles which forbid Riba (usury) in the form of interest, unjustified rewards or unlawful gain. Furthermore, it discourages Gharar, or uncertainty. All investments must be Halal and cannot engage in Haram transactions or activities, that is, those which transgress Shariah law. Other aspects of Islamic finance include Qard-al-Hasana and Al-Wadi-a (Abdul Rahman, 2004).

In accordance with the principles of Shariah law, Shariah-compliant real estate investment funds are not permitted to invest in companies which trade in:

pork products;
adult entertainment;
financial services (conventional);
arms or munitions;
cinema;
tobacco;
gambling;
alcoholic liquor.

Concepts and growth of Shariah methods of finance and investment

Islamic finance is one of the most rapidly growing areas of international finance today. The increasing popularity and press coverage of Islamic finance has further clarified the topic but misconceptions are still common. There are those who equate anything Islamic as financing terrorism. The Western world has very strange visions of what is going on in the Islamic world. Another myth is that Shariah-compliant products cannot provide returns similar to those of more conventional financial instruments. This view is rapidly fading due to the Sukuk sector's popularity and its market efficiency, coupled with a realization of the competitive returns that are possible, which have encouraged the non-Muslim investors to chose Shariah-compliant products as a way to 'sin-screen' their portfolio and invest ethically.

Meyer (2007) argues that Shariah-compliant funds are just another strand of socially responsible investing. Nevertheless, he asserts that performance does count. You always get back to the golden question: 'How are you doing in the market'? Meyer, for his part, has seen enthusiasm for Islamic finance products percolate and, in association with Barclays, has launched a Shariah-compliant trading platform acting as the sole prime broker. Meyer calls the new platform a 'historic' achievement for the market as it represents an opportunity for investment managers to offer a Shariah-compliant equivalent to their conventional portfolios without fundamentally altering their strategies or processes. With the establishment of such platforms, increasing number of hedge fund managers, including Boston-based GRT Capital, have signed up.

Now that concepts are being translated into actual platforms, Meyer believes that the market for Islamic finance is finally 'coming of age'. He adds, 'In 2007, it has arrived in Dubai, London and New York, and it's going to be taken much more seriously going forward' (Ibid, 2007). Islamic banking is flourishing as Islamic banks currently manage between $200 and $300 billion, an amount that has been increasing between 12% and 15% each year. As the world's fastest growing major religion, with over a billion adherents worldwide, Islamic finance proves an even more lucrative market. The International Islamic Financial Services Board has predicted that assets managed under Islamic rules will almost triple to $2.38 trillion by 2015. There are now 300 Shariah-compliant financial services providers globally compared to only one in 1975. Shah (2007) cites two major reasons for the increasing popularity of Islamic finance: 'The growth of Islamic finance is linked to the surge in petrodollars and the related opportunity for financial institutions to create Islamic financial products'. Subsequently, an increasing number of Western banks have introduced Islamic-compliant products. These include the UK-based HSBC and Lloyds TSB banks, which began to offer Islamic mortgages in 2005. With sizable Muslim communities in countries in Europe and North America, the potential for Islamic-compliant products and services is very high. For example, Muslims make up 3% of the British population, but in some cities, such as Leicester, they make up as much as 20%. There are also estimated to be about half a million regular Muslim visitors to the UK and approximately 12 million Muslims living in the EU, principally in France and Germany. However, according to Shah, Islamic finance still remains a niche market (Shah, 2007) although, according to market researchers Datamonitor, demand for Islamic mortgages in the UK is so strong that gross advances could reach £4.5 billion ($7 billion) in 2006 (Datamonitor, 2006).

The development of Shariah-compliant financial products and services is at different stages of development in Europe. According to Brugnoni (2006), the first *murabaha* transaction ever done in Italy was achieved in October 2006 with increasing number of 'ijarah wa iqtinah' deals in the pipeline. Furthermore, he cites the perception that many finacial institutions and existing institutional settings view Islamic finace as a challenge to the establishment. These are amongst the barriers to the development of Islamic finance and products in Europe.

In addition to the real estate market, there are other sectors of the economy that have considered Islamic finance for their activities. Seeking to expand its fleet, the Abu Dhabi–based career Etihad Airline utilized a mixture of Islamic and conventional finance to raise $900 million. The fund-raising included a $400 million Islamic finance facility, the largest transaction of its type by an airline. Etihad has also launched another fund-raising initiative which many international banks are hoping to facilitate for a $500 million. The airline has also implemented a fuel hedge to reduce its exposure to price fluctuations. According to its Chief Financial Officer, 'We were keen to tap into the Islamic market, which we had not done before, to diversify our sources of finance' (MEED, 2007a).

Meyer Fund Management established in 2005 offering Islamic financial products had previously experimented with socially responsible investment (SRI) funds in the 1990s. The founder of Meyer Fund Management, citing the enormous potential for growth of Shariah funds, explains: 'My main message to investors is not to put all your eggs into one basket like real estate. We have good hedge fund managers who delivered a 15% return in 2005 and 25% in 2006. We can also arrange for investors to pick their own hedge fund managers who then run on our Shariah screen, something which has proven popular' (Meyer, 2007).

The evolution of Islamic finance is a huge opportunity for South East Asian financial centres and, according to Standard & Poors credit rating agency, Islamic financial services now comprise a roughly $1 trillion market worldwide. Assets management under mortgages and investment products abiding by Shariah law are growing at an average of 23% per annum, or more than twice the pace of conventional global financial services assets, which grew nearly 10% in 2006 (Figure 10.1).

Today, more than 250 Islamic banks are operating from China to USA, managing funds to the tune of $200 billion. Western banks, through their Islamic units in the UK, Germany, Switzerland, Luxembourg, etc. also

Banks and Islamic Finance Institutions Operating in the UK
Albaraka International Ltd,
Albaraka Investment Co. Ltd,
Al Rajhi Investment Corporation,
Al Safa Investment Fund
Bank Sepah, Iran
Dallah Al Baraka (UK) Ltd.,
Takafol (UK) Ltd,
Barclays Capital
HSBC Amanah Finance
ABCIB Islamic Asset Management, Arab Banking Corp

Banks with Islamic windows
ABC International Bank,
Islamic Bank of Britain
European Islamic Bank
Europe Arab Bank Plc,
Riyadh Bank
Citibank International Plc,
Cedel International,
Dawnay Day Global Investment Ltd
Global Islamic Finance, HSBC Investment Bank Plc
Gulf International Bank Bsc, Bahrain
The Halal Mutual Investment Company Plc
IBJ International, (Subsidiary of Industrial Bank of Japan)
J. Aron & Co. (Goldman Sachs International Finance) Ltd.,
Islamic Investment Banking Unit (IIBU), United Bank of Kuwait,

Figure 10.1   Islamic financial institutions.

practice Islamic banking. Besides, Islamic funds have found a flourishing market in the USA and Europe (International Directory of Islamic Banks and Institutions, 2000).

Islamic banking assets already account for 12.2% of total banking assets in Malaysia, and by 2010, the government aims to have 20% of all banking assets in Malaysia under Islamic banks. 'Islamic financial services are one of the key growth engines for Malaysia', says Second Finance Minister Nor Mohammed Yakcop. 'We realize that we can not compete with big financial centres like New York, London, or Hong Kong, but we are trying to carve a niche for ourselves in the area of Islamic finance' (Bremner & Shameen, 2007). According to the Chief Executive of the Islamic Banking and Finance Institute of Malaysia, the country is managing some 30–40% of assets in the global Islamic financial system, amounting to $0.85 trillion, and this may rise further through aggressive promotion and innovations. It is also speculated that assets managed by the Malaysian Islamic financial system may one day even surpass those of the local conventional banking system. 'It is possible, if we can attract "petro dollars" from the Middle East and Africa, as well as demand for Islamic financial products and services through innovation' (Adnan Alias, 2007). To lure foreign institutions in the Islamic financial services arena, Malaysia has given out tax breaks and other incentives as well as relaxed rules. Middle Eastern Islamic financial concerns like Kuwait Finance House, Qatar's Asian Finance Bank, Saudi Arabia's Al-Rajhi and Dubai Investment Group's Bank Islam all now have big footprints in Malaysia (Jobst, 2007).

Singapore financial players are also attracted into this arena. South East Asia's biggest bank, Singapore-based DBS (DBSM), recently teamed with more than 20 Middle East investors to create the Islamic Bank of Asia. The initial capital base of this bank was set about $418 million and focuses on commercial and private banking, as well as corporate finance. This is also an indication of the fierce competition between different countries and cities to become a hub for Islamic finance and investment.

To get help for upgrading its energy infrastructure, China is attracting strategic investments from the Middle East. Development of a port in Tianjin has received a funding of $500 million from Dubai-based DPW, while a $5 billion refinery in the Guangdong province will be funded by Kuwaiti investors. China is assumed to be a money magnet for Middle East investment in future. Beijing is trying to shore up its energy infra-structure, and Gulf countries view China and India as among their most critical customers in the 21st century. This was further reinforced by the fact that major oil-producing countries like Iran, Saudi Arabia and Sudan have become major trade partners for both China and India through major political and economic exchanges in recent years. The Middle East Asia economic relationship is set to expand substantially.

Globalization of Shariah property investment

The rapid growth of the diverse international property investment over the last decade has brought about a belief that property investment through Shariah compliance has an assured return that cannot be achieved by invest-ment in other sectors such as stocks, bonds and equity markets. Islamic banking and finance market has been one of the fastest growing financial niche markets globally in the past decade. This might be due to the fact that there has been significant flight of capital originating from the Middle East and other Islamic nations in the aftermath of 9/11 in the US. According to the Dubai International Financial Centre (DIFC), the global market for Islamic financial products is worth over $200 billion and is expected to grow at 12–15% a year over the next 10 years. The outgoing amount of Islamic real estate fund from GCC has also reached $1.8 billion (Table 10.1). It is likely to account for some 50–60% of the total savings of the world's 1.2 bil-lion Muslims within the next decade (http://www.difc.ae).

Table 10.1   List of Islamic Real Estate Funds as of June 2006.

Fund manager/ Distributor	Name of fund	Country	Size $ million	Type	Investor advisor	Description
Kuwait Finance House	Baitak Asia Real Estate Fund	South Asia	600	Commercial Residential	Pacific Star Group	A $600 million Islamic real estate fund. The Baitak Asia Real Estate fund will invest in residential and commercial sites in Asian countries. This will be the first real estate deal in Asia for KFH, which is 49% owned by Gulfs.
Kuwait Finance House	Islamic European Real Estate Fund	Europe	486	Commercial Residential	Equity Estate Bv	The fund intends to invest Euro 400 million in European property concentrating in high yielding office, logistics and light industrial properties in the Benelux, France and Germany.
Dubai Islamic Bank, Cheung Kong Group	Al Islamic Far Eastern Real Estate Fund	Far Far East	450	Commercial Retail Residential	ARA Asset Management	The new fund will be managed by ARA Asset Management and jointly promoted by DIB and Cheung Kong Group. The Islamic compliant investment vehicle has set aside $450 million to invest in commercial, retail and residential projects in major Asian cities.
Guidance Financial Group	Guidance Fixed Income Fund	USA	200	Residential	Freddie Mae	The fund will hold securities that are backed by Shariah-compliant real estate finance assets. The securities will be issued and guaranteed by the Federal Home Loan Mortgage Corporation ('Freddie Mac').
Shamil Bank	China Realty Fund	China	150	Commercial	International Assets Management Co.Ltd (CITICIAM)	Shamil Bank Bahrain entered into a Memorandum of Understanding (MOU) with prominent Chinese financial institution CITIC International Asset Management Co. Ltd (CITICIAM) to set up and launch $ 150 million closed-end China Realty Fund.

Source: Ibrahim and Ong (2006).

Affected by globalization, the diverse real estate markets have attracted a wide range of investors from remote areas of the world into UK's real estate market. In June 2006, Gordon Brown, the present PM and former Chancellor of the Exchequer for the UK government, said that he wants to see London become the global centre for Islamic finance, by offering regulatory and tax regime measures to support the creation of products that comply with Shariah law. Why would this be an aim, and what would be necessary to achieve it? There can be no doubt as to the motivation – the flow of funds from Muslim countries is estimated to be somewhere in the region of $300–$400 billion annually, growing at a rate of some 15% annually. With the oil price currently at about $78 a barrel, this global flow of funds seems set to continue.

Real estate investments have proved to be a popular home for Shariah-compliant funds, and Middle Eastern money accounted for some 11% of the total foreign investment in the UK commercial property, having grown from about 4% in 2004 (RICS, 2005). The report also named UK as the top location for Shariah-compliant real estate investment. Investors from the Middle East invested £827 million in European property in 2001, a 225% increase over the previous year. Of this amount, some 91% was invested in the UK. In the first 9 months of 2002 alone, Middle Eastern investment in the UK commercial property totalled £875 million, which is 15% up on the entire 2001 total. With rental yields falling in many Western countries, there are, however, a growing number of Middle Eastern investors seeking higher returns from investments in Eastern Europe property (and also outside the EU), emerging markets outside Europe and also riskier property development.

Although Middle Eastern investors have been active in different international markets, there has been a substantial flow of funds in the real estate markets within the region. Over the past 5 years, Islamic project finance has grown from next to nothing to take a significant share of the region's massive project finance market. Despite uncertainty over the extent of the liquidity pool, political and investor pressure has meant that this growth is certain to continue. Within the Middle East, there are growing numbers of infrastructure projects requiring Islamic compliant finance. This has created a considerable demand for specialist advisory services offered by a limited but growing number of lawyers, bankers and real estate investment advisors. However, despite such growth, the market is still under-developed and fragmented due to the restriction of property ownership rights. To address these issues, a number of countries in the Middle East have embarked on liberalization of their property markets in terms of ownership restriction and activities of international real estate investors. For example, in its effort to diversify its economy, the United Arab Emirates has removed restrictions concerning real estate ownership of foreign and expatriate nationals from outside the GCC. In 2002, the Dubai

Emirate passed a law allowing foreign entities (persons, institutions, etc.) to own and usufruct property.

With increasing appetite for knowledge and information on Islamic-compliant finance, there has been a surge in dedicated conferences, seminars and events in different parts of the world. It is in such events that key trends and opportunities in the market are examined. Borrower-led case studies have explored lessons learnt from major Shariah-compliant deals, including the Islamic financing of the $1 billion Al Waha Petrochemicals project and the Shuq aiq IWPP $150 million Islamic tranches, helping those interested in Shariah compliance to gain a better understanding of this complex market (IPF, 2007).

US-based Guidance Financial Group has recently set up a Shariah-compliant housing finance company with local investors in Saudi Arabia. Investment companies already offer housing finance in the Kingdom but the market is set to expand, with the issue of mortgage regulations expected by the end of the year. Guidance Financial already offers Islamic mortgages in the USA. Nevertheless, investment diversity needs to be tailored with methods of investment and portfolio management. Achieving this target requires a clear understanding of how Shariah funds differ from conventional funds. While in some areas there are no great differences, however, the major area where they are seen to differ and sets them apart is in the monitoring of compliance. The introduction of Shariah-compliant Real Estate Investment Trusts (REITs) is seen to be a future possibility in terms of developments.

With growing demand for Shariah-compliant investment, an increasing number of funds have been established. For example, Munshaat Real Estate Projects (MREP) recently launched the first Shariah-compliant REITs in Kuwait. It has announced the offering of 254.448 million shares of Al Mahrab Tower (MREIT) for private placement. MREIT is currently under incorporation as a Kuwaiti closed shareholding company with an expected paid-up capital of KD26.784 million (approximately $93 million). MREIT will operate in accordance with the regulations of the Ministry of Commerce and Industry in Kuwait and MREIT's business activities will be Shariah-compliant (http://www.zawya.com).

'We are getting permission. It is not a licensed activity today', says executive chairman Mohamad Hammour. 'The Saudi [mortgage] market will be slower to develop than people expect. Real estate development and finance companies have to go hand in hand. Residential developers need a lot of experience and growth will be gradual, but there are very robust housing needs' (MEED, 2007b). Guidance Financial also plans to enter the secondary mortgage market in the region. 'At the moment, there is not much to feed [into a secondary market], but there is an opportunity for it to develop', asserts Hammour (Ibid, 2007b).

In a separate move, Guidance Financial was managing a hospitality fund that was expected to reach $200 million by June 2007. It was earmarked for funding the development of a chain of Shariah-compliant hotels in partnership with Kempinski Hotel Group. The fund has plans to launch a total of 30 hotels and the first is planned to open in Dubai in 2009 (Ibid, 2007b).

Finance methods for Shariah-compliant real estate investment

Based on the principles of Shariah law, there are a number of methods of financing real estate investment that are permitted and are fully compatible. The most important financial vehicles used in property finance are: Murabaha, Musharakah, Sukuk, Gharar, Ijarah and Mudarabah, among which the Sukuk method is most favoured (Newell, 2006). However, all such finance methods have to be certified by a panel of experts, the 'Shariah board', whose members are drawn from respected Shariah scholars with the expertise to interpret Islamic law. Similarly, every single transaction will have to be scrutinized by the Shariah board to ensure full compliance with the Islamic principles (Ibrahim *et al.*, 2007). Middle Eastern investors prefer using the Murabaha and Ijarah vehicles to invest in the USA. This is the method most consistent with the standard real estate process (Abdulkader *et al.*, 2005). In light of these moral impediments to 'passive' investment and secured interest as form of compensation, Shariah-compliant lending in Islamic finance requires the replication of interest-bearing, conventional finance via more complex structural arrangements of contingent claims (Mirakhor & Iqbal, 1988). A recent study by Parsa and McIntosh (2006) conducted a survey of a number of UK-based Shariah real estate active banks, investment funds, real estate advisors and lawyers. The report found that the majority of the respondents (74%) appeared to use the 'Ijiara' method of financing. Murabaha method was used by 65% whilst 'Sukuk' has been utilized by 57%. This was followed by 54% using Musharakah and a further 51% having used 'mudarabah'.

Sukuk

As a Shariah-compliant product, Sukuks were developed to provide borrowers with development and restructuring capital while offering stable income to Muslim investors. Islamic law, which outlaws the use of interest and other practices generating money from debt, requires all lent money be tied to a tangible asset. This condition is being steadily overcome by ingenuity in Islamic finance.

Although the religious prohibition of the exchange of debt and the required conferral of ownership interest to participate in business risk still poses challenges to further development of Islamic securitization, the gradual acceptance of Islamic investment certificates, the so-called *Sukuk* bonds, represents a successful attempt to overcome these impediments based on the adequate interpretation and analogical reasoning of Shariah principles applied in Islamic finance (Jobst, 2007). Sukuks are Shariah-compliant and tradable asset-backed, medium-term notes, which have been issued internationally by governments, quasi-sovereign agencies and corporations after their legitimization by the ruling of the *Fiqh Academy* of the *Organization of the Islamic Conference* in February of 1988. Over the last 5 years, the Sukuk has evolved as a viable form of capital market-based Islamic structured finance, which reconciles the concept of securitization and principles of the Shariah law on the provision and use of financial products and services in a risk-mitigation structure subject to competitive pricing (El-Qorchi, 2005). According to Jobst (2007), The *Accounting and Auditing Organization of Islamic Finance Institutions* (AAOIFI) currently recognizes 14 different types of Sukuks, which are traded on the *Scripless Securities Trading System* (SSTS) in Malaysia. Only appropriate Islamic bodies, the 'Shariah boards', may adjudicate the Shariah compliance of the terms of any Sukuk issuance.

Institutional investors and funds have become increasingly attracted to Sukuks. According to one such fund manager (Meyer, 2007), 'We are also looking to diversify ourselves into Sukuks in the US with the idea being to issue Islamic debt finance for US companies. And we are helping NYSE and Toronto companies that want to establish independent, Shariah-compliant business units for this purpose' (Meyer, 2007).

Until recently, Sukuk bonds have been an illiquid market, but when Encore Management devoted $70 million of its $100 Sanad Sukuk as a commitment to GCC, Sukuk has become a remarkable Islamic vehicle. The first Sukuk listing outside the Muslim world took place in July 2006 when Abu Dhabi's National Central Cooling Company (Tabreed) listed a $200 million offering on the London Stock Exchange (LSE). The same steps have been taken by Kuwait's National Industries Company for Building Materials which listed a $100 million Sukuk on the Irish Stock Exchange in October. Sharjah Islamic Bank has also listed a $225 million on the LSE at the same month. Nakheel, a Dubai-based property developer has entered the market with a $2.5 billion exchange-appropriate offering, which sources say should be oversubscribed. Furthermore, the recent establishment of the Dow Jones Citigroup Sukuk Index and the decision by Moody's Investors Service to rate Sukuk should both be regarded as positive indicators that the industry is bullish on Sukuk potential. The Sanad fund serves as the latest sign that the market is maturing (IDD 7, 2006).

Another structure that is gaining popularity in the market is the *Sukuk al Musharaka*. This structure involves an SPV issuer entering into a joint venture *Musharaka* agreement with the finance seeking party (*Musharaka* Party). The purpose of the *Musharaka* is to generate profits.

The parties' respective interests in the *Musharaka* are represented by contractual 'Units' held by each party. The Issuer will make a funding contribution to the *Musharaka* from funds it raises from the *Sukuk* issue (Dechert, 2006). The *Musharaka* Party will make an in-kind contribution to the *Musharaka* (usually including some tangible assets). In recent years, Malaysia has become the pacemaker and champion for the development of capital market–based, fixed - income instruments under Islamic law in the form of Sukuks. It hosts the world's largest Islamic bond market, estimated at $300 billion, which has grown at an average rate of 20% per year over the last 3 years. Although Sukuks have been issued by governments, government agencies, international development organizations and private corporations, private debt securities dominate and constitute the largest segment (70%) of Malaysia's Islamic bond market. The most common type of Sukuks are based on *bai bithaman ajil* (BBA) and *murabaha* (ca. 90%), while government entities tend to issue *istina* Sukuks, which are also considered pricing benchmarks (Jobst, 2007). The Issuer and the *Musharaka* Party also enter into a Purchase Undertaking pursuant to which the Issuer can require the *Musharaka* Party to purchase a set amount of Units on set dates during the term of the *Sukuk*. The Issuer will receive profit distributions from the *Musharaka* and proceeds from sales of the Units to the *Musharaka* Party. The amounts received are distributed to the *Sukuk* holders in accordance with a set formula. This structure is viable when the *Musharaka* Party can use its in-kind contribution for a profit-generating venture. The structure is diagrammed in Figure 10.2.

Primary market opportunities should not be a problem, with more than 100 companies in the Middle East preparing Sukuk, according to Sanad.

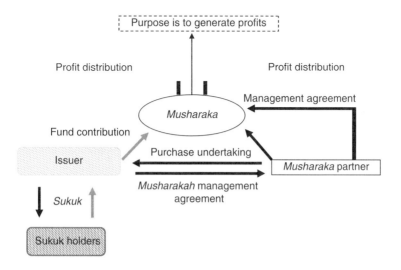

Figure 10.2 Musharakah Sukuk structure. *Source:* Dechert (2006).

Some German states, including Saxony-Anhalt, have recently issued Sukuk to finance public works, and Japan, China and Indonesia are preparing Sukuk for 2007. 'More of the world's Muslims are looking to further integrate the principles [of Shariah] into their life', cites Maples and Calder's senior lawyer. 'Seeing this, non-Islamic entities are seeing the benefits of issuing Sukuks to appeal to the largest possible pool of investors'. So, with increased interest from Muslim and non-Muslim investors alike, how long could it be before maturity is reached in the Sukuk secondary market? He further speculated that in 3–4 years, 'it will be a truly deep market'. And the manner in which investment banks and houses around the world approach the maturing Sukuk market in that period will have a significant impact on the huge pool of unemployed capital in the Middle East (IDD 7, 2006).

Ijarah

This is an Islamic lease agreement. Instead of lending money and earning interest, Ijarah allows the bank to earn profits by charging rentals on the asset leased to the customer. Ijarah wa iqtinah extends the concept of Ijarah to a hire and purchase agreement. The *Ijarah* (which is a word derived from the term 'rental' in Arabic) is a structure that utilizes an asset's rental stream to produce a return to the owner of the asset. Economically, an *Ijarah* financing works and operates like an amortizing or bullet repayment loan in many respects. However, Shariah scholars have become comfortable with the arrangement being a sale and an Islamic-compliant lease of an asset as opposed to a loan under which principal and interest are payable. The traditional *Ijarah* structure had been in use for some time before Islamic capital market instruments started to appear on the scene (Dechert, 2006) (Figure 10.3).

Ijarah or instalment leasing agreement is a vehicle of Shariah finance that is contractually enforceable in Islamic courts – it allows the purchase of assets for subsequent leasing at a mutually agreed periodic rent. Again, a bank actually buys the asset from the seller and rents it to the buyer at

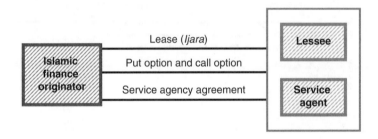

Figure 10.3   Ijarah or Islamic leasing structure. *Source:* Kamalpour (2006).

an agreed price plus profit (an instalment leasing agreement in which own-ership of fixed assets is not actually transferred). The lessee may agree at the outset to purchase the assets on termination of the lease, an alterna-tive known as Ijarah wa iqtinah (lease and ownership).

Mudarabah

A Mudarabah is an investment partnership, whereby the investor (Rab ul Mal) provides capital to another party/entrepreneur (the Mudarib) in order to undertake a business/investment activity. While profits are shared on a pre-agreed ratio, loss of investment is borne by the investor only. The mudarib loses its share of the expected income. The mudarib is the entre-preneur or investment manager in a mudarabah who invests the investor's funds in a project or portfolio in exchange for a share of the profits. For example, a mudarabah is essentially similar to a diversified pool of assets held in a Discretionary Asset Management Portfolio. It is important to separate the activities of speculators and legitimate investors in Islamic finance. The use of knowledge and information is rewarding as such investment will be fruitful if it is based upon rational use of knowledge and knowing how to use the information. On the contrary, speculation is associated with risk (Keon, 1989). There are rewards for risk sharing in a mudarabah finance deal, but this activity of taking on the risk of others is different in nature from deliberately seeking risk. Speculators can actu-ally increase risk for those who enter the market by churning stock, or by manipulating supply and demand and destabilizing the market. Yet it is impossible to prevent speculative investment in equity and bond markets through regulation (Yusoff, 1992).

Murabaha

Murabaha is the purchase and resale of a commodity instead of lending out money. In this method of Islamic finance, the capital provider purchases the desired commodity (for which the loan would have been taken out) from a third party and resells it at a predetermined higher price to the cap-ital user. By paying this higher price over instalments, the capital user has effectively obtained credit without paying interest. It is also called 'dimin-ishing Murabaha' because the interests in the property owning partnership will be transferred in instalments from the bank to the investor.

Cost-plus financing is another term used for explaining Murabaha finance. This term often appears as a form of trade financing based on letters of credit. Murabaha is a cost-plus 'trust sale' in which the buyer trusts that the seller is divulging its true costs, so a profit margin can be agreed on accurately. In such a sale to an Islamic importer, the exporter actually sells the goods to a bank, which then sells them to the importer at an agreed profit margin and on deferred payment terms (typically 3–12 months). Weist, who has structured a number of investment vehicles for financing assets in a Shariah-compliant and tax-efficient manner, explains that such contracts 'are usually drawn up under UK or US law' and are legally enforceable (Weist, 2007) (Figure 10.4).

According to Shariah principles, a Murabaha may only be used if:

- the goods are bought by the financial institution, or its agent, from a third party other than the client or related entities, thus avoiding the prohibited sale and lease back of goods;
- the financial institution, or its agent, acquires title to the goods before passing them on to the client;
- the financial institution bears the risk that the client will comply with his or her obligations to buy goods as agreed.

Musharakah

This is profit and loss sharing. It is a partnership where profits are shared according to an agreed ratio, whereas the losses are shared in proportion to the capital/investment of each partner. In a musharakah, all partners to a business undertaking contribute funds and have the right, but not the obligation, to exercise executive powers in that project, which is similar to a conventional partnership structure and the holding of voting stock in a limited company. This equity financing arrangement is widely regarded as the purest form of Islamic financing. Traditional musharakah can be looked on as a type of venture capital financing, with relatively high risks involved for the provider of the funding. The risks are greater today given the much more competitive international conditions than they were in

Figure 10.4   Murabaha real estate financing structure. *Source*: Kamalpour (2006).

the isolated and, to a large degree, sheltered markets of Muslim countries historically. In this modern context, the number of individuals who are in a position to provide musharakah financing is limited, although modern musharakah funding through equity market participation may have much smaller risks because of the ease of divestment. Perhaps, the best method of musharakah financing in a modern financial context is through Islamic banks. Because the banks have the resources to build up diversified musharakah portfolios, they are able to engage in such financing at much lower risk to themselves. Yet Islamic banks appear to concentrate excessively on short-term murabaha financing, and have neglected to a considerable extent the possibility of musharakah.

Shariah funds in the research agenda

Recent research by King Sturge and London South Bank University carried out by Parsa and McIntosh in 2006 examined the growing importance of Shariah property investment funds in Europe. The project considered the role of Shariah property funds in comparison with other international property funds, including: pension funds, life insurance funds, open-ended German funds, USA based and other structured funds and joint venture partnerships.

The approach was based on a programme of interviews with 34 key players in the field of Islamic finance. The interviewees were based in the UK and representing international funds: specialist property investment companies, trading companies, banks equity and debt lenders, international consultants, fund/ asset managers, legal advisors and accountants based in London, but all international. The aim was to ascertain their attitude towards Islamic finance and more specifically the important role the Shariah funds can play in enhancing property investment funds.

Prerequisites for investment decisions

Although compliance with Shariah principles is fundamentally important for Shariah funds investment, equal attention is paid to other criteria such as tax efficiency and risk assessment, in line with the requirements of other conventional investments. Over 65% of the respondents view tax efficiency as being very important. Availability of specialist advice is also seen as very important by 61% of the respondents whilst 47% view investment regulation is being vital with similar number of respondents requiring risk assessment regulation for Shariah-compliant real estate investment.

According to the King Sturge and London South Bank University's research findings, 85% of the respondents seem to be using debt financing with 44% determined to use it in the future. At the same time, 79% of those interviewed made use of equity finance.

Geographical locations favoured for Shariah investment

Shariah investors appear to follow similar locational decision strategies to conventional investors. Within Europe, the focus has, over the last 3 years, been on the more established real estate markets in north and west Europe, with the UK being the prime market. The most favoured countries, outside the UK, are Germany and France. While the same countries are expected to dominate, there seems to be an appetite to explore more emerging markets over the next few years. The greater interest seems to be in countries in the peripheries and in central and eastern Europe. Although Poland and Hungary were the only countries in eastern Europe for investment in the last few years, nevertheless, investors are now looking more seriously at other emerging economies including the Czech Republic, Slovenia and Slovakia. Outside Europe, the USA remains the prime investment focus, both now and in the future.

The work by Parsa and McIntosh (2006) also confirms that the majority of Shariah investment funds or 94% of the respondents to their survey consider the UK as the most favored location with 85% citing Europe and 47% the USA as potential locations for such investment funds. Furthermore, 62% of respondents consider the Middle East a good location for investments. Only 38% view South East Asia as potential locations for investment. This is rather interesting as Malaysia and Indonesia are both populous Islamic countries whilst Singapore, Thailand and the Philippines also have sizable Muslim populations.

One clear message to emerge from the research is that the UK and, in particular, London, is a popular place to do business. Parsa and McIntosh (2006) commented, 'We find that in all the issues – political environment, legal and institutional framework and access to skills – London leads the world'. One thing that seems to be certain, however, is that the amount of money being invested through Shariah-compliant funds is going to increase. At the moment, the organizations interviewed had about Euro 650 million available, and almost everyone interviewed was of the view that their Shariah-related investment activity was going to increase over the next 12 months.

As to whether Shariah funds will also start to engage with the REITs market – the answer was unequivocal – 'why not'? was the almost universal response. So, as Angus McIntosh commented, 'Once we have REITs in the UK, one of the first ones may be a Shariah-compliant REIT'.

Differences to conventional and ethical funds

Does this make much of a difference to the way in which they behave, if we compare them with purely conventional funds and to ethical funds? In some areas, there is little difference. Their approach to portfolio management is

	Don't know	Not different	Somewhat different	Very different
Finance and investment	0	4	64	32
Portfolio selection	4	11	74	11
Costs	4	12	65	19
Monitoring of compliance	7	19	52	22
Payment of dividends	11	25	39	25
Taxation structure	11	25	46	18
Regulation	4	51	30	15
Portfolio management	0	57	36	7

Figure 10.5   Differences between Shariah and conventional funds.

seen to be little different to conventional funds. In this respect, they are seen to be even more similar to conventional funds than ethical funds. In most other areas, there is little difference between Shariah-compliant funds and other funds, whether conventional or ethical (Figure 10.5).

Saleh Amin Dawood (2005) argues against the contention that Islamic finance can be just as effective as conventional finance. There are concerns on the threat posed by the increasing Western influence in the field of finance, which may place restrictions in the orthodox version of Islamic finance by, for example, the increased use of derivatives. He postulates that 'Agree or Disagree: Islamic finance can be just as effective and sophisticated as conventional finance'.

Shariah Funds: do they understand the importance of decision making?

It might be thought that with the more complex structures used in Shariah finance, these funds may be disadvantaged by the time taken to make decisions. The survey by Parsa and McIntosh seemed to indicate that this was not a problem. The respondents to their survey said that these funds did understand the need for clear and efficient decision making – although some did say that not all funds actually delivered this. Decisions are taken in weeks rather than days, although it rarely takes more than a month for decisions to be made. There was an even split between those wanting to invest direct into property and those preferring using a third-party investment fund. A fund manager interviewed mentioned that it is often the lack of available expertise (Shariah scholars) that affects the time taken for decisions rather than slow decision making.

Market efficiency requires reliable and speedy decision making in the context of rapidly changing market conditions. As with ethical investment, all property transactions, portfolio selection and tenant selection require constant scrutiny by an advisory Shariah board. The respondents were asked to comment on whether in their view Shariah boards understood the importance of decision making and time taken to make such decisions. It appears that 47% of the respondents believe this to be the case. The speed and reliability of decision making was considered to be a prerequisite for all companies involved in Shariah transactions. However, this depends on the level of sophistication of the investment fund manager or sponsor.

Understanding Shariah funds

Despite the phenomenal growth of Shariah funds in recent years, there is still a real lack of understanding of Shariah funds in well-established markets such as London. This appears to be mainly due to unfamiliarity of the general public and ignorance about the Shariah-compliant funds. Therefore, more education of the general public would overcome such problems in the long run. It is assumed that with more exposure, over time, this will improve. Other respondents believe that there is a need for 'dispersing the myths and suspicions'. This is compounded by the fact that very few understand the structuring of such funds, as they think it is harder than it actually is, possibly out of fear. Therefore, the role of regulative institutions such as FSA and HM Treasury in the UK in supporting and facilitating the development of new financial products such as SCIs is crucial.

Availability of human capital and expertise

The contribution of human capital and expertise is a prerequisite to the overall success of cities and market places where constant innovation and product development is vital. In today's competitive global financial services, London plays a dominant role in offering new and diverse financial products. This is due to the availability of an internationally diverse and unrivalled human expertise capable of developing new financial products (Figure 10.6). The survey by Parsa and McIntosh confirms London as

	Human capital and expertise
UK	83
Germany	29
France	25
Scandanavia	0
Luxembourg	0
Others	0

Figure 10.6 Human capital and expertise.

centre of innovation for financial services and products. According to the
survey, London offers the best in human capital and expertise in Shariah-
compliant real estate investment within Europe. This is confirmed by
almost 90% of the respondents who identify London where relevant expertise can be found. This has important implications for the future development of this niche market as part of the overall financial services industry
in Europe and globally. France and Germany are cited by just fewer than
30% and 20% of respondents, respectively, as having the relevant human
capital and expertise in Islamic finance and SCI.

Operating environment for Shariah investment in Europe

The ultimate success of any new financial product on offer is dependent
on the overall operating environment or the market's ability to provide
the necessary, political environment, human capital and expertise, overall regulative and legislative framework and institutional framework.
Furthermore, the ability of investors to operate in different markets is
dependent on how well such markets can accommodate the operation
of international firms and can offer diverse financial products (D'Arcy
& Keogh, 1996). Within northern Europe, UK is shown to be the most
favoured location for Shariah investors. Some 88% of those interviewed
view UK as the country offering the best environment for Shariah-
compliant real estate investment. France and Germany are seen as most
favoured countries after UK for Shariah investment funds. Other countries cited by respondents as potential locations for Shariah investment

are Turkey and Russia. Turkey is seen as an Islamic country suitable for investment by 30% of the respondents whilst Russia is considered by 26% of those interviewed.

With the development of the real estate markets in the transition economies, more opportunities are created for investment. With increased maturity of real estate markets in Poland, Czech Republic and Hungary, new destinations are available for real estate investors (McGreal *et al.*, 2002). Furthermore, with the availability of more diverse real estate investment products, Shariah investment funds are willing to operate in new markets and geographical diverse locations.

Within central Europe, 47% of the respondents wish to invest in the Czech Republic. Poland and Hungary are selected by 44% of the respondents who would wish to invest in their capital cities of Warsaw and Budapest.

Real estate sectors favoured by Shariah investors

As previously discussed, stock selection, tenancy and portfolio management of Shariah-compliant real estate investment must be scrutinized and authorized by the Shariah board. Although restrictions are imposed concerning investment in office, retail, hotel and leisure property due to the type of activity, there is still substantial investment by Shariah funds in these sectors. Parsa and McIntosh (2006) argue that a great majority of investors (76% of their respondents) would invest in commercial office sector and over 46% would also consider investing in retail property. The retail property sector provides a more challenging investment sector for Shariah funds due to diverse retail operations including leisure (betting shops, pubs and restaurants) and sales outlets (alcohol, specialist media and meat products) which are not approved by Shariah scholars.

The industrial sector, including logistics and warehousing, seems to be the most popular sector for investment by Shariah funds. Seventy-nine percent of those interviewed by Parsa and McIntosh (2006) invest in industrial property with 53% likely to continue investing. This is mostly due to the fact that the industrial sector, due to the nature of its activities, is much better suited for stock selection and approval by the Shariah board. Other preferred sectors include logistics and distribution.

The residential sector is a well-suited market for Shariah funds as it poses no difficulty in terms of compliance and approval by the Shariah board. The majority of those interviewed by Parsa and McIntosh are of the view that there will be substantial increase in Shariah investment since there is a lot of available capital in the Muslim world, therefore more money to invest in the foreseeable future.

Global credit professionals whose companies do business in the Middle East and many parts of Asia, Africa, and the Pacific Rim can improve their competitive position by understanding the fundamental principles of Shariah-compliant financing. While Islamic finance tools may initially seem quite alien to many global credit professionals, Shariah-compliant financing is, according to Khan, 'largely compatible with conventional banking'.

Social responsibility

According to Quran, the Earth belongs to Allah and that humans are merely custodians. Anything deemed harmful to the planet's welfare is considered a violation of Shariah law and, by extension, anything that benefits the environment is viewed favourably.

According to Metcalf (2007), Shariah favours productive, SRIs. According to Ibrahim and Ong (2006), it is worth drawing some similarities and differences between SRI and SCI. The motivation for SRI may be divided into two categories that are not mutually exclusive – subjective and objective motivations (Dupre *et al.*, 2003). Personal ethics usually underpin subjective motivations for SRI, where moral principles are applied for which there can be no compromise. In such a context, profitability and financial or social costs have no relevance. Objective motivations reflect apprehension or aversion to activities that have social and/or environmental costs, such as pollution, smoking, etc. Clearly, SCI are defined by religious beliefs and may be viewed as ethical motivations. Nevertheless, SRI and SCI place various (different) constraints on the investment universe.

Conclusion

In essence, Muslims' view of economics is based on Man's obligation as representative of God and his vice-regent on earth. The goal is not equality but avoiding inequality. Islamic finance is firmly embedded in the commercial, real value–producing domain.

Shariah funds is another ethical, indigenous and equitable mode of Islamic finance, which, like other Islamic activities, derives its principles from the Quran and the Sunnah. Shariah law governs Islamic finance. It is an ethical mode of broadening ownership, creating more stakeholders and stabilizing the Muslim communities worldwide. Resource allocation in the Islamic economic system not only takes into consideration the best of both worlds, that is the capitalist and socialist economic systems, but also includes some additional criteria based on Islamic social and moral welfare functions. The real allocation of resources depends more upon subjective criteria. The subjective criteria are expressed in terms of welfare criteria which are intermixed with the criteria of investment.

The relentless flow of funds from Middle Eastern countries to be invested in compliance with Shariah, which forbids the paying of interest, shows the bright future of the Shariah investment. Real estate has proved to be an attractive home for SCI. Ultimately, the success or failure of any investment is dependent on the overall performance, taking into consideration such factors such as risks, transaction costs and security of investment. Clearly, the same rules as conventional investments apply, including diversification strategy in terms of market sector and geographical spread. Recent evidence from a number of Shariah real estate investment funds in Europe suggests that the performance of the funds has been within the range of the market as a whole with some reporting total returns on investments between 10% and 18%, very much in line with the marketplace as a whole.

With globalization of SCIs, different countries are competing to establish themselves as the global centre for such investments by introducing financial, tax and regulative reforms. London, Kuala Lumpur, Singapore, Bahrain and Dubai are amongst the top centres for Islamic finance products. Although Shariah-compliant funds have invested in Europe, Asia, North America and the Middle East, their greatest challenge for growth is to reach the small investor. SCIs are still within reach only of an exclusive elite of large investors.

References

Abdulkader, T. *et al.* (2005) Structuring Islamic Finance Transactions, Euromoney Institutional Investor PLC.

Abdul Rahman, Y. (2004) *Lariba Banking.* American Finance House.

Adnan Alias (2007) Key-note speech 2-day 5th International Finance Conference in Kuala Lumpur, 3–5 September 2007.

Aggarwal, R. & Yousef, T. (2000) Islamic banks and Investment Financing. *Journal of Money, Credit and Banking, 32* (1), 93–120.

Ahmad, K. (ed.) (1980) *Studies in Islamic Economics.* Islamic Foundation, London.

Ahmad, M.A. (2007) Developing the Islamic Financial Services Industry and the Role of Regulation and Supervision. Credit & Collections Benchmarking Report www.ioma. com/CREDIT.

Akram Khan, M. (2007) *An Introduction to Islamic Economics.* Islamic Book Service, Idara Islamiyat-e-Diniyat, or Kitab Bhavan (India).

Al-Ashkar, A. (1987) *The Islamic Business Enterprise.* Croom Helm, London.

Al-Mubarak, M. (1974) *Nizam Al-Islam Al-Iqtisadi wa Qwaaid Al-Ammah.* Dar- Al-Fikr, Beirut. (in Arabic).

Al-Sadr, M.B. (1968) *Iqtisadona (our economy).* Darul-Fikr, Beirut. (in Arabic).

Bremner, B. & Shameen, A. (2007) The ties that bind the Middle East and Asia. *Middle East Economic Digest, 51* (18).

Brugnoni, A. (2006) A case study: Italy and Islamic finance. From a borderline actor to a land of opportunities. International Islamic Finance and Investment Symposium, *Karachi* 6–7 December 2006.

Choudhury, M.A. (1991) *The Unity Precept and the Socio-Scientific Order.* University Press of America, Lanham, MD.

D'Arcy, E. & Keogh, G. (1996) Towards a property market paradigm of urban change. *Environment and Planning A, 28*, 685–706.

Datamonitor (2006) http://www.datamonitor.com (accessed September 2007).

Dawood, S.A. (2005) Islamic finance: a look behind the practice of merging faith and financials. *CFA Magazine, 16* (2), 48.

Dechert (2006) Dechert On Point Structured Finance Report, Spring, Issue 3.

Dupre, D., Gererd-Potin, I. & Kassoua, R. (2003) Adding an ethical Dimension to Portfolio Management. University of Wharton Working Paper.

El-Qorchi, M. (2005) Islamic finance gears up. *Finance & Development*, International Monetary Fund, Washington, DC, December, 46–49.

Hamid, A.H. & Norization, A.M.H. (2001) A study on Islamic banking education and strategy for the new millennium: Malaysian Experience. *International Journal for Islamic Financial Service, 2* (4), 3–11.

Hasanuz Zaman, S.M. (2007) *Economic Functions of an Islamic State.* The Islamic Foundation (July 12, 2007).

Ibrahim, M.F., Ong, S.E. & Parsa A. (2007) Shariah Property Investment in Asia. National University of Singapore Research Project.

Ibrahim, M.F. & Ong, S.E. (2006) Shariah Compliance in Real Estate Investment. Department of Real Estate, National University of Singapore.

IDD (Investment Dealers' Digest 4) (2006) http://iddmagazine.com/idd/index.cfm

International Directory of Islamic Banks and Institutions (2000) http://www.islamic-banking.com/ibanking/ifi.php

Jobst, A.A. (2007) The Economics of Islamic Finance and Securitization. Monetary and Capital Markets Department. IMF Working Paper, Washington DC.

Kahf, M. (1978) *Islamic Economic System: A Review.* Al- itahad, Indiana, USA. Conference on Islamic Project Finance (2007). 24–25 June 2007, Dubai.

Kahf, M. (1989) The theory of consumption. In: Sayyid Tahir, Aidit Ghazali, and Syed Omar Agil (eds), *Readings in Micro Economics.*Long man, Kuala Lumpur.

Kahf, M. (1994) The economic role of state in Islam. *Journal of Objective Studies, 6.*

Kamalpour, A. (2006) Islamic Real Estate Securitisation. Paper presented at the Middle East Business Forum Conference, November, London.

Keon, N.S. (1989) *Stock Market Investment*, pp. 138–139. Berita Publishing, Kuala Lumpur.

Mannan, M.A. (1984) *The Making of Islamic Economic Society*. International Centre for Research in Islamic Economics, Jed dah, Saudi Arabia, King Abdul Aziz University.

Mannan, M.A. (1999) Resource allocation, investment decision and economic welfare: capitalism, socialism and Islam. *Managerial Finance, 25.*

McGreal, W.S., Parsa, A. & Keivani, R. (2002) Evolution of property investment markets in Central Europe: opportunities and constraints. *Journal of Property Research, 19* (3), 213–230.

MEED (2007a) Etihad secures aircraft finance. Middle East Business Intelligence, 30 November 2007.

MEED (2007b) Guidance Financial enters kingdom's housing market. Middle East Business Intelligence, 4 May 2007.

Metcalf, A. (2007) *The Shari'a: Islamic Finance in Theory and Practice*, Managing Credit, Receivables and collections Issue 07-06, 2007. www.ioma.com.

Meyer, E. (2007) President & CEO, Shariah Capital on www.shariahcapital.com.

Mirakhor, Abbas & Zaidi Iqbal (1988) Stabilization and Growth in an Open Islamic Economy, IMF Working Paper No. 88/22, International Monetary Fund (IMF), Washington, DC.

Naqavi, S.N.H. (1981) *Ethics and Economics: An Islamic Synthesis*. Robert Maclehouse and Co.Ltd., Great Britain, London.

Newell, R. (2006) Dubai City and the Arabian Gulf. IPE Real Estate, January/February 2006, Dubai.

Newell, R. (2007) Dubai City and the Arabian Gulf. Islamic Project Finance (IPF) 24–25 June 2007, Dubai.

Parsa, A. & McIntosh, A. (2006) Current trends in Shariah property investment. RICS Findings in Built and Rural Environments, October.

Parsa, A. & McIntosh, A. (2005) Shariah Property Investment: Developing an International Strategy, RICS.

Rosser, J.B. & Rosser, M. V. (2004) *Comparative Economics in a Transforming World Economy* (2nd ed.). MIT Press.

Shah, M.P. (2007) Writing the rule: the need for standardized regulation of Islamic finance. *Harvard International Review*, 29.

Weist, D. (2007) The Shari'a: Islamic Finance in Theory and Practice, Managing Credit, Receiveables and collections Issue 06-07 www.ioma.com.

Yusoff, N.Z. (1992) *An Islamic Perspective of the Stock Market*. Dian Darulnaim, Kuala Lumpur.

Appendix 1

List of Most Active Players in the Shariah-compliant Real Estate Market

Name of Fund/Bank (rank by importance)	Place of Origin	Location (registered)	Operating Market	Value (approx)
Crescent Capital/First Islamic	Bahrain	Bahrain	USA/Europe, GCC	$1.5 billion
Crescent Capital/First Islamic			Germany	£100 millions
Kuwait Finance House	Kuwait	Kuwait	USA/UK, Europe, GCC, Malaysia	$2–3 billion overall
Kuwait Finance House		Cayman, Guernsey	UK	£140/£160 million, aim to reach £250 million, looking up for Europe to commit another £150 million
Gulf Finance House	Bahrain	Bahrain	USA/UK, France, Spain, GCC	$1 billion
Gulf Finance House	Bahrain	Cayman	Sweden/UK (Europe)	Euro 250 million Sweden/£150 million UK= approx Euro 500 millions (Europe)
Gulf Atlantic Real Estate – GFH	Bahrain		UK/France	
Qatar Islamic Bank	Qatar	Qatar	USA/UK, GCC	$500 million
Bank Islam Malaysia	Malaysia	Malaysia	Malaysia	$20.5 billion in the RE sector (2003)
Dubai Islamic Bank	Dubai	Dubai	GCC	$2–3 billion
National Commercial Bank	KSA	KSA	USA/Europe, GCC	$3–4 billion
UBS/NORIBA Bank	Bahrain			£160 million
Albaraka	Bahrain			£50 million
ABC Bank/Credit Suisse				£50 million
Al Bait/Al Beyt Fund (ABC Arab Bank)		Cayman, Guernsey	UK	£44–80 million

Appendix 2

Definitions of the Most Commonly Used Terms in Shariah and Islamic Banking

Amanah = Al-Wadi-a: Trust and 'safekeeping': Trust, with associated meanings of trustworthiness, faithfulness and honesty. As an important secondary meaning, the term also identifies a transaction where one party keeps another's funds or property in trust. This is in fact the most widely understood and used application of the term, and has a long history of use in Islamic commercial law. By extension, the term can also be used to describe different financial or commercial activities such as deposit taking, custody or goods on consignment.

Arbun: Earnest money/down payment; a non-refundable deposit paid by the client (buyer) to the seller upon concluding a contract of sale, with the provision that the contract will be completed during the prescribed period.

Gharar: Uncertainty. One of three fundamental prohibitions in Islamic finance (the other two being riba and maysir). Gharar is a sophisticated concept that covers certain types of uncertainty or contingency in a contract. The prohibition on Gharar is often used as the grounds for criticism of conventional financial practices such as short selling, speculation and derivatives.

Halal: Religiously permissible.

Haram: Religiously not permissible.

Ijarah: An Islamic lease agreement. Instead of lending money and earning interest, Ijarah allows the bank to earn profits by charging rentals on the asset leased to the customer. Ijarah wa iqtinah extends the concept of Ijarah to a hire and purchase agreement.

Ijtihad: A technical term of Islamic law that describes the process of making a legal decision by independent interpretation of the legal sources, the Quran and the Sunnah. The opposite of ijtihad is taqlid, Arabic for 'imitation'. A person who applies ijtihad is called a mujtahid, and traditionally had to be a scholar of Islamic law, an Islamic lawyer or alim.

Islamic banking: Financial services that meet the requirements of the Shariah, or Islamic law. While designed to meet the specific religious requirements of Muslim customers, Islamic banking is not restricted to Muslims: both the financial services provider and the customer can be non-Muslim as well as Muslim. Also called Islamic finance or Islamic financial services.

Istisna: A contract to acquire goods on behalf of a third party where the price is paid to the manufacturer in advance and the goods are produced and delivered at a later date.

Maysir: Gambling. One of three fundamental prohibitions in Islamic finance (the other two being riba and Gharar). The prohibition on maysir is often used as the grounds for criticism of conventional financial practices such as speculation, conventional insurance and derivatives.

Mudarabah: A Mudarabah is an Investment partnership, whereby the investor (the Rab ul Mal) provides capital to another party/entrepreneur (the Mudarib) in order to undertake a business/investment activity. While profits are shared on a pre-agreed ratio, loss of investment is born by the investor only. The mudarib loses its share of the profit.

Mudarib: The mudarib is the entrepreneur or investment manager in a mudarabah who invests the investor's funds in a project or portfolio in exchange for a share of the profits. For example, a mudarabah is essentially similar to a diversified pool of assets held in a Discretionary Asset Management Portfolio.

Murabaha: Purchase and resale. Instead of lending out money, the capital provider purchases the desired commodity (for which the loan would have been taken out) from a third party and resells it at a predetermined higher price to the capital user. By paying this higher price over instalments, the capital user has effectively obtained credit without paying interest.

Musharakah: Profit and loss sharing. It is a partnership where profits are shared as per an agreed ratio, whereas the losses are shared in proportion to the capital/investment of each partner. In a Musharakah, all partners to a business undertaking contribute funds and have the right, but not the obligation, to exercise executive powers in that project, which is similar to a conventional partnership structure and the holding of voting stock in a limited company. This equity financing arrangement is widely regarded as the purest form of Islamic financing.

Qard-al- Hasana: Loan without interest.

Qiyas: The process of analogical reasoning from a known injunction (nass) to a new injunction. According to this method, the ruling of the Quran and the Sunnah may be extended to a new problem provided that the precedent and the new problem share the same operative or effective cause. Sunni Islam uses qiyas as the fourth source, whereas Shi'a Islam uses 'aql' (intellect).

Riba: usery or Interest. The legal notion extends beyond just interest, but in simple terms riba covers any return of money on money – whether the interest is fixed or floating, simple or compounded, and at whatever the rate. Riba is strictly prohibited in the Islamic tradition.

Shariah: Islamic law as revealed in the Quran and through the example of Prophet Muhammad (PBUH). A Shariah-compliant product meets the requirements of Islamic law. A Shariah board is the committee of Islamic scholars available to an Islamic financial institution for guidance and supervision in the development of Shariah-compliant products.

Shariah advisor: An independent professional, usually a classically trained Islamic legal scholar, who advises an Islamic bank on the compliance of its products and services with the Shariah, or Islamic law.

Shariah-compliant: An act or activity that complies with the requirements of the Shariah, or Islamic law. The term is often used in the Islamic banking industry as a synonym for 'Islamic' – for example, Shariah-compliant financing or SCI.

Sukuk: Plural of sakk ('legal instrument, deed, check'), Sukuk is the Arabic name for a financial certificate but can be seen as an Islamic equivalent of bond. However, fixed income, interest-bearing bonds are not permissible in Islam, hence Sukuk are securities that comply with the Islamic law and its investment principles, which prohibits the charging, or paying of interest. Similar characteristics to that of a conventional bond with the difference being that they are asset-backed. A Sukuk represents proportionate beneficial ownership in the underlying asset. The asset will be leased to the client to yield the return on the Sukuk.

Takaful: Islamic insurance. Structured as charitable collective pool of funds based on the idea of mutual assistance, takaful schemes are designed to avoid the elements of conventional insurance (i.e. interest and gambling) that are problematic for Muslims.

Tawarruq: Reverse murabaha. As used in personal financing, a customer with a genuine need buys something on credit from the bank on a deferred payment basis and then immediately resells it for cash to a third party. In this way, the customer can obtain cash without taking an interest-based loan (http://www.hsbcamanah.com).

Notes

1.   Note that this and other technical terms relating specifically to Shariah-compliant finance are defined in Appendix 2 at the end of this chapter.

Part II

Processes

11

Socially Responsible Property Investment – Background, Trends and Consequences

Thomas Lützkendorf and David Lorenz

Introduction

In this chapter, the authors discuss current questions concerning socially responsible property investment (SRPI) against the background of a growing debate on the implementation of principles of sustainable development within the property and construction sector. For the description of the basics of SRPI, the analysis of current trends and the discussion of possible consequences for the actors concerned, the authors' use, amongst other resources, results and insights from participation in international and European standardisation activities on sustainable construction as well as from research on the integration sustainability issues into property valuation and property rating.

One precondition for taking responsibility towards society and the environment within the scope of investment decision making in the property sector is that the contribution of buildings to sustainable development can be recognised, described and assessed. In this regard, technical, functional, aesthetic, economic, environmental and social aspects are treated simultaneously and equally. At the same time, it is required that SRPI not only does not hamper the economic goals of individual and institutional actors, but also that SRPI can actually improve the prospects for higher returns and increases in property values. On the one hand, the authors therefore concentrate on the description of the interrelation between sustainability-related characteristics and attributes of buildings and the development of a building's income stream or value respectively, and on the other hand, they discuss how aspects of social responsibility and the principles of sustainable development can be both translated for major actors of property and construction markets and integrated into their methods, instruments and decision-making processes. In this regard, the authors' aim is to highlight the important and growing role of property valuation and property valuers.

Nonetheless, the major intention of this chapter is to describe the key fundamentals of and the rationale for SRPI. Furthermore, the chapter aims to characterise SRPIs by identifying appropriate investment strategies and products as well as by explaining the methodological basis for their assessment and evaluation. The chapter also reports on the current stage of development of the market and gives examples of early adopters of SRPI strategies.

The research undertaken for writing this chapter was completed in January 2007.

Social responsibility and sustainable development – background

SRI as an element of social responsibility

Within the process of property investment decision making, increasing attention is being given to the relationship between property valuation and financing and the growing interest and responsibility that the property industry is taking towards society and the environment. The property industry is also becoming aware of the need to actively communicate this attitude to the wider public, as well as seeing the increasing demand for property assets and investment opportunities that are in compliance with the principles of sustainable development or that follow ethical maxims as a major opportunity.

The growing acceptance of social responsibility by organisations, corporations and other actors has an impact not only on investment, planning and financing PROCESSES, but also on the demand for and the provisioning of PRODUCTS (e.g. buildings, property investment products, financing and insurance products). This chapter is therefore also closely connected to the sections on new investment products that have been dealt with in Part A of this book (e.g. in connection with 'green' REITs). Within Part B of this book, connections exist to the chapter on 'performance measurement' (in the sense of measuring not only the performance of corporations and investment products and strategies, but also the technical, functional, economic, environmental and sociocultural advantageousness of buildings), to the chapter on 'corporate governance' (in the sense of a practical realisation of corporate social responsibility (CSR) within single companies), to the chapter on 'market transparency' (in the sense of portraying additional requirements for the description and analysis of property assets and transactions), and to the chapter on 'skills, requirements – education' (in the sense of formulating proposals for the integration of sustainability issues into the education and further training of major groups of actors in property and construction markets).

The main topic of this chapter, Socially Responsible Property Investment, can be seen as one facet of a general trend towards Social Responsibility. The terms Social Responsibility or CSR are used by organisations, investors and companies to commit themselves to the protection of social and environmental interests. CSR (sometimes referred to as 'good' corporate governance) is defined as an open and transparent business practice that is based on ethical values and respect for employees, communities and the environment. It is designed to deliver sustainable value to society at large, as well as to shareholders (US SIF, 2006). A new international standard on Social Responsibility (ISO 26 000) is currently under development which is intended to serve as a guideline and provide a universal basis for introducing and implementing social responsibility into corporations and organisations; the standard will be available by 2010 at the earliest. The current draft of the standard lists the following topics that are to be taken into account by organisations in connection with Social Responsibility (Margot, 2006): Human Rights, Labour Practices, Organisational Governance, Consumer Issues, Community Involvement, Fair Operating Practices and Environment.

Usually, corporations and organisations aim to communicate their contribution to sustainable development by publishing Sustainability Reports. In this regard, the Global Reporting Initiative (www.globalreporting.org) or AccountAbility (www.accountability21.net) offer a basis for the standardised description of economic, environmental and social performance aspects of corporations and organisations. Examples of such sustainability reports are available, for example, for the building products industry[1] and for the construction industry[2]. In the meantime, a number of insurance companies[3], banks[4], firms from the property sector, fund managers and professional organisations (e.g. RICS[5]) have accepted their social responsibility and have committed themselves to adhere to principles of sustainable development.

CSR impacts on all business activities including investment policies. Such policies and investment practices can be grouped under the term Socially Responsible Investment (SRI). Socially Responsible Investment as a strategy and Socially Responsible Investing as a process characterise the behaviour of investors who not only focus on mere economic aspects of an investment, but also follow ethical principles and take into account environmental and social aspects. Such investors either avoid investments into particular companies and products or they systematically select and support other companies and products through their investment. In addition, such investors sometimes use their shareholder rights in order to positively impact on the development of a particular company. A framework for this is provided by the Principles for Responsible Investment (Figure 11.1).

The principles for responsible investment

As institutional investors, we have a duty to act in the best long- term interests of our beneficiaries. In this fiduciary role, we believe that environmental, social, and corporate governance (ESG) issues can affect the performance of investment portfolios (to varying degrees across companies, sectors, regions, asset classes and through time). We also recognise that applying these Principles may better align investors with broader objectives of society. Therefore, where consistent with our fiduciary responsibilities, we commit to the following:

1   We will incorporate ESG issues into investment analyses and decision-making processes.
2   We will be active owners and incorporate ESG issues into our ownership policies and practices.
3   We will seek appropriate disclosure on ESG issues by the entities in which we invest.
4   We will promote acceptance and implementation of the Principles within the investment industry.
5   We will work together to enhance our effectiveness in implementing the Principles
6   We will each report on our activities and progress towards implementing the Principles.

Figure 11.1   The principles for responsible investment, excerpt (PRI, 2006).

The principles for responsible investment

As institutional investors, we have a duty to act in the best long-term interests of our beneficiaries. In this fiduciary role, we believe that environmental, social and corporate governance (ESG) issues can affect the performance of investment portfolios (to varying degrees across companies, sectors, regions, asset classes and through time). We also recognise that applying these Principles may better align investors with broader objectives of society. Therefore, where consistent with our fiduciaryresponsibilities, we commit to the following.

1 We will incorporate ESG issues into investment analyses and decision-making processes.
2 We will be active owners and incorporate ESG issues into our ownership policies and practices.
3 We will seek appropriate disclosure on ESG issues by the entities in which we invest.
4 We will promote acceptance and implementation of the Principles within the investment industry.
5 We will work together to enhance our effectiveness in implementing the Principles.
6 We will each report on our activities and progress towards implementing the Principles.

In a general sense, SRI can be viewed from the viewpoint of two groups of actors, those who act as investors and those who communicate both their positive attitude towards taking social responsibility as well as the environmental and social advantageousness of their products and services. In between these two groups, rating agencies and analysts act as mediators who assess the contribution of companies and products to sustainable development.

The issue of SRI appears to attract a growing number of corporations, financial institutions and private investors worldwide since there is a growing awareness that ignoring environmental and social concerns within investment decision making can be financially risky. A number of stock-listed companies have therefore made CSR programmes to an element of their risk and reputation management. It is also increasingly clear that SRI can result in higher returns and is not only financially beneficial from a long-term perspective, but also can produce financial gains in the short term, as well. For example, a survey of 195 fund managers from around the world revealed that the use of positive screening for environmental, social and ethical factors is entering mainstream investment analysis, particularly where such screening may potentially yield superior financial performance by targeting companies that adopt socially responsible practices and thereby avoid future liabilities and losses (Ambachtsheer, 2005). Thus, the attractiveness of sustainable investment opportunities is increasingly rising not only for those investors who primarily follow ethical goals (ethically driven approach), but also for those who use sustainable investment opportunities as an instrument for minimising or diversifying risk and for safeguarding an average to above-average performance (performance-driven approach).

The trend towards the mainstreaming of SRI is driven by and closely linked to the efforts undertaken by the global community to achieve more sustainable development. Sustainable development means development that meets the needs of the present without compromising the ability of future generations to meet their own needs (WCED, 1987). While sustainability is usually interpreted today as the overarching goal or target of having a durable balance between the economy, environment and society, sustainable development means an ongoing process directed towards achieving this goal. In this context, taking responsibility towards society and the environment can be seen as a precondition and measure for implementing the principles of sustainable development; and SRI represents a major instrument in this regard.

The urgency of undertaking action in order to achieve more sustainable development can be highlighted by referring, for example, to two recent publications. First, the Millennium Ecosystem Assessment Report – a study involving the work of more than 1 360 experts worldwide – which revealed that 'human activity is putting such strain on the natural functions of Earth that the ability of the planet's ecosystems to sustain future generations can no longer be taken for granted' (MA, 2005, p. 2). And second, the Stern Review on the Economics of Climate Change which argued that climate change is the greatest and widest-ranging market failure ever seen and that its overall costs will be equivalent to losing between 5% and 20% or more of global Gross Domestic Product each year (now and in the future) if prompt and strong action is not undertaken (Stern, 2006).

The extent and consequences of these trends require us to look for options that allow for both a stronger commitment to the principles of sustainable development and an improved uptake of social responsibility within all branches, companies and asset classes.

Role of the property and construction sector for sustainable development

One key justification for seeking to encourage action in the property and construction sector is that no other sector has such a great potential role in contributing to sustainable development. For this reason, buildings and the property and construction sector have been termed the *cornerstone of sustainability* (OECD, 2003). Buildings can be viewed and assessed from a number of different perspectives; for example, as physical/material assets representing embodied resources, as a factor of production, as an investment vehicle or as a provider of human needs like protection, identity and culture. The property and construction sector's economic, environmental and social impacts are immense.

Estimates vary but it has been suggested that the investment volume in new and existing buildings per annum in Europe is around US$ 1.2 trillion, in the USA around US$ 1.1 trillion and in Asia around US$ 0.9 trillion. Construction represents over 50% of national fixed capital formation in most countries. For example, in Germany alone, the net value (at current replacement costs) of the national building stock has been estimated by the Federal Statistical Office to be on the order of €5.9 trillion at the beginning of 2006, representing almost 90% of the net stock of fixed assets of the country.

Investment in construction accounts for approximately 10 % of global GDP and 111 million people worldwide are directly employed within this sector (UNEP, 2003, 2006; European Commission, 2004a). Furthermore, the share of the built environment in global resource use and pollution emission is substantial: in OECD countries, the built environment is responsible for around 25–40% of total energy use, 30% of raw material use, 30–40% of global greenhouse gas emissions and for 30–40% of solid waste generation (OECD, 2003; UNEP, 2006). In addition, property investment decisions and the ways that buildings and the built environment are designed, constructed, operated, renovated and demolished significantly impact on the economic performance of towns, cities and regions and on the quality of life of urban and rural citizens because:

- almost 50 % of all humans live in cities, and this figure is expected to rise up to 60% by 2030; around 9% of the world's urban population – about 280 million people – currently live in megacities, and this figure is likely to rise to 350 million over the next 10 years; approximately 80% of Europe's citizens live in urban areas;
- people spend almost 90% of their time inside buildings;
- the built environment represents a substantial and relatively stable resource. Most buildings survive for several decades, and very many survive for centuries; and
- repair and maintenance activities to buildings can account for between approximately 6.5% (for housing estates) and 30% (for schools and hospitals) of initial construction costs each year (OECD, 2003; Bruhns, 2003; European Commission, 2004b; Munich Re, 2005; Porritt, 2006).

Consequences and duties for single actors

As shown above, implementing the principles of sustainable development in the property and construction sector is of paramount importance for creating more sustainable communities and economies. A huge responsibility exists for all those groups of actors who jointly shape and design the built environment since there is much room for both reducing the property and construction sector's negative impacts and for dramatically increasing its positive effects. This is particularly true for actors within the property investment sector who drive the market and determine 'best practice' in planning, construction, management, refurbishment and demolition of buildings. However, while several actors within the property and construction markets, such as constructors, designers, engineers, researchers, governmental authorities or certain occupiers and clients, have been concerned with aspects of sustainable development for some considerable time, those involved in the property investment markets such as fund and asset managers, institutional and private investors, estate agents, valuers and analysts have responded more slowly to the challenges imposed by sustainable development. Only very recently has the notion of SRPI emerged on property investment agendas.

In order to advance the situation, it is necessary to:

- improve and intensify the communication of the reasons, goals and benefits of SRPI;
- develop special investment strategies for property assets and investment products through transfer and adaptation of existing SRI concepts;

- develop, harmonise and apply generally accepted assessment or rating methods for the description and evaluation of both the environmental and social performance of individual buildings, buildings stocks and property investment products as well as of the environmental and social performance of construction and property companies;
- improve the supply of design and planning services, building products and processes as well as of property investment products that demonstrably contribute positively to sustainable development;
- investigate more thoroughly the relationship between buildings' technical, functional, environmental and social characteristics and attributes on the one hand and their economic performance on the other hand;
- integrate aspects of social responsibility and of sustainable development into the education and further training of all actors within the construction and property sector;
- strengthen the role model function of the public authorities; and
- discuss possibilities for tax schemes that reward the reduction of social/external costs.
- In the following, the current stage of discussion and possible future trends are portrayed and discussed for selected questions.

Trends and concepts within the property market

Within property and construction markets, three different developments or streams of action and research can be observed which are concerned with the environmental, social and economic impacts of property-related decision making. Besides the notion of SRPI, these are the sustainable building and the performance-based building approach. To a greater or lesser extent, all three are indicative of a more responsible attitude being taken towards societal and environmental issues. From the authors' point of view, an examination of the requirements for sustainable buildings as well as of the performance-based building approach are important starting points for the discussion on SRPIs.

The 'Sustainable Building' approach

The concept of and requirements for sustainable buildings can be found in an understanding of the concept of sustainable development. A large number of formal definitions of sustainable development can be found in literature; Parkin (2000) refers to more than 200. However, the most prominent and universal definition can be found in the *Brundtland Report* which was published in 1987 and represented the outcome of 4 years of study and debate by the World Commission on Environment and Development led by the former Prime Minister of Norway, Gro Harlem Brundtland. The Commission defined sustainable development asdevelopment which meets the needs of the present without compromising the ability of future generations to meet their own needs. Sustainable development can be seen as a journey towards a destination: 'sustainability'. Although it is difficult to define 'sustainability' from a scientific perspective, Porritt (2006) argues that the realisation of sustainability can be measured against a set of four 'system conditions'.

1 Finite materials (including fossil fuels) should not be extracted at a faster rate than they can be redeposited in the Earth's crust.
2 Artificial materials (including plastics) should not be produced at a faster rate than they can be broken down by natural processes.
3 The biodiversity of ecosystems should be maintained, whilst renewable resources should only be consumed at a slower rate than they can be naturally replenished.
4 Human needs must be met in an equitable and efficient manner.

In this context, the authors interpret the term 'sustainable development' as a desirable model or overall concept for the process of economies', societies' and individual humans' development or evolution respectively. Questions related to the description and assessment of sustainable development can – for example – be applied to corporate processes. In this regard, the contribution of products and services to sustainable development is increasingly being described and assessed. This is usually done by an assessment of both their ability to meet current and future requirements as well as their capability of keeping current and future impacts, expenses and risks within certain limits or boundaries. If the assessment results are positive, such products and services are colloquially named 'sustainable'. This also applies to buildings and constructed works. In order to classify sustainable buildings, it is necessary to start with the general areas of protection which can be deduced from the five dimensions of sustainable development. These are as follows:

• protection of the natural environment/ecosystem;
• protection of basic natural resources;
• protection of human health and well-being;
• protection of social values and of public goods;
• protection and preservation of capital and material goods.

Transferred to buildings and their associated plots of land, several requirements can be formulated that help to classify sustainable buildings. These requirements are shown in the upper part of Table 11.1.

Table 11.1   Requirements for sustainable buildings.

Minimisation of life-cycle costs/cost-effectiveness from a full financial cost-return perspective	
• Reduction of land use and use of hard surfaces	
• Reduction of raw material/resource depletion	
• Closing of material flows	
• Avoidance/reduction of the use of hazardous substances	
• Reduction of CO_2 emissions and other pollutants	
• Reduction of impacts on the environment	
• Protection of health and comfort of building occupants/ users as well as of neighbours	
• Preservation of buildings' cultural value	Economic, environmental and social aspects
• Maximisation of the building's serviceability	Aspects related to the fulfilment of users' and occupants' needs
• Maximisation of the building's functionality	

The requirements formulated in the lower part of Table 11.1 are not always explicitly addressed within international discussions on sustainable buildings. However, in regard to Brundtland's definition of sustainable development, it is apparent that the issue of satisfying users' and occupants' needs (i.e. the maximisation of the building's serviceability and functionality) is another central requirement for the classification of sustainable buildings. Taking all these requirements mentioned above into account allows property to be viewed from a full 'cost-benefit' or 'input–output' perspective respectively, including commonly accepted values and the interests of all stakeholders involved. In short, a sustainable building squeezes the maximum utility for owners, users and the wider public out of the lowest possible throughput of energy and raw materials and with minimum impacts on and risks for the environment and human health. Sustainable buildings – or to be more precise, buildings that contribute positively to sustainable development through their characteristics and attributes – are the result of sustainability-oriented design, construction, use and management of buildings. Sustainable design and construction can be traced back to different roots. These are, amongst others, energy-saving design and construction, building biology, design for the environment/low-carbon design and design for deconstruction. As a result of this development, the environmental aspects have come to dominate, and the resulting buildings are frequently termed 'green' buildings instead of sustainable buildings. However, little by little, a shift towards an integral design can be observed which takes into account the full building life cycle as well as aesthetic, functional, technical, economic, environmental and sociocultural aspects. The assessment of a single building's contribution to sustainable development is usually based on the methods of life-cycle costing/whole-life costing and life-cycle assessment/life-cycle impact assessment in order to describe and assess its resource consumption and the impacts on the environment. Thereby, the fulfilment of functional requirements is presupposed but not assessed; furthermore, effects on cash flow and development of value are barely investigated.

The issue of sustainable design and construction is part of several concepts and strategies (e.g. the EU thematic strategy on the urban environment) and a topic of current standardisation activities at international (ISO TC 59 SC 17 Sustainability in Building Construction), European (CENT C 350 Sustainability of Construction Works) and national level. At the moment, these standardisation activities are mainly focused on the description and assessment of a building's environmental performance. The ability to assess and communicate the energy and environmental quality of buildings in the design phase as well as within the existing stock is one major precondition for establishing new SRI products in the property sector.

The performance-based/high-performance building approach

The assessment of a building's contribution to sustainable development involves the measurement of its performance. Property performance is a very broad concept and performance means different things to different people. But in a very general sense, performance can be defined as behaviour in use. Regarding the performance-based building approach, performance is understood as the degree of compliance of user/owner requirements with corresponding building characteristics and attributes. This notion of performance has its seeds in the area of describing and assessing the fulfilment of functional requirements (functionality and serviceability) and its development has strongly been influenced and affected by F. Szigeti and G. Davis (Szigeti & Davis, 2003; Szigeti *et al.*, 2004). Developments in the area of performance-based building can be retraced within the literature; see, for example, Lee and Barrett (2003), Meacham *et al.* (2005), Bakens *et al.* (2005) and Huovila (2005). A recent overview and summary can also be found in Lützkendorf *et al.* (2005). Currently, a variety of efforts are being made at an international and European level to define criteria and indicators that determine several aspects of property performance. These criteria and indicators no longer simply relate to aspects of functionality and serviceability, and the updating of performance assessment criteria is currently extending user demands into the realm of societal and environmental requirements.

The developments in the area of performance-based building are influenced and promoted, amongst others, through the CIB (see: http://www.cibworld.nl) and the Performance Based Building Thematic Network (see: http://www.pebbu.nl). The description and assessment of the full building life cycle under particular adherence to issues of functionality and serviceability is currently a topic of ISO TC 59 SC 14 'Design life'. Approaches for harmonising the description and assessment of the performance of smaller housing facilities are currently discussed within ISO TC 59 SC 15 'Performance criteria for single family attached and detached dwellings'.

Independent from the performance-based building approach – which aims in particular at improving the communication on functionalities and qualities between principals and agents – a so called 'high-performance building' approach has been developed particularly in the USA. According to the US Department of Energy (2006), 'a high-performance commercial building is a building with energy, economic, and environmental performance that is substantially better than standard practice. It's energy efficient, so it saves money and natural resources. It's a healthy place to live and work for its occupants and has relatively low impact on the environment. All this is achieved through a process called whole-building design'. This design approach comes close to the sustainable building approach. In practice, however, high-performance buildings are currently focused on improving aspects of energy efficiency and on utilising the interrelated economic and environmental advantages.

Within the EU, progresses towards more sustainable building practices are made through the introduction of the assessment of the energy performance of buildings. The EU directive on the energy performance of buildings puts forward requirements, which will then be translated into national law by each member country (European Commission, 2002). Amongst other issues, the directive requires that an energy passport/energy certificate containing information on the building's energy performance and efficiency is made available for prospective buyers or tenants within the scope of each property transaction. In connection with the financing of measures to improve a building's energy efficiency, the business segment of 'energy performance contracting'[6] has been growing over the past few years.

A building's energy performance represents an aspect of its environmental performance, which is in turn one part of the integrated building performance of sustainable buildings. The developments which either follow a sustainable building approach or a performance-based building approach are currently moving towards one another.

SRPI approach

While the sustainable building approach and the performance-based building approach are predominantly concerned with improving the design, construction, use and management of buildings and building stocks as well as with the methodological basics of describing, assessing and communicating the contribution of buildings to sustainable development, the SRPI approach is mainly concerned with investment strategies.

Buildings and building stocks, particularly in the commercial sector, are predominantly regarded as investment assets or asset classes respectively.

A number of different motives for the development towards SRPI can be identified. These are:

- the interest in buildings and buildings stocks as sustainable investment assets is growing; however, in comparison to the general development within the SRI market, this trend is slower to take root;
- fund managers of SRI funds (particularly the managers of SRI-oriented pension funds) wish to diversify their portfolios by investing in property assets directly or through indirect investment in respective property investment products;
- a wide range of actors in property markets (including investors, planning and regulatory authorities, occupiers and tenants) aim to minimise risks, cut down costs and improve their image and reputation through the ownership in construction, use and letting of sustainable buildings;
- a general concern (e.g. expressed through the European Commission) to increase the demand for energy efficient, environmentally friendly and healthy buildings with high functionality as well as a high level of aesthetic and urban quality.

Pivo and McNamara (2005, p. 129) defined responsible property investing as a business practice that is aimed at 'maximising the positive effects and minimizing the negative effects of property ownership, management and development on society and the natural environment in a way that is consistent with investor goals and fiduciary responsibilities'. This definition implies that a responsibility towards the environment and society does not only exist for those who buy property assets or property investment products, but also for those who are concerned with the facilities and portfolio management. However, it also becomes clear that actors are particularly keen on following SRPI approaches if this can be combined with the minimisation of risks and an improvement in financial performance. In this regard, the number of publications and studies investigating the relationship between costs and benefits of green/sustainable buildings is constantly growing – see also Chapter 3.

Within the United Nations Environment Program (UNEP) and in connection with UNEP-FI 'Innovative Financing for Sustainability' (see: http://www.unepfi.org) and UNEP-SBCI 'Sustainable Buildings & Construction Initiative' (see: http://www.unepsbci.org), a 'responsible property investment working group' has been formed which also investigates-related issues.

The measurement of property performance represents one key requirement for SRIs within the property sector, since SRI can be defined as 'an investment process that considers the social and environmental consequences of investments, both positive and negative, within the context of rigorous financial analysis' (O'Rourke, 2003, p. 684). SRI is a process of identifying and investing in assets and/or companies that meet certain baseline standards or criteria of CSR which includes issues such as environment, health and safety, diversity, human resource policies, human rights and the supply chain. Although no common definition exists for the SRI market, it can nevertheless be described by referring to its central actors and to the four prevailing investment strategies. In addition to private and institutional investors, the SRI market's central actors are: (1) financial institutions and fund companies that develop, market, trade and manage environmentally and socially advantageous investment products; (2) agencies and services providers that screen companies' environmental and social performance and (3) companies which voluntarily expose themselves as well as their products to such screening processes and which publish relevant information. The prevailing investment strategies, which are sometimes applied in combination, are:

- ethical exclusions;
- positive screening;
- best in class;
- pioneer screening/thematic investment propositions;
- norms-based screening;
- simple screens/simple exclusions;
- engagement;
- integration (Eurosif, 2006).

The untapped market potential for SRPI products can be estimated on the basis of the current volume of SRI markets. The most recent estimates on the volume of the institutional European SRI market report a market size of up to €1.03 trillion by the end of 2005 (Eurosif, 2006), while the size of the European retail SRI market has been estimated to be around €34 billion by the end of the second quarter of 2006 (Avanzi SRI Research, 2006). While SRI in Europe has grown rapidly over the last few years, the US market is more mature. According to the US Social Investment Forum (US SIF, 2006), SRI assets in the USA grew more than 258% from US$ 639 billion in 1995 to US$ 2.29 trillion in 2005 (representing 9.4% of all assets), while the broader investment universe of assets under professional management increased by less than 249% from US$ 7 trillion to US$ 24.4 trillion over the same time period. The largest share of SRI assets (US$ 1.5 trillion) in the USA were found in separate accounts (i.e. portfolios privately managed for individuals and institutions); assets in screened retail funds and other pooled products rose to US$ 179 billion in 2005; this represents a 15-fold increase compared to US$ 12 billion in 1995.

Astonishingly, the SRI community has not yet fully recognised the diversification benefits offered through investments in property assets.

Table 11.2 Untapped market potential for publicly offered sustainable property investment products in million € (based on data provided by Avanzi SRI Research, 2006 and US SIF, 2006).

USA	22 000–44 000	Europe	3 400–6 800
UK	948–1 896	The Netherlands	221–442
France	653–1 306	Swiss	312–624
Italy	258–516	Germany	149–298
Sweden	308–616	Austria	135–270
Belgium	376–752	Spain	17–34

Apparently, none of the over 200 stated retail SRI funds in the USA as well as none of the 388 funds in Europe offer investors a screened and professionally managed property portfolio. Furthermore, Gary Pivo (2005) stated that none of the over 300 REITs in the USA makes social responsibility or sustainability an explicit goal. He goes on to argue 'that neither the real estate research firms that evaluate real estate funds nor the SRI screening firms that evaluate all kinds of companies collect or distribute information on the social or environmental practices of the many retail or institutional real estate investments that are offered in the USA. This is not to say that no real estate investment firms may be constructively engaged in these issues. But if they do exist, they're simply too hard to find' (Pivo, 2005, p. 17). The situation is very similar in Europe; only very few property investment firms or funds make sustainability an explicit goal. Given that an optimal share of property (direct or indirect investment) within a mixed-asset portfolio is somewhere between 10 and 20% (Sirmans & Worzala, 2003; Worzala & Sirmans, 2003), the retail SRI market as a whole is significantly underallocated from the perspective of optimal asset allocation. Consequently, the untapped market potential for publicly offered sustainable property investment products is huge and can be easily calculated: it is simply 10–20% of the volume of the current retail SRI market; that is between US\$ 17.9 and US\$ 35.8 billion in the USA and between €3.4 and €6.8 billion in Europe. Table 11.2 gives an overview of the market potential within individual countries.

The same calculation cannot, however, be made for the institutional SRI market because little is known about the share of property owned by SRI-engaged institutional investors. However, given the worldwide lack of sustainable property investment products and given the fact that sustainable building is not yet a mainstream activity, it may be reasonable to assume that those buildings or property investment products owned by institutional investors may not be the most sustainable ones. Thus, if only 10% of the more than US\$ 3.3 trillion now in SRI (Europe and USA) is moved to sustainable property assets, it would equal to approximately one half of the current free-float market capitalisation of the FTSE EPRA/NAREIT global listed real estate index which was US$ 686 billion at the end of 2006. A possible reason for this lack of appropriate investment products might be the absence of both knowledge and common understanding of the benefits and constituents of sustainable buildings in general and of sustainable property investment products in particular as well as of appropriate systems or frameworks to assess and report their performance.

Characterisation of the status quo

In 2007, the *status quo* can be described as follows: On the part of the building products industry, the construction industry and among designers and facilities managers, the intense engagement in questions relating to sustainable design and construction during recent years has led to a situation in which building products, technologies, design schemes and concepts for energy efficient, environmentally friendly and healthy buildings are available on an international basis. At the same time, researchers have developed methods for the description and assessment of the economic and environmental benefits of buildings over their full building life cycle. In particular, the description and portrayal of the energy characteristics of buildings is becoming standardised and is now mandatory within the EU. Assessment approaches and methods for assessing the environmental performance as well as for the integrated building performance (which covers all aspects of sustainable development) are currently under development and are also an issue of international standardisation activities.

As well as governmental regulation, market forces further promote the certification of buildings that fulfil sustainable design and construction requirements. Public authorities increasingly support and require sustainable construction activities and increasingly take a leading role in this regard. Banks (e.g. the Co-operative Bank) and insurance companies (e.g. Firemen's Fund Insurance Company) offer preferential conditions for sustainable buildings; and property funds and companies (e.g. Hermes) are engaged in the area of sustainable building. An overview on the pioneers in financing, developing and managing sustainable buildings can be found, for example, in Lorenz (2006).

In spite of this positive situation, a number of deficits can also be observed. At the moment, there is not an adequate supply of sustainable buildings to satisfy the demand from individual and institutional investors (e.g. sustainable property investment funds, green REITs and so on). A number of possible reasons for this shortcoming have been identified and are as follows.

- Possible initiators of sustainable property investment products do not yet have clear answers to the following questions: who can assess and certify the sustainability of buildings, how can this be done and what is the appropriate information basis?

- There is a concern as to whether there are a sufficient number of sustainable buildings already (or becoming) available in the marketplace in order to satisfy the demand from property funds.
- A commonly held misconception is that the construction of sustainable buildings is more expensive than the construction of their conventional counterparts.
- Another prejudice is that the range of products, components and systems that are used within sustainable buildings are not yet appropriately tested and free of risks.
- Information on major building characteristics and attributes (which form the basis for the assessment of a building's contribution to sustainable development) is not yet available or appropriately described. This hampers the investigation of the relationship between environmental quality and economic advantageousness.
- Existing SRI strategies have not yet been transferred and adjusted to property assets and respective investment products.

In order the address these misconceptions and information deficiencies, the next section provides an overview on the economic advantages of sustainable buildings and an overview of the trends in property performance measurement and risk assessment. Following on from that, a proposal for the deduction of appropriate investment strategies is offered.

The benefits of sustainable buildings and of SRIs

The environmental, social and (to some extent) economic benefits of sustainable buildings are extensively researched, documented and illustrated in the literature. It is now generally agreed that sustainable buildings are more cost and energy efficient, functionally effective, profitable and marketable than conventional buildings and that they exhibit increased functionality, serviceability and adaptability as well as increased comfort and well-being of occupants while at the same time offering loss prevention benefits[7], risk reduction potential (see Table 11.3) as well as reduced negative impacts on the natural environment (Wilson *et al.*, 1998; Yates, 2001; Heerwagen, 2002; Mills, 2003a,b; Kats *et al.*, 2003; RICS, 2004, 2005).

From the authors' point of view, the issue of avoiding and reducing property-specific risks is of particular interest in connection with SRPI. Besides taking responsibility towards society and the environment, investors are primarily interested in the financial advantages of sustainable

Table 11.3   Links between sustainable design features and reduced property-specific risks (examples).

Characteristics and attributes of sustainable buildings	Examples for reductions in/avoidance of property-specific risks
Flexibility and adaptability	Reduction of risks through changes market participants' preferences (obsolescence) and through restricted usability by third parties
Energy efficiency and savings in water usage	Reduction of risks through changes in energy and water prices; reduced business interruption risks (e.g. caused by power outages) through facilities that derive energy from on-site resources and/or have energy efficiency features
Use of environmentally friendly and healthy building products and materials	Reduction of litigation risks and of being held liable for paying compensations to construction workers and building occupants
High functionality in connection with comfort and health of user and occupants	Reduction of vacancy risks or of losing the tenant(s)
Construction quality, systematic maintenance and market acceptance	Lower risks of changes in property values
Compliance with/overcompliance of legal requirements in the areas of environmental and health protection	Reduction of risks from increasingly stringent legislation (e.g. expensive retrofitting or losses in property values)

buildings and respective investment options. However, the quantification of these financial advantages in monetary terms is not yet always possible. Therefore, one possible approach consists in the description and portrayal of reduced property-specific risks, which can also be economically assessed by using appropriate methods and tools such as property rating systems (Lützkendorf & Lorenz, 2007). Examples for the relationship between characteristics and attributes of sustainable buildings and reduced property-specific risks can be found in Table 11.3.

Kats (2003) and Kats *et al.* (2003) produced a comprehensive and well-documented cost-benefit analysis of sustainable buildings and investigated the direct financial gains associated with incorporating sustainable design features into new building projects. They concluded that minimal increases in upfront costs of about 2% to support sustainable design would, on average, result in life-cycle savings of 20% of total construction costs. For example, an initial upfront investment of up to €100.000 to incorporate sustainable building features into a €5 million project would result in a saving of €1 million at current prices (discounted by a 5% interest rate) over the life of the building, assumed conservatively to be 20 years. 'From a life cycle savings standpoint, savings resulting from investment in sustainable design and construction dramatically exceed any additional upfront costs' (Kats *et al.*, 2003, p. vii).

Other financial benefits such as increases in market value due to improved marketability or occupant productivity gains are more difficult to prove empirically. However, this evidence exists: One of the first came from an American study by Nevin and Watson (1998), who calculated that market values of residential homes increases by US$ 20 for every US$ 1 decrease in annual utility cost and that cost-effective energy efficiency investments do appear to be reflected in residential housing market values. Furthermore, extensive research conducted by Kumar and Fisk (2002), Heerwagen (2002), Heerwagen *et al.* (2004) and Kampschroer and Heerwagen (2005) identified strong correlations between sustainable design features (e.g. natural lighting, thermal comfort, air quality, worker-controlled temperature and ventilation etc.) and reduced illness symptoms, reduced absenteeism and significant increases in the measured productivity of the workforce. These findings support earlier results of the Probe studies (Bordass *et al.*, 1999) and a resulting statement by Leaman and Bordass (1999) that losses or gains of up to 15% of turnover in a typical office organisation might be attributable to the design, management and use of the indoor environment.

In addition, there are now a number of studies available which refute the commonly held misbelief that sustainable buildings cost up to 15% more in terms of capital cost to build from the outset than conventional buildings. For example, Matthiessen and Morris (2003) found that many building projects can be built to a sustainable design within their initial budget, or with very small supplemental funding (< 3% of initial budget). Other sources for information on the costs of sustainable construction are: Bartlett and Howard (2000), Bordass (2000) and Mackley (2002). To conclude, there can be no doubt that sustainable buildings can clearly outperform their conventional counterparts. Figure 11.2 represents the authors' view of the effects and benefits of sustainable buildings. It is also shown that an evaluation of economic benefits is always influenced through the perception of the individual actor concerned. The authors attempt to assign the different effects and benefits to investors, users, society and the environment. Furthermore, interdependencies and interactions between different effects are indicated.

Obviously, sustainable design features positively impact on a building's worth and market value. This is now beginning to be accepted and recognised outside research circles and academia. Recently, a report published by the RICS concluded that a clear 'link is beginning to emerge between the market value of a building and its green features and related performance' (RICS, 2005, p. 3).

In addition to research on the benefits of sustainable buildings, there exists a variety of studies carried out during the last decade investigating the correlation between corporate profitability or investment performance

Effects and benefits on …	Developer/Owner/Landlord										User/Tenant			Society			Environment		
	Increased marketability	Reduction of vacancy risks	Reduction of maintenance costs	Image and reputation gains	Advantages in tendering processes	Inclusion in sustainable property investment funds/indexes	Trading of CO_2-certificates	Access to better financing conditions, subsidy programmes and tax credits	Higher prices/rents; more stable cash flow; profit maximisation	Stability of value and worth/ Increases in value and worth	Occupant satisfaction and productivity gains	Reduction of operating costs	Image and reputation gains	Urban design quality/cultural quality	Fewer Sick-Building Syndromes/ lower costs for health care system	Reduction of 'external costs' through environmental damages	Lower resource use and raw material depletion	Reduction of impacts on the environment	Preservation of biodiversity
Building																			
B1 Energy efficiency/energy saving	■	■		■	■	■	■	■	■	■		■	■		■	■	■	■	□
B2 Reduction of water cons./waste water	■			■	■	■		■	■	■	■	■	■			■	■	■	■
B3 Environmental friendly material selection	■	■	■	■	■	■		■	■	■	■				■	■	■	■	□
B4 Air quality/thermal comfort	■	■	■	■		■		■	■	■	■		■		■				
B5 Functionality	■	■		■				■	■	■	■								
B6 Adaptability																			
B7 Longevity/durability			■																
B8 Design/aesthetic quality				■						■	□		■	■					
Process																			
P1 Integral design	■	■									□	□		□			□	□	□
P2 User participation	□	□		□					□		□	□	□	■			□	□	□
P3 Systematic maintenance	□		■	□							■			□	□	■	■	■	■

Figure 11.2 Effects and benefits of sustainable buildings (Lützkendorf & Lorenz, 2007); ■ = strong/direct impact; □ = weak/indirect impact.

on the one hand, and environmental and social performance of businesses and investment products on the other hand. In particular, three publications need to be mentioned that contain reviews of a large number of relevant studies on this issue:

(1) Murphy (2002) concluded – based on an extensive literature review – that companies that score well according to objective environmental criteria deliver stronger financial returns than the overall market, and companies that score poorly have weaker returns. Furthermore, Murphy stated that companies that go beyond legal compliance deliver stronger stock price gains and market value growth than the overall S&P 500. In contrast, laggard companies that are threatened by actual or impending environmental laws have been shown to experience weaker returns. (2) Schröder (2003) reviewed literature on the comparison between the financial performance of SRI funds and indexes and the performance of conventional funds and stock indexes. He concluded that SRI assets do not show weaker returns in comparison to other assets. (3) The investment management company Phillips *et al.* (2005) reviewed the literature on the performance of sustainability indexes versus traditional stock indexes, of SRI funds versus conventional funds, as well as of the financial performance of companies that score high on one or more measures of good corporate governance versus those that do not. Their main finding is that the literature does not provide any evidence that socially responsible investing or the adoption of good corporate governance policies result in lower investment returns or financial performance respectively.

In summary, a vast body of credible evidence now indicates that there are no financial disadvantages, and in some cases, positive financial effects associated with the adoption of SRI and CSR polices. Furthermore, it is likely that the range of environmental and social advantages of such policies are not yet fully expressed in investment value since they cannot yet be truly reflected through the traditional approaches to investment analysis that focus on internal financial returns only and do not capture the external costs and benefits. Consequently, the question is no longer if, but when will it be possible to clearly demonstrate that SRI and CSR approaches outperform the conventional modes of business and investment practice from any relevant point of view; that is economically, environmentally and socially?

Unfortunately, empirical evidence on the investment performance of SRPIs does not yet exist due to the absence of a SRPI index. However, given the research on single buildings and on non-property SRI assets reviewed above, it can be assumed that increasing economic returns, sustaining the natural environment and protecting social values can be accommodated within property investment markets.

Criteria and assessment tools

With regard to the required assessment of buildings' contribution to sustainable development, two clear trends become apparent. One the one hand, assessment tools for evaluating building performance are being developed and applied within the green/sustainable building and construction community. One the other hand, however, sustainability issues are being increasingly integrated into decision support and risk assessment tools and into decision-making processes by banks and rating agencies.

Assessment tools for green buildings and information transfer

Methodological approaches and frameworks for assessing the performance of single buildings are currently being developed and standardised by the International Standardisation Organisation (ISO) within the scope of ISO TC 59 'Building Construction' (notably SC 14 'Design Life' and SC 17 'Sustainability in building construction') and ISO TC 207 'Environmental Management'. Furthermore, standardisation activities in this area are carried out by CEN (the European Committee for Standardization) within the scope of TC 350 'Sustainability of Construction Works'. Amongst others, current standardisation activities are concerned with the following issues.

- Translation and adjustment of the principles of sustainable development to the assessment object construction works.
- Development and selection of criteria and indicators for assessing the contribution of buildings to sustainable development (with a focus on environmental building performance); including agreement on a minimal list of relevant criteria and indicators.
- Classification of aspects of sustainability within an integrated building performance approach through the combination of environmental, social and economic performance aspects with issues of functional and technical quality.
- Further development of the methodological basics for estimating the service life of building products and components.
- Further development of the methodological basics for life-cycle assessment and life-cycle costing.
- Development of the basics for providing environmentally relevant information on building products in the form of environmental product declarations (EPDs).
- Development of harmonised basics for the description of the full life cycle of buildings and for assessing energy and mass flows or for conducting inventory analyses respectively.

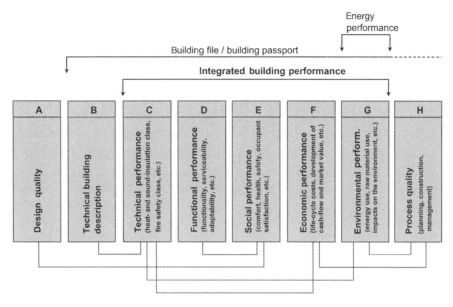

Figure 11.3 Different aspects of property performance within an overall framework (Lützkendorf & Lorenz, 2006a).

One important issue which is not yet covered by standardisation activities is the development of commonly accepted benchmarks for assessing the contribution of buildings to sustainable development. In summary, however, current standardisation activities involve technical, functional, social, environmental and economic aspects. These activities and proposals can be arranged into an overall system of building performance. Figure 11.3 depicts different aspects of property performance within a framework of building-related information. It should be noted that the activities at ISO and CEN do not cover all aspects portrayed in Figure 11.3. On the basis of these building performance characteristics, the contribution of single buildings to sustainable development becomes measurable and distinguishable.

Ideally, this performance information is contained within a so-called building file or building passport. But building files are currently only rarely issued, and on a voluntary basis, and mainly relate to residential property.

One good example for the commercial property sector, however, is the electronic data exchange standard called PISCES which is currently being developed by major UK property market players (PISCES, 2004). The standard (which could be interpreted as an electronic building file for commercial property assets) does not yet contain references to sustainability performance aspects; however, since the standard is flexible and intended to evolve over time, these issues could and should be integrated.

One precondition for the realisation of SRPIs is the availability of appropriate assessment methods and tools that allow evidencing a positive contribution to sustainable development. To a certain extent, this is already
possible with existing methods and tools. However, within the process of
further developing assessment methods and tools, it is necessary to find
a balance between quantitative and qualitative measures and to develop
clear rules and guidelines. Also, in order to assure comparability of different assessment approaches and to assure a certain degree of quality
and amount of required information, it is essential to reach agreement on
a 'minimal list' of indicators within an international or European framework respectively. Furthermore, it is necessary to develop appropriate
schemes and software tools that allow for a simultaneous assessment of
these indicators.

Existing performance assessment tools for single buildings have been
frequently described, evaluated and comparatively analysed in the literature; for example, in IEA Annex31 (2001); in Todd *et al.* (2001); in Kats
et al. (2003) and recently in Cole (2005) and in Peuportier and Putzeys
(2005); furthermore, assessment tools are under continuous review of
the European Thematic Network on Practical Recommendations for
Sustainable Construction (PRESCO)[8]. Examples for tools are: BREEAM
and ENVEST (UK); GBTool; LEED (US); Eco-Quantum (NL); Okoprofil
(NOR); ESCALE (FR) and LEGEP (D), to mention only a few.

Up to date, the only assessment approach suitable as a basis for a worldwide application is represented through the SBTool[9] which has emerged
from the former GBTool and which has been developed under the leadership of the International Initiative for a Sustainable Built Environment
(iiSBE). A schematic overview of the tool is represented in Figure 11.4.

But most of these tools assess buildings after they are designed and do
not account for future life-cycle costs of the building. Due to the com-
plexity involved, only a few tools exist that allow for a combined determination and assessment of cost, environmental and (to some extent)
occupational health and other social issues in the planning phase. The
basic goal of these combined assessment approaches is to allow professionals to assess a design or building solution simultaneously from different
points of view and within different life-cycle scenarios. Early examples
of such combined tools are LEGEP (Germany) and OGIP (Switzerland).
One major problem, however, associated with combined or/and simple
LCA-based assessment approaches is the lack of standardisation in terms
of scope, definition of performance indicators and weighting of different
aspects (Todd *et al.*, 2001).

Given the variety of existing assessment tools available in the marketplace, it seems reasonable to provide a classification of assessment tools.
They can be classified according to the following aspects.

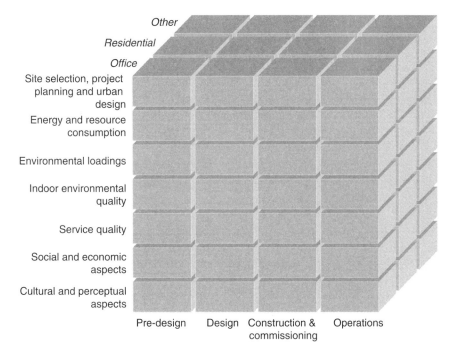

Figure 11.4   Overview of the structure of the SBTool (Larsson, 2005).

- Dimensions of sustainable development (i.e. does the tool solely focus on environmental aspects, or does it additionally assess economic, social, technical and functional aspects?)
- Phases of the building life cycle (i.e. does the tool cover all phases of the building life cycle, or is it focused on single parts or time frames respectively?)
- Integration of design and assessment issues (i.e. does the tool focus on the assessment process only, or is it linked to CAD-software and therefore capable of internally calculating assessment inputs?)
- Nature of the assessment (i.e. does the tool predominantly use qualitative, quantitative information or a balanced combination of the two?)
- Level of detail or extent of aggregation respectively (i.e. to what extent does the tool summarise or aggregate assessment results?)
- Nature and breadth of assessment results (i.e. does the tool deliver an energy certificate, building file and/or an assessment report and does it additionally provide any label for building products or construction works?)
- Applicability for the assessment of existing buildings (i.e. is it possible to use the tool to assess already existing buildings and/or does it even allow for an application accompanying the entire building life cycle?)

A more detailed description and explanation of different tools can be found in IEA Annex31 (2004). The results of applying these building assessment tools can then be seen as one aspect of the assessment of SRPIs. As it was said before, further aspects that need to be considered are the regional and wider social impacts of investments as well as company level issues.

Developments in the area of property rating/risk assessment

The methodologies and processes by which banks assess and monitor the risks associated with property lending are currently undergoing major changes. Until very recently, banks' internal risk assessments did not distinguish between sustainable buildings and conventional ones. However, this is no longer the case anymore. The application of new, international banking capital adequacy rules called Basel II requires banks to take a much more sophisticated approach with regard to the risks they take in lending (BCBS, 2004). As a consequence, the so-called property ratings will increasingly be conducted for lending purposes. In a very general sense, a rating can be defined as a procedure which illustrates the assessment of a thing, a person or situation, etc. on a scale in order to improve the informational basis for the predicttion of future outcomes. Rating is not a new concept; it is has been used since the beginning of the 20th century by companies like Moody's and Standard & Poors in order to provide information on the financial strengths and willingness of companies to comply with liabilities completely and in time (TEGoVA, 2003). The European Group of Valuers Associations (TEGoVA) has recently developed a property and market rating system which is likely to become influential for European property lending practice. TEGoVA's rating system contains four different criteria classes (market, location, property and quality of the property cash flow), up to four levels of subcriteria classes and employs a rating scale that ranges from 1 (excellent) to 10 (disastrous). Table 11.4 shows that the criteria class 3 'property' contains the rating criterion 'ecological sustainability'.

Unfortunately, what is meant by ecological sustainability and the issue of how to assess it is neither defined nor explained within TEGoVA's publications. However, the rating proposal of the German association of public banks (VÖB), currently being implemented by public banks across Germany, defines three subcriteria of ecological sustainability which will have to be assessed: building materials, energy performance and emissions (VÖB, 2005). Critics may argue that 10 out of 20% is a very modest start. However, both rating approaches contain (slightly different) 'dynamic risk weight functions'; that is, the basic weighting assigned to each indicator or subcriteria class is flexible; the more the rating score deviates from the average, the more significantly it impacts on the overall rating results. This is done to reflect the fact that a high level of exposure to one particular hazard is usually perceived to have a greater impact on the outcome

Table 11.4 TEGoVA's property and market rating, criteria class 3 'property' (TEGoVA, 2003).

Subcriteria		Weighting (subcriterion) (%)	Weighting (criteria class)
3.1	Architecture	20	
3.2	Fitout	10	
3.3	Structural condition	15	Criteria class 3
3.4	Plot situation	25	20%
3.5	Ecological sustainability	10	
3.6	Profitability of the building concept	20	
Result for the property rating		100	

of a property investment or on the property's selling or letting prospects respectively (e.g. a property with very good overall structural condition and fitout, etc. would achieve a good rating for the criteria class 'property'; however, if the property's location is 'disastrous', then this fact deserves more attention). As a result of applying dynamic risk weights, a particular indicator that is originally assigned secondary importance can have a great impact on the overall rating result. For example, a 'disastrous' or 'excellent' rating of the criterion ecological sustainability can change the overall result by several points. Given that the rating scale ranges from 1 to 10, sustainability issues can, indeed, have a strong impact on the banks' assessment of the risks associated with property lending and thus, on lending decisions as well as conditions.

Outlook

It is becoming clear that the methods, instruments and tools that have been developed by the sustainable building community in order to assess individual buildings' quality and contribution to sustainable development such as 'green' building rating systems, LCA-based assessment tools, post-occupancy evaluations, energy labels, etc. have the potential to be used to inform the processes of property financing and risk analysis.

This will increase the demand for such methods and instruments. As a consequence, their future role within property markets (which has been recently discussed within a special issue of *Building Research and Information*, see Lorch and Cole (2006)) can be extended and more precisely described within an overall system of measures and instruments that contribute to the market transformation of the construction and property sectors.

If the results of building assessment tools are to be used to support the rating and risk analysis process, then the flow of information can be organised in different ways. The question arises whether partial results of

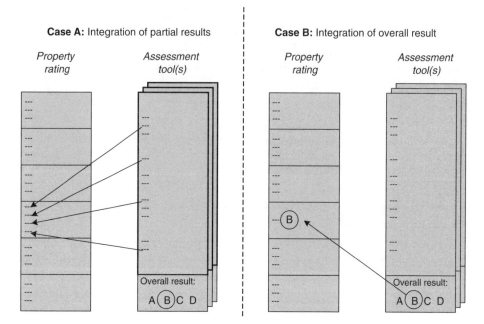

Figure 11.5   Different forms of integrating building assessment results into property ratings.

building assessments should be used to provide the informational basis for certain aspects of property ratings or whether the overall building assessment result should be integrated into property ratings as a separate rating category. These different forms of integrating building assessment results into property ratings are depict in Figure 11.5.

The opportunity exists for the built environment research community to work together with the financial community to discuss, develop, monitor and refine these mechanisms and to use these to accelerate the market transformation towards more sustainable buildings. However, it is unclear at the moment which assessment approaches and which possible combinations of different approaches will achieve acceptance in the market.

Realisation of SRPIs

Basics

One of the basic questions for the development of SRPI options is concerned with the interpretation of the manner and scope of the responsibility that has to be taken towards society and the environment. The assessment and performance measurement of SRPIs may require the investigation of a variety of different criteria and indicators at a number of different levels. Pivo (2005, p. 22) suggested that 'it may be best to evaluate investments in terms of a variety of dimensions or criteria and to offer a range of choices that investors can select among, allowing the individual investor to determine what they consider to be acceptable investments'. The extent to which different criteria and indicators at different levels are investigated will depend on what is both demanded by investors and feasible for analysts and rating agencies to deliver. It becomes clear that if different assessment approaches emerge – which is very likely to happen – then the assessment results will not be comparable. Thus, a very similar development will take place which can already be observed within the general SRI market. As to how far the introduction of respective labels[10] represents a possible solution remains to be seen.

Within the scope of assessing socially responsible or sustainable property investments, the authors therefore suggest following a clear system of criteria and signalling the respective assessment basics. They suggest distinguishing between:

- characteristics and attributes of the building (e.g. energy efficiency, use of renewable construction materials, thermal and acoustic comfort, appearance of building-related illness, cultural value, etc.);
- quality of design, operating and management processes (e.g. stakeholder participation during the planning stage, quality and appropriateness of services available);
- the building's location (e.g. the characteristics and the conditions of inclusive environments, access and/or distance to other facilities, brownfield regeneration);
- regional circumstances (e.g. biodiversity and ecological integrity, settlement efficiency, urban sprawl, heritage protection and so on);
- wider social circumstances (e.g. equal opportunities, justice, human rights, safety, avoidance of social segregation and so on) and
- company level issues (e.g. labour practices, staff training and education, supply chain management, financial soundness and so on).

For each of these areas, different criteria, indicators and assessment tools apply, and discussing all of them is not feasible within the scope of this chapter. A discussion of criteria, indicators and assessment tools for regional and wider social circumstances is contained within Bentivegna *et al.* (2002), Brindley (2003) and Baines and Morgan (2004); for information on the assessment and reporting of company level issues, see Lamberton (2005), GRI (2005) and AccountAbility (2006).

Strategies and products

In general, socially responsible property investing can be realised either through direct or indirect investment. From the authors' point of view, socially responsible property investing can encompass four main investment strategies. In the case of indirect property investment, it would mean investing only into such property investment products that are committed to one ore more of these four main strategies which are as follows.

1 *Selection/Screening:* Purchase and/or disposal of property assets that meet/do not meet predefined environmental and social performance requirements.
2 *Build and operate/Build and sell:* Investments into new building projects that are designed, constructed and subsequently managed according to the requirements of sustainable buildings as outlined above.
3 *Optimisation:* Investments into the existing building stock in order to systematically improve sustainability performance.
4 *Cause-based investment:* Investments into community projects such as affordable housing and urban revitalisation or into property projects that support urban infill, preservation of historic buildings, etc. in order to foster sustainability at large.

What becomes clear from these strategies is that the scope of targets and goals of SRPI can be focused on both single buildings and their immediate surroundings as well as on broader urban development and community level issues. This makes it difficult to determine whether a property investment can actually be classified as socially responsible or not. Furthermore, a distinction can be made between investment strategies and products that directly increase the market share of sustainable buildings and those that do not. For example, while pursuing the selection/screening strategy, an open-end fund provider could identify all buildings within his portfolio that fulfil the requirements for sustainable buildings (it is, indeed, not impossible that existing funds do contain sustainable buildings) and offer a specialised fund made up exclusively of these buildings. But this approach does not result in the creation of new sustainable buildings; there are no direct benefits for the environment and society.

While, in contrast, the offering of sustainable project development funds (build and sell strategy) can make a direct contribution to the protection of natural resources and environmental relief. These projects can be tailored to fulfil the requirements for sustainable construction and management right from the predesign phase. However, since project development funds regularly sell the buildings short after completion, the question remains if a high-sustainability performance can also be maintained during the subsequent occupation and management phase.

In terms of implementing the principles of sustainable development, pursuing the build and operate strategy appears particularly advantageous. For example, the compilation of BOT (build-operate-transfer) or PPP (public-private-partnership) models into distinct funds could represent an attractive SRPI product. In this regard, relatively long contractual arrangements (30 years or more) provide an excellent basis for safeguarding a high-sustainability performance also during the occupation phase.

Also, the introduction of energy performance certificates within the EU opens up the possibility for effectively pursuing a selection/screening strategy and for offering specialised funds that focus on one or more aspects of sustainable development; in this case, on energy efficiency. Energy performance certificates will allow investors or fund providers to easily identify the most energy efficient buildings in the marketplace.

In general, all indirect property investment forms could be used to offer private and institutional investors the opportunity to invest in sustainable buildings. Figure 11.6 gives an overview on possible investment products and strategies. In addition, the preconditions for assessing the environmental, economic and social benefits of such products are listed.

The provision of SRPI products requires considering the entire building life cycle including upstream and downstream as well as construction, acquisition, use, management and ongoing maintenance. It requires that actions are undertaken which are entirely different from current 'best practice' in property investment, for example, integrated sustainability assessment of property assets; true sustainability accounting and reporting at the building/portfolio as well as company level (which means no 'creative writing exercises') and promoting next-generation construction approaches such as closed-loop design and the use of organic materials in order to reach breakthroughs in energy efficiency. This does, of course, not mean that socially responsible property investors cannot also be highly profitable. In fact, current experience suggests that these innovative or 'radical' approaches to

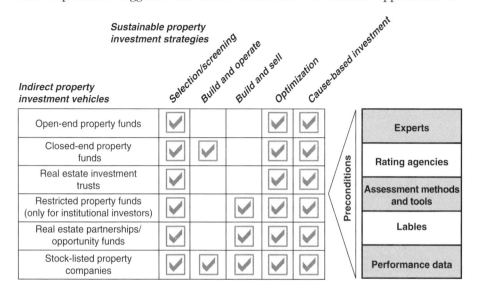

Figure 11.6 SRPI strategies and indirect investment vehicles.

construction are the most profitable ones (McDonough & Braungart, 2003, p. 16) and that those investors or companies who take the most proactive approach are the most successful ones (Murphy, 2002). Socially responsible property investing involves adjusting or 'fine-tuning' actions at the following levels or areas: strategy, business processes, building/portfolio level and stakeholder level. A proposal for possible adjustments to current practice in property investing is portrayed in Figure 11.7.

Implications for property professionals

Practice

The current lack of sustainable practices in property investment bears the great risk for society that property (and other) values are in fact being

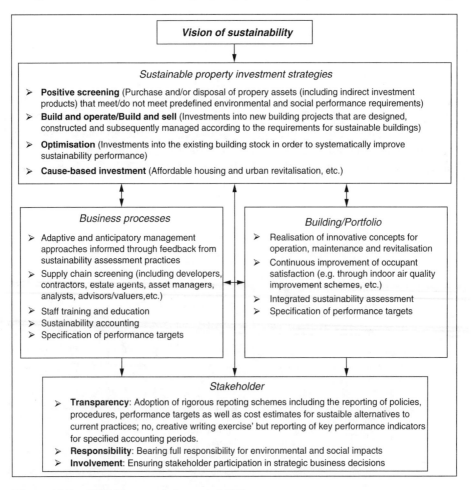

Figure 11.7   SRPI framework (Lorenz, 2006).

destroyed through irresponsible or unsustainable behaviour among property investors and others. As a consequence, the property investment industry as a whole or certain actors of it may be held liable – first, morally and later, financially (see the 'changing landscape of liability' as described in SustainAbility, 2004) – by the court of public opinion for violating the principles of sustainable development and for all the adverse side effects of such behaviour; for example, hostile public spaces[11], social conflicts, occupational diseases, contaminated land[12]; contribution to climate change, brownfield sites[13] within cities and throughout the countryside.

Given this and the significance of the built environment and its huge potential to contribute to sustainable development, it can be argued that concerted and carefully coordinated approaches that involve major groups of stakeholders are required in order to move SRPI quickly into the mainstream. The principles of sustainable development need to be translated or operationalised into the areas of responsibility of the different actors concerned. However, the multitude of activities that take place in the property sector reflects the complex nature of buildings and of property markets which involve a huge number of social, political, economic and physical factors, impacts and processes as well as many different groups of actors, each group with different motivations, goals and perceptions.

Key groups of actors in property markets can be classified into the following six clusters.

- Ownership-related actors (property management companies, owners and investors).
- Design- and consultancy-related actors (design team, property agents, valuers, advisors and analysts).
- Production-related actors (developers, contractors and manufacturers).
- Policy-related actors (urban planners, governments, municipalities, local authorities and intergovernmental institutions).
- Market-related actors (occupiers, researchers, teachers, property index and data providers and the media).
- Finance-related actors (banks, mortgage institutions and insurance companies).

Concerning the mainstreaming of SRPIs, property valuers play a crucial role. Property valuation represents the major mechanism to align economic returns with the environmental and social performance of property assets. Since the material impact of sustainability issues on the financial performance of residential and commercial property investments has not yet been fully captured within the financial world, mainstream financial professionals will not account for sustainability issues in property investment and financing decisions unless sustainable building features and related performance are integrated into property valuations; that is, unless 'the financial sector understands the benefits of green to the net value of an asset' (RICS, 2005, p. 17). Also, if property valuations do not attempt to account for major factors that actually determine or destroy value, these valuations can be misleading since they fail to reflect the full range of benefits and risks that accrue to the one who has ownership- or use-rights in a particular property asset.

If conducted appropriately, a property valuation (i.e. the attempt to provide a monetary measure of the utility derived through ownership and/or use of property) should be understood by everyone; regardless if the end user of a valuation is committed to sustainable building or even aware of its benefits. However, this does not mean that property valuation has to account for sustainability issues in every case and to the widest possible extent. Since one form of property valuation – market valuation – requires estimating the most likely sale price, these valuations need to account for sustainability issues only to the extent to which these issues impact on the competitive position of property assets in the marketplace. As there already is growing awareness of the benefits of sustainable buildings – and market valuations need to reflect this circumstance since they would produce misleading price estimates otherwise – valuers need to find effective measures to monitor and account for the increasing change in market participants' preferences for certain building features. This in return can lead to a positive feedback loop: as market participants see the specific benefits of sustainable buildings (e.g. energy efficiency) reflected in the price estimates produced by property valuers, they are encouraged to become more sustainable in order to achieve higher price estimates for the buildings they own or aim to sell.

Regarding another form of property valuation which is equally important as a basis for investment decision making – calculation of worth – the case is, however, entirely different. Here, the potential for integrating sustainability issues into property valuation depends on subjective investment objectives. As shown above, subjective investment objectives can definitely be shaped by strict sustainability requirements. As a consequence, and in order to avoid producing misleading calculations of worth, valuers need to find measures to account for a wider range of benefits of sustainable buildings (such as environmental impact, occupant productivity, loss prevention, risk reduction or image/reputation gains). This, however, requires a deeper understanding of the differences between conventional and sustainable buildings, on how sustainable building features affect property risk and returns and on how the utility derived from these buildings adds value for individuals or groups of individuals.

The work of the Sustainable Property Appraisal Project in the UK (Sayce *et al.*, 2004; Kingston University, 2005) has developed a methodology for integrating sustainability issues into calculations of property worth and an explanation of the rationale for this. Initial suggestions for reflecting sustainability considerations in property market valuations are addressed, for example, in Lützkendorf and Bachofner (2002), Guidry (2004), Lützkendorf and Lorenz (2005), McNamara (2005) and Lorenz (2006).

In any case, property valuers will need to provide clients with information on the different aspects of building performance – as an extra service that complements the value estimate or an integral part of the valuation process – because it is likely that clients will sooner or later pay for and request it: 'By providing the client with advice that goes beyond the scope of the original information requested, the valuer may actually be providing something of greater benefit than what was requested. This is about valuers helping their clients make the best possible property decisions. The more clients are aware that this service is available, the more they will be willing to pay a fair price for it' (Gilbertson & Preston, 2005, p. 135). Property performance assessment adds a new and potentially desirable quality to the services the valuation profession has to offer. And simply because valuers do not *yet* offer such services and clients do not *yet* pay for them, does not mean that this will not change in future years. This is because 'quality in a product or service is not what the supplier puts in. It is what the customer gets out [...] Customers pay only for what is of use to them and gives them value' (Peter Drucker, cited in Gilbertson & Preston, 2005, p. 135). What gives clients value is not fixed, and it depends on, amongst other issues, the business environment. Given that the business environment is currently changing to favour more sustainable products and services, it is likely that information on the sustainability performance of property assets will in the future become highly valuable for clients.

Education

The importance of *education for sustainable development* has often been emphasised in the literature (Ahlberg, 2005; Marshall & Harry, 2005; Haigh, 2005). In addition, the United Nations Decade of Education for Sustainable Development (2005–2014) was launched on 1 March 2005. There is no universal model or educational strategy, but this concept of education emphasises a holistic, interdisciplinary approach to developing the knowledge and skills needed for a sustainable future as well as changes in values, behaviour and lifestyles.

Education for sustainable development is particularly important within the property and construction sectors. However, efforts and debates are usually focused on the development of educational programmes tailored to the needs of architects, engineers and construction managers (Graham,

2000; Myers, 2003; Lourdel *et al.*, 2005). Also, many of these programmes do not adequately address issues of cost-efficient construction, of planning and construction within the existing building stock or of the systematic maintenance and management of construction works. Furthermore, educational programmes and teaching materials tailored to the needs of property professionals such as valuers and estate agents apparently do not yet exist.

A possible educational strategy to overcome these shortcomings is currently pursued at the Chair of Sustainable Management of Housing and Real Estate, School of Economics, University of Karlsruhe. The chair's concept of combining economic, environmental and social aspects in order to offer a complex teaching profile is (so far) unique in Germany. Starting from the basic principles of sustainable development (overall concept, areas of protection, management rules and guidelines), the teaching profile involves introducing aspects of describing and assessing buildings' contribution to sustainable development into both the design-oriented as well as into the assessment-oriented areas. Here, a distinction is made between basics for undergraduate and for postgraduate education; while the former requires an educational top-down approach, a bottom-up approach is suggested for the latter. Within undergraduate education, students should, first of all, be taught general principles of sustainable development; afterwards, the connection can be made to a particular industry sector or branch as well as to specific problems, methodologies and methods of resolution. In contrast to undergraduate students, the participants of postgraduate university courses or seminars would normally already have a body of knowledge to build on. In most cases, these postgraduate students and seminar participants are interested in updating their knowledge or in achieving additional skills and qualifications. In either case, educational contents need to bear clear references to the students' professional activities; that is, the knowledge provided shall be applicable in practice. In addition, the completion of postgraduate courses shall lead to improved career opportunities. Consequently, the offering of educational contents that provide an overview on the issues and aspects of sustainability only has not proven to be of any great value. Thus, a bottom-up approach is suggested for postgraduate education and training. The starting point is formed by precise problems or procedures which can be related to specific professions or occupational images respectively. Subsequently, these problems and procedures can be classified within an overall context of sustainable development.

A more detailed description of this educational strategy is contained in Lützkendorf and Lorenz (2006b); an overview of contents offered to students is provided in Figure 11.8.

The actors in property and construction markets need to be sensitised for their role, responsibility and options in contributing to sustainable

Design-related contents	Basics/assessment methods
Energy efficient design	Sustainability basics
Design for environment	Energy demand calculation
Low energy house/passive house	Life-cycle assessment (LCA)
Solar energy use (active/passive)	Assessment of surface areas/
Rainwater use	Ecological footprint
Green roof	Assessment of environmental risks
Selection of building materials	Assessment of health risks
Selection of heating systems	Analysis of user requirements
Design for deconstruction	Assessment of user satisfaction/
User-oriented design	Post occupancy evaluation (POE)
Design for senior citizens	Life-cycle costing (LCC)
	Property valuation

Figure 11.8 Building blocks of education for sustainable development in property and construction (Lützkendorf & Lorenz, 2006b).

development. One possible option to achieve this quickly among property professionals is to include elements of education for sustainable development into the Assessment of Professional Competence (APC) procedures of the large professional bodies. This has recently been done by the RICS[14]. Introducing elements of education for sustainable development into these procedures means that one can only become a property professional if one has understood the importance of sustainable development and knows what to do to contribute towards achieving it.

Conclusion and recommendations

There is no doubt that there is an untapped market potential for SRPI products. This represents a huge opportunity for the property industry, not only in terms of making short-term profit, but also in terms of increasing the industry's reputation within the business world and among the general public. Furthermore, the necessity to implement the principles of sustainable development in the property sector and to offer SRPI products and associated consulting services does not only result from the property industry's huge responsibility to society at large, but also addresses the industry's need to safeguard and increase competitiveness and long-term profit.

Also, the perception of property as a commodity is changing to emphasise sustainable design features and performance characteristics as important determinants of a property's worth and market value. Private and corporate market participants are becoming more aware and informed of the quality and performance of the space they use and occupy. Furthermore, poor environmental and social performance is increasingly being seen as an investment risk, and a change in investment paradigms can be observed. Increasingly, investors no longer see a conflict between acting in a sustainable fashion and making a profit (Figure 11.9). Going further, sustainable behaviour and responsible business practices are increasingly seen as a precondition for achieving better investment returns.

At the moment, however, conceptual and technical difficulties mean that it is difficult to empirically prove the financial benefits as well as the risk reduction potential of sustainable buildings. This hampers the integration of sustainability issues into property investment, valuation and risk assessment processes. One primary research objective, therefore, consists in demonstrating that SRPIs enhance investment returns or, at least, do not lead to financial losses. This requires collecting environmental, social and financial performance data for the creation of more sophisticated transaction databases and of a SRPI index.

In the meantime, property professionals (particularly valuers) can focus on and report value creation through sustainable design. In doing so, they can incentivise change and more sustainable behaviour in property markets. This will create a positive, self-perpetuating loop, encouraging more change and sustainable behaviour.

However, focussing on value creation through sustainable design requires an understanding of the concept of sustainable development and of its implications for the property and construction sector. Distinguishing more clearly between conventional buildings and sustainable ones is a major challenge for property professionals, their professional bodies and their educational institutions. Making these distinctions by quantifying the positive impacts of sustainable design will not only move sustainable construction quickly into the mainstream, it will also apply greater pressure

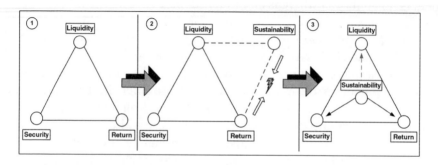

Figure 11.9 Changing investment paradigm.

on investors and investment managers (who traditionally relied simply on financial performance information) to include sustainability issues in their decisions in order to boost property returns.

Notes

1. HeidelbergZement – see: http://www.corporateregister.com/data/showp.pl?num=12799
2. HOCHTIEF – see: http://www.corporateregister.com/data/showp.pl?num=14153
3. See http://www.unepfi.org/signatories/statements/fi/index.html
4. See http://www.unepfi.org/signatories/statements/ii/index.html
5. See http://www.rics.org/Builtenvironment/Sustainableconstruction/rics+view+su stainable+construction.htm
6. See, for example, http://www.eere.energy.gov/buildings/info/plan/ financing/contracts.html or http://www.researchandmarkets.com/reportinfo. asp?report_id=363623
7. Many sustainable design features reduce the likelihood of physical damages and losses in facilities. For example, Mills (2003a) identified a wide a range of energy efficient and renewable energy technologies that offer such loss prevention benefits; for example, water pipe insulation; this is a simple retrofit that saves energy and reduces the likelihood of freeze damage (frozen water pipes have been identified as an important cause of losses in Europe and North America). Furthermore, a subset of energy efficient and renewable energy technologies make buildings less vulnerable to natural disasters, especially heat catastrophes (Mills, 2003b).
8. See www.etn-presco.net
9. See http://greenbuilding.ca/down/gbc2008/SBTool/SBTool_Notes_Jan07.pdf
10. See, for example, http://www.ethibel.org/
11. See a recent RICS publication titled *What kind of world are we building? – The privatisation of public space* (Minton, 2006).
12. Contaminated land can have adverse effects on human health; quality of surface and groundwater; viability of ecosystems; condition of buildings and archaeological artefacts within the ground and on the visual amenity of an area (CLARINET, 2002, p. 4).
13. Brownfield sites have been affected by the former uses of the site and surrounding land; are derelict or underused; have real or perceived contamination problems; are mainly in developed urban areas and require intervention to bring them back to beneficial use (Bardos, 2003, p. 5).
14. www.rics.org/Careerseducationandtraining/Assessmentoftechnicalcompetence/ the2006_apcatc.html
15. SBCI Sustainable Buildings & Construction Initiative
16. International Initiative for a Sustainable Built Environment

References

AccountAbility (2006) *AA1000 Series* [online]. Published by: The Institute of Social and Ethical AccountAbility. URL: http://www.accountability.org.uk/aa1000/default.asp [accessed on 14 April 2006]

Ahlberg, M. (2005) Integrating education for sustainable development. In: W.L. Filho (ed.), *Handbook of Sustainability Research*. Peter Lang Verlag, Frankfurt.

Ambachtsheer, J. (2005) *Socially Responsible Investing – Moving into the Mainstream* [online], Published by: Mercer Investment Consulting. URL: http://www.merceric. com/summary.jhtml/dynamic/idContent/1181715 [accessed on 08 December 2005]

Avanzi SRI Research (2006) *Green, Social and Ethical Funds in Europe 2006* [online]. URL: http://www.avanzi-sri.org/pdf/complete_report_2006_final.pdf [accessed on 15 March 2007]

Baines, J. & Morgan, B. (2004) Sustainability appraisal: a social perspective. In: B. Dalal-Clayton & B. Sadler (eds), *Sustainability Appraisal – A Review of International Experience and Practice* [online]. Published by: International Institute for Environment and Development. URL: http://www.iied.org/Gov/spa/docs.html [accessed on 01 March 2006], pp. 95–111.

Bakens, W., Foliente, G. & Jasuja, M. (2005) Engaging stakeholders in performance-based building: lessons form the Performance-Based Building (PeBBu) Network. *Building Research and Information*, 33 (2), 149–158.

Bardos, P. (2003) *The Contaminated Land Rehabilitation Network for Environmental Technologies – Managing and Developing the UK Interface with CLARINET* [online]. Published by: The Department for Environment, Food and Rural Affairs. URL: http:// www.defra.gov.uk/ENVIRONMENT/land/contaminated/pdf/clarinet-report.pdf [accessed on 22 March 2006]

Bartlett, E. & Howard, N. (2000) Informing the decision makers on the cost and value of green building. *Building Research and Information*, 28 (5/6), 315–324.

BCBS (2004) *International Convergence of Capital Measurement and Capital Standards – A Revised Framework* [online]. Published by: Bank for International Settlements. URL: http://www.bis.org/publ/bcbs107.htm [accessed on 25 July 2004]

Bentivegna, V., Curwell. S., Deakin, M., Lombardi, P., Mitchell, G. & Nijkamp, P. (2002) A vision and methodology for integrated sustainable urban development: BEQUEST. *Building Research and Information*, 30 (2), 83–94.

Bordass, B., Leaman, A. & Ruyssevelt, P. (1999) *Probe Strategic Review 1999 – Report 4: Strategic Conclusions* [online]. URL: http://www.usablebuildings.co.uk [accessed on 12 May 2003]

Bordass, B. (2000) Cost and value: fact and fiction. *Building Research and Information*, 28 (5/6), 338–352.

Brindley, T. (2003) The social dimension of the urban village: a comparison of models for sustainable urban development. *Urban Design International*, 8 (1–2), 53–65.

Bruhns, H. (2003) *The Role of Information in a Sustainable Property Market* [online]. Published by: RICS Foundation. URL: http://www.rics-foundation.org/publish/download.aspx?did=3160 [accessed on 13 June 2004]

CLARINET (2002a) *Sustainable Management of Contaminated Land: An Overview* [online]. Published by: Contaminated Land Rehabilitation Network for Environmental Technologies. URL: http://www.clarinet.at/library/rblm_report.pdf [accessed on 19 April 2006]

Cole, R.J. (2005) Building environmental assessment methods: redefining intentions and roles. *Building Research and Information*, 33 (5), 455–467.

European Commission (2002) *Directive of the European Parliament and of the Council on the energy performance of buildings*, 2002/91/EC, Official Journal of the European Communities, December, 2002, L1 pp. 65–71.

European Commission (2004a) *Construction Sector Overview* [online]. URL: http://europa. eu.int/comm/enterprise/construction/index_en.htm [accessed on 05 January 2005]

European Commission (2004b) *Towards a Thematic Strategy on the Urban Environment* [online]. COM(2004)60, Brussels, 2004. URL: http://europa.eu.int/ comm/environment/urban/thematic_strategy.htm [accessed on 05 September 2004]

Eurosif (2006) *European SRI Study 2006* [online]. Published by: European Social Investment Forum. URL: http://www.eurosif.org/media/files/eurosif_sristudy_2006_complete [accessed on 28 January 2007]

Gilbertson, B. & Preston, D. (2005) A vision for valuation. *Journal of Property Investment and Finance, 23* (2), 123–140.

GRI (2005) *G3 – Global Reporting Guidelines* [online]. Published by: Global Reporting Initiative. URL: http://www.grig3.org/index.html [accessed on 30 March 2006]

Graham, P. (2000) Building education for the next industrial revolution: teaching and learning environmental literacy for the building professions. *Construction Management and Economics, 18,* 917–925.

Guidry, K. (2004) How green is your building? An appraiser's guide to sustainable design. *The Appraisal Journal,* Winter, 57–68.

Haigh, M. (2005) Greening the University Curriculum: appraising an international movement. *Journal of Geography in Higher Education, 29* (1), 31–48.

Heerwagen, J. (2002) *Sustainable Design Can Be an Asset to the Bottom Line – expanded internet edition* [online]. *Environmental Design and Construction.* URL: http://www.edcmag.com/CDA/ArticleInformation/features/BNP__Features__Item/0,4120,80724,00.html [accessed on 10 April 2004]

Heerwagen, J.H., Kampschroer, K., Powell, K.M. & Loftness, V. (2004) Collaborative knowledge work environments. *Building Research and Information, 32* (6), 510–528.

Huovila, P. (ed.) (2005) Performance based building. *Advancing Facilities Management and Construction through Innovation Series,* Published by: Technical Research Centre Finland (VTT) and Association of Finnish Civil Engineers (RIL), Helsinki.

IEA Annex31 (2001) *Directory of Tools – A survey of LCA Tools, Assessment Frameworks, Rating Systems, Technical Guidelines, Catalogues, Checklists and Certificates* [online]. URL: http://annex31.wiwi.uni-karlsruhe.de/INDEX.HTM [accessed on 15 January 2005]

IEA Annex31 (2004) *Types of Tools* [online]. URL: http://www.iisbe.org/annex31/pdf/D_types_tools.pdf [accessed on 15 December 2004]

Kampschroer, K. & Heerwagen, J.H. (2005) The strategic workplace: development and evaluation. *Building Research and Information, 33* (4), 326–337.

Katz, G. (2003) *Green Building Costs and Financial Benefits* [online]. http://www.cap-e.com/ewebeditpro/items/O59F3481.pdf [accessed on 16 May 2007]

Kats, G., Alevantis, L., Berman, A., Mills, E. & Perlman, J. (2003) *The Costs and Financial Benefits of Green Buildings – A Report to California's Sustainable Building Task Force* [online]. URL: http://www.usgbc.org/Docs/News/News477.pdf [accessed on 22 January 2004]

Kingston University (2005) *The Sustainable Property Appraisal Project, Closing Report to DTI, December 2005.* URL: http://www.spongenet.org/library/SPA%20PART%201%20closing%20report%2012%2005%20Inc%20cover%20sheet.pdf [accessed on 22 April 2006]

Kumar, S. & Fisk, W. (2002) *The Role of Emerging Energy-Efficient Technology in Promoting Workplace Productivity and Health: Final Report* [online]. URL: http://www.ihpcental.org [accessed on 9 March 2004]

Lamberton, G. (2005) Sustainability accounting – a brief history and conceptual framework. *Accounting Forum, 29,* 7–26.

Larsson, N. (2005) *The SBTool – An Overview,* Speech held at the World Sustainable Building Conference (SB05), Tokyo, Japan, 27–29 September 2005.

Leaman, A. & Bordass, B. (1999) Productivity in buildings: the 'killer' variables. *Building Research and Information, 27* (1), 4–19.

Lee, A. & Barrett, P. (2003) *Performance Based Building: First International State-of-the-Art Report* [online]. Published by: International Council for Research and

Innovation in Building and Construction (CIB). URL:http://cibworld.xs4all.nl/pebbu_dl/resources/pebbupublications/downloads/01SotaPart1.pdf [accessed on 15 December 2004]

Lorch, R. & Cole, J.R. (eds) (2006) Building environmental assessment: changing the culture of practice, Special Issue. *Building Research and Information, 34* (4).

Lorenz, D. (2006) *The Application of Sustainable Development Principles to the Theory and Practice of Property Valuation*, Dissertation, Karlsruher Schriften zur Bau-, Wohnungs- und Immobilienwirtschaft, Band 1, Universitätsverlag Karlsruhe, Karlsruhe.

Lourdel, N., Gondran, N., Laforest, V. & Brodhag, C. (2005) Introduction of sustainable development in engineers' curricula: problematic and evaluation methods. *International Journal of Sustainability in Higher Education, 6* (3), 254–264.

Lützkendorf, T. & Bachofner, M. (2002) *The consideration of ecological quality in the valuation and funding of buildings – a methodological overview*, Proceedings of the International Sustainable Building Conference, Oslo, 2002.

Lützkendorf, T. & Lorenz, D. (2005) Sustainable property investment: valuing sustainable buildings through property performance assessment. Building Research & Information, Vol. 33, No. 3, pp. 212-234

Lützkendorf, T. & Lorenz, D. (2006a) Using an integrated performance approach in building assessment tools. *Building Research and Information, 34* (4), 334–356.

Lützkendorf, T. & Lorenz, D. (2006b) *The issue of 'Sustainability' in Education and Training of Real Estate Economists*, Proceedings of the International Conference on Building Education and Research, BEAR 2006, Hong Kong, 10–13 April 2006.

Lützkendorf, T. & Lorenz, D. (2007) Integrating sustainability into property risk assessments for market transformation. *Building Research and Information* (In press).

Lützkendorf, T., Speer, T., Szigeti, F., Davis, G., le Roux, P., Kato, A. & Tsunekawa, K. (2005) *A comparison of international classifications for performance requirements and building performance categories used in evaluation methods*, Proceedings of the 11th Joint CIB International Symposium; Helsinki, Finland; June 2005.

MA (2005) *Millennium Ecosystem Assessments – Living Beyond our Means, Natural Assets and Human Well-Being, Statement from the Board* [online]. URL: http://www.millenniumassessment.org/proxy/document.429.aspx [accessed on 01 February 2006]

Mackley, C.J. (2002) *Unlocking the Value in Sustainable Buildings*, Sustainable Building 2002, Summary book of the 3rd International Conference on Sustainable Building, Pettersen, T. (ed.) EcoBuild, Oslo.

Margot, C. (2006) *Wo steht ISO 26000?* In: Umwelt-Perspektiven Nr. 6/2006, S. 16–17.

Marshall, R.S. & Harry, S.P. (2005) Introducing a new business course: "Global business and sustainability". *International Journal of Sustainability in Higher Education, 6* (2), 179–196.

Matthiessen, L. & Morris P. (2003) *Costing Green: A Comprehensive Cost Database and Budgeting Methodology* [online]. Published by: Davis Langdon Adamson. URL: http://www.davislangdon-usa.com/images/pdf_files/costinggreen.pdf [accessed on 22 June 2004]

McDonough, W. & Braungart, M. (2003) Towards a sustaining architecture for the 21st century: the promise of cradle-to-cradle design. In: UNEP (2003) Sustainable building and construction. *Industry and Environment, 26* (2–3). Published by: United Nations Environment Programme Division of Technology, Industry and Economics, Paris, pp. 13–16.

McNamara, P. (2005) *Sustainable Property Investment – Balancing the Commercial Pressures of Today with the Realities of the Future* [online]. Presentation held at the RICS Valuation conference 2005, 29 December 2005, London. URL: http://www.rics.

org/NR/rdonlyres/DAF0FD53-23F1-4A56-B05A-739A4A41E77B/0/PaulMcNamara. pdf [accessed on 01 February 2006]

Meacham, B., Bowen, R., Traw, J. & Moore, A. (2005) Performance-based building regulation: current situation and future needs. *Building Research and Information*, 33 (2), 91–106.

Mills, E. (2003a) The insurance and risk management industries: new players in the delivery of energy-efficient and renewable energy products and services. *Energy Policy*, 31, 1257–1272.

Mills, E. (2003b) Climate change, insurance and the buildings sector: technological synergisms between adaptation and mitigation. *Building Research and Information*, 31 (3–4), 257–277.

Minton, A. (2006) *What Kind of World Are we Building – The Privatisation of Public Space* [online]. Published by: The Royal Institution of Chartered Surveyors. URL: http://www.rics.org/RICSservices/RICSresearch/privatisation_public230306.html [accessed on 21 May 2006]

Munich Re (2005) *Megacities – Megarisks: Trends and Challenges for Insurance and Risk Management* [online]. Published by: Munich Re Group. URL: http://www.muenchener-rueck.de/publications/302-04271_en.pdf?rdm=61251 [accessed on 21 April 2006]

Murphy, C.J. (2002) *The Profitable Correlation – Between Environmental and Financial Performance: A Review of the Research* [online]. Published by: Light Green Advisors. URL: http://www.lightgreen.com/files/pc.pdf [accessed on 28 January 2003]

Myers, D. (2003) The future of construction economics as an academic discipline. *Construction Management and Economics*, 21, 103–106.

Nevin, R. & Watson, G. (1998) *Evidence of Rational Market Valuations for Home Energy Efficiency* [online]. The Appraisal Journal, October 1998. URL: http://www. natresnet.org/herseems/appraisal.htm [accessed on 26 June 2002]

OECD (2003) *Environmentally Sustainable Buildings – Challenges and Policies*. OECD Publications, Paris.

O'Rourke, A. (2003) The message and methods of ethical investment. *Journal of Cleaner Production*, 11, 683–693.

Parkin, S. (2000) Sustainable development: the concept and the practical challenge. *Proceedings of the Institution of Civil Engineers, Civil Engineering*, 138, 3–8.

Peuportier, B. & Putzeys, K. (2005) *Inter-Comparison and Benchmarking of LCA-Based Environmental Assessment and Design Tools – Final Report* [online]. Published by: The European Thematic Network on Practical Recommendations for Sustainable Construction (PRESCO). URL: http://www.etn-presco.net/generalinfo/PRESCO_WP2_Report.pdf [accessed on 08 August 2005]

Phillips, Hager & North (2005) *Does Socially Responsible Investing Hurt Investment Returns?* [online]. URL: http://www.phn.com/pdfs/SRI%20Articles/does_sri_hurt.pdf [accessed on 01 January 2006]

PISCES (2004) *PISCES – Property Information Systems Common Exchange Standard, Version 1.6.1* [online]. URL: http://www.pisces.co.uk/ [accessed on 30 March 2006]

Pivo, G. (2005) Is There a Future for Socially Responsible Property Investments? *Real Estate Issues*, Fall, 16–26.

Pivo, G. & McNamara, P. (2005) Responsible property investing. *International Real Estate Review*, 8 (1), 128–143.

Porritt, J. (2006) *Capitalism as if the World Matters*. Earthscan, London.

PRI (2006) *Principles for Responsible Investment* [online]. Published by: UN Environment Programme Finance Initiative in cooperation with UN Global Compact. URL: http://www.unpri.org/files/pri.pdf [accessed on 28 April 2006]

RICS (2004) *Sustainability and the Built Environment – An Agenda for Action* [online]. Published by: The Royal Institution of Chartered Surveyors. URL:http://www.rics.

org/NR/rdonlyres/DE2FC8A1-9600-46F4-9673-D13D6B686023/0/Sustainability_and_built_environment.pdf [accessed on 10 November 2004]

RICS (2005) *Green Value – Green Buildings, Growing Assets* [online]. Published by: The Royal Institution of Chartered Surveyors. URL: http://www.rics.org/NR/rdonlyres/93B20864-E89E-4641-AB11-028387737058/0/GreenValueReport.pdf [accessed on 18 November 2005]

Sayce, S., Ellison, L. & Smith, J. (2004) *Incorporating Sustainability in Commercial Property Appraisal: Evidence from the UK*. Proceedings of the 11th European Real Estate Society Conference (ERES 2004), Milan, 2004.

Schröder, M. (2003) S*ocially Responsible Investments in Germany, Switzerland and the United States – An Analysis of Investment Funds and Indices* [online]. Published by: Zentrum für Europäische Wirtschaftsforschung. URL: ftp://ftp.zew.de/pub/zew-docs/dp/dp0310.pdf [accessed on 11 November 2004]

Sirmans, C.F. & Worzala, E. (2003) International direct real estate investment: a review of the literature. *Urban Studies, 40* (5–6), 1081–1114.

Stern, N. (2006) *Stern Review on the Economics of Climate Change* [online]. URL: http://www.hm-treasury.gov.uk/independent_reviews/stern_review_economics_climate_change/sternreview_index.cfm [accessed on 24 December 2006]

SustainAbility (2004) *The Changing Landscape of Liability – A Director's Guide to Trends in Corporate Environmental, Social and Economic Liability* [online]. Published by: SustainAbility Ltd. URL: http://www.sustainability.com/compass/register.asp?type=download&articleid=23 [accessed on 21 March 2006]

Szigeti, F. & Davis, G. (2003) *Matching People and their Facilities: Using the ASTM/ANSI Standards on Whole Building Functionality and Serviceability* [online]. Published by: Performance Based Building Thematic Network. URL: http://www.pebbu.nl/resources/literature/ [accessed on 10 April 2004]

Szigeti, F., Davis, G., Dempsey, J., Hammond, D., Davis, D., Colombard-Prout, M. & Catarina, O. (2004) *Defining Performance Requirements to Assess the Suitability of Constructed Assets in Support of the Mission of the Organization*, Proceedings of the CIB World Congress 2004, Toronto, Canada.

TEGoVA (2003) *European Property and Market Rating* [online]. Published by: The European Group of Valuers Associations. URL: http://www.tegova.org/reports/EPMR.pdf [accessed on 10 January 2004]

Todd, J.A., Crawley U., Geissler, S. & Lindsey, G. (2001) Comparative assessment of environmental performance tools and the role of the Green Building Challenge. *Building Research and Information, 29* (5), 324–335.

UNEP (2003) Sustainable building and construction. *Industry and Environment, 26* (23), Published by: United Nations Environment Programme Division of Technology, Industry and Economics, Paris.

UNEP (2006) *Sustainable Building & Construction Initiative – Information Note* [online], Published by: United Nations Environment Programme Division of Technology, Industry and Economics. URL: http://www.unep.fr/pc/pc/SBCI/SBCI_2006_InformationNote.pdf [accessed on 24 March 2006]

US SIF (2006) *Report on Socially Responsible Investing Trends in the United States – 10 Year Review* [online]. Published by: US Social Investment Forum. URL: http://www.socialinvest.org/areas/research/trends/SRI_Trends_Report_2005.pdf [accessed on 28 February 2006]

US Department of Energy (2006) *High Performance Buildings – Design Approach* [online]. Published by: US Department of Energy. URL: http://www.eere.energy.gov/buildings/highperformance/design_approach.html [accessed on 28 December 2006]

VÖB (2005) *VÖB-Immobilienanalyse - Instrument zur Beurteilung des Chance-Risikoprofils von Immobilien* [online]. Published by: Bundesverband Öffentlicher Banken Deutschlands (VÖB). URL: http://www.voeb.de/content_frame/downloads/them_fach_immo.pdf [accessed on 12 November 2005]

WCED (1987) *Our Common Future.* Published by: World Commission on Environment and Development, Oxford University Press, New York.

Wilson, A., Uncapher, J., McManigal, L., Hunter Lovins, L., Cureton, M. & Browning, W.D. (1998) *Green Development: Integrating Ecology and Real Estate.* John Wiley & Sons, New York.

Worzala, E. & Sirmans, C.F. (2003) Investing in international real estate stocks: a review of the literature. *Urban Studies, 40* (5–6) 1115–1149.

Yates, A. (2001) *Quantifying the Business Benefits of Sustainable Buildings* [online]. Published by: The Building Research Establishment. URL: http://www.bre.co.uk [accessed on 22 November 2001]

Further reading

Lorch, R. & Meikle, J. (eds) (2006) Sustainable development: understanding the social and economic value of construction, Special Issue. *Building Research and Information, 34* (3) May–June 2006.

Useful resources

Social Investment Forum	http://www.socialinvest.org
European Social Investment Forum	http://www.eurosif.org/
Global Reporting Initiative	http://www.globalreporting.org
IEA Annex 31	http://www.greenbuilding.ca/annex31/index.html
Equator Principles	http://www.equator-principles.com
Principles for Responsible Investment	http://www.unpri.org
International Finance Corporation	http://www.ifc.org/sustainability
UNEP Finance Initiative	http://www.unepfi.org
UNEP Property Working Group	http://www.unepfi.org/work_streams/index.html
UNEP SBCI[15]	http://www.unepsbci.org
iiSBE[16]	http://www.iisbe.org
RICS	http://www.rics.org/Builtenvironment/Sustainableconstruction/
OGC	http://www.ogc.gov.uk/ppm_documents_construction.asp
Performance based building thematic network	http://www.pebbu.nl/
Energy Building Performance Directive	http://www.diag.org.uk/
Energy Building Performance Directive	http://www.buildingsplatform.org/cms/
Sustainable Buildings Industry Council	http://www.sbicouncil.org/about.htm

High Performance Buildings	http://www.eere.energy. gov/buildings/highperformance/
Energy Performance of Buildings Directive Implementation Advisory Group	www.diag.org.uk
International Institute for Sustainable Development	www.iisd.org
World Green Building Council	http://www.worldgbc.org/
Sustainable Property Appraisal Project	www.sustainableproperty.ac.uk
Green Building Finance Consortium	www.greenbuildingfc.com
World Business Council for Sustainable Development	http://www.wbcsd.ch

12

Corporate Governance in the Real Estate Industry

Nicolas Kohl, Wolfgang Schäfers
and Karl-Werner Schulte

Introduction

In a changing corporate finance environment, characterized by globalizing debt and equity capital markets, deeper market integration as well as stronger competition for international capital, it has become crucial for companies to diligently respond to the needs of investors. In recent years, shareholders, particularly institutional investors, increasingly demand higher transparency and more effective control mechanisms for corporate action.

In this context, the term 'corporate governance' has attracted major attention in the professional sphere and across different areas of academic research, such as law and economics. Even though a generally accepted definition does not exist, numerous varying definitions of the term can be found in the literature. A representative selection is provided below:

> 'Corporate governance is the system by which companies are directed and controlled'. (Cadbury, 1992, p. 15)

> 'Corporate governance ... involves a set of relationships between a company's management, its board, its shareholders and other stakeholders. Corporate governance also provides the structure through which the objectives of the company are set, and the means of attaining those objectives and monitoring performance are determined. Good corporate governance should provide proper incentives for the board and management to pursue objectives that are in the interests of the company and

shareholders and should facilitate effective monitoring, thereby encouraging firms to use resources more efficiently'. (OECD, 1999, p. 11)

'Corporate governance deals with the ways in which suppliers of finance to corporations assure themselves of getting a return on their investment'. (Shleifer/Vishny, 1997, p. 737)

'Corporate governance particularly concerns the functionality of management bodies, their cooperation and the control of their conduct'. (Baums, 2001, p. 20)

'Corporate Governance refers to the entire system by which a company is managed and monitored, its corporate principles and guidelines and the system of internal and external controls and supervision to which its operations are subjected. Good, transparent Corporate Governance ensures that our company is managed and monitored in a responsible manner geared to value creation. This is a prerequisite for maintaining the confidence of investors, customers and business associates and for ensuring that the market puts an appropriate value on the company's shares'. (IVG, 2006, p. 14)

The need for a well-functioning corporate governance system stems from the separation of corporate ownership and corporate control and the related conflicts of interest between shareholders and managers of a firm, which are subject to the agency theory (Figure 12.1).

Managers are supposed to run the company on behalf of the shareholders with the objective to maximize shareholder value on a long-term basis[1]. However, they do not always act in the best interest of their

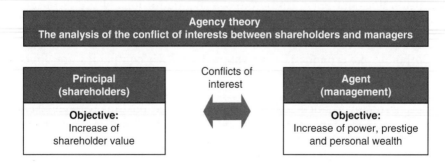

Figure 12.1 Illustration of the conflicts of interest between shareholders and management. *Source*: Own illustration following Jensen (1986), p. 323; Jensen & Meckling (1976), p. 308, 309; Shleifer & Vishny (1997), p. 742, 743.

shareholders[2] and hence destroy corporate value. In order to mitigate shareholder– manager conflicts, appropriate governance mechanisms have to be implemented. Thus, the primary objective of effective corporate governance is to solve agency problems associated with the separation of ownership and control.

Following corporate governance reforms in the USA, numerous countries worldwide have introduced the so-called corporate governance codes since the early 1990s, supplementing the respective legal framework. Corporate governance codes are legally non-binding best practice guidelines intending to establish 'good' corporate governance and to foster transparency in international capital markets.

In addition to other sectors, the real estate industry has become aware of the significance of corporate governance issues. As a consequence, national and supranational corporate governance codes that take into account the particularities of real estate companies have been developed.

Reasons for the rising importance of corporate governance

Within the last two decades, there have been three major capital market trends that have significantly contributed to an increasing relevance of corporate governance issues worldwide.

Firstly, there is the trend toward institutionalization of shareholdings[3] which refers to the process of accumulation and managing of capital by professional investors, such as insurance companies, mutual and pension funds. Institutional investors have become significant players in global equity markets. Between 1990 and 2001, financial assets controlled by this category of investors have increased by approximately 193% in the USA, by 146% in the UK and by 213% in Continental Europe (Figure 12.2).

Some of this growth can be attributed to reforms of national pension systems (e.g. in Germany and Italy) which require individuals to increasingly deal with growing capital resources for retirement rather than relying on the state. Institutional investors professionally manage the capital assets of private individuals on the principle of diversification using the most modern techniques in pursuing their investment strategies. In this context, good firm-specific corporate governance has become a critical screening criterion for institutional investors when evaluating investment opportunities. According to the 'Global Investor Opinion Survey' conducted by McKinsey & Company in 2002, corporate governance is considered equally or more important than financial figures in North America as well as in Western Europe by approximately 55% of all institutional investors being addressed (Figure 12.3). In addition, roughly 75% of

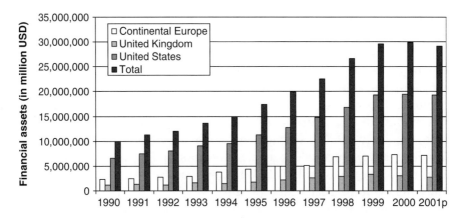

Figure 12.2 International development of financial assets held by institutional investors between 1990 and 2001. *Source*: OECD (2003).

the respondents claimed that they were willing to pay an average premium of 20% for well-governed companies (see Figures 12.4 and 12.5).

As asset gatherers, institutional investors have large capital resources at hand and consequently are very influential in capital markets. They are able to exert great pressure especially on publicly traded (real estate) companies either directly by exercising control rights or indirectly by selling shares of companies that do not comply with internationally recognized corporate governance standards.

Secondly, the integration of international capital markets and the competition for international funds can be considered as another reason for an increasing awareness of corporate governance[4]. Based on the idea of diversification benefits, institutional investors increasingly tend to allocate a certain percentage of their funds to international equities instead of holding a purely domestic portfolio. At the same time, certain companies desire to attract foreign capital. Fast-growing companies in Europe, for instance, have been increasingly raising capital by cross-listing on foreign exchanges[5], since national capital markets were too small to cost-efficiently provide enough capital to finance their growth. However, the decision to broaden the investor base on an international scale requires the respective companies to commit to international investment values and standards, predominantly set by institutional investors from the USA and the UK. This includes Anglo-Saxon corporate governance standards, which are generally regarded as a role model. The financial strength and dominant presence of US and UK institutional investors in international capital markets have contributed to a spread of shareholder value orientation and equity culture outside the Anglo-Saxon countries and have fostered a process of cross-national convergence of corporate governance principles.

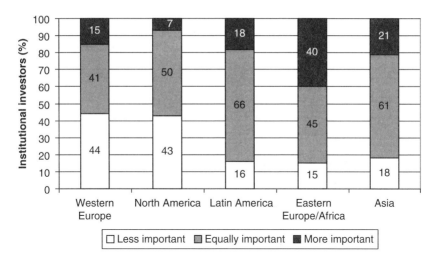

Figure 12.3 Significance of corporate governance relative to financial figures for the decision-making process of institutional investors by region. *Source*: McKinsey & Company (2002).

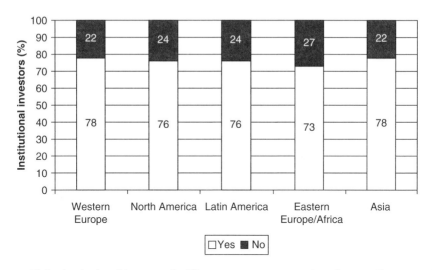

Figure 12.4 Institutional investors' willingness to pay a premium for a well-governed company by region. *Source*: McKinsey & Company (2002).

Thirdly, numerous examples of financial and accounting scandals of the recent past (e.g. Enron, Worldcom, Tyco, Parmalat) caused by malpractice of corporate management[6] intensified the discussion on corporate governance issues. In many of these cases, management manipulated financial statements to overstate earnings. By the time these practices of financial fraud were revealed, the equity value of the respective companies declined dramatically. Some companies were even forced into bankruptcy[7]. As

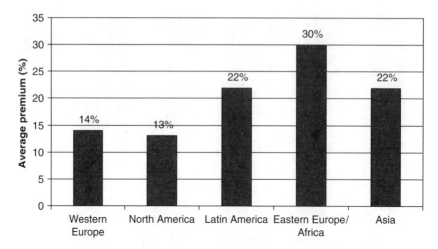

Figure 12.5 Size of the premium institutional investors who are willing to pay by region. *Source*: McKinsey & Company (2002).

a consequence, investors increasingly demanded higher transparency and better control mechanisms in order to protect their invested funds.

In response to the widespread failure in financial reporting, four fundamental changes could be observed. First, audit firms started to divest or to spin off their consulting business in order to avoid potential conflicts of interest. Second, Arthur Andersen, one of the 'Big Five' audit firms, went out of business due to financial fraud accusations. Third, the Sarbanes-Oxley Bill, imposing a number of corporate governance rules on all publicly traded companies in the USA, was signed into US law in 2002. Finally, in 2003, the New York Stock Exchange (NYSE) and NASDAQ introduced an additional set of corporate governance rules, applicable to most publicly traded companies in the USA[8]. These US corporate governance reforms have accelerated corporate governance activity around the world[9].

The developments described above indicate that it has become crucial for (real estate) companies to adapt to internationally recognized corporate governance standards in order to be able to compete with peers for international capital on a long-term basis[10].

Existing corporate governance principles for the real estate industry

For corporate governance to happen, one needs to have infrastructure in terms of industry associations. This is an important requirement and should be discussed. If one did not have these industry associations, then corporate governance would not even get to first base.

Considering the importance of corporate governance, the following sections amine the extend to which highly reputed international real estate organizations, such as the Royal Institution of Chartered Surveyors (RICS), the European Public Real Estate Association (EPRA), the National Association of Real Estate Investment Trusts (NAREIT) and the European Association for Investors in Non-listed Real Estate Vehicles (INREV), have dealt with corporate governance issues. Therefore, it is of particular interest whether or not the respective institutions have defined or published corporate governance principles and guidelines.

Furthermore, the activities of the Initiative Corporate Governance for the German Real Estate Industry are presented in order to provide an example for a national real estate–related corporate governance code.

Corporate governance and RICS

'The Royal Institution of Chartered Surveyors is one of the most respected and high profile global "standards and membership" organizations for professionals involved in land, property, construction and environmental issues with:

- 136 years of representing property professionalism;
- 120 000 full and trainee members across 120 countries worldwide;
- 400 degree level courses approved worldwide;
- 50 national associations, linked groups and societies;
- 160 diverse "specialisms" represented across 17 "faculties"'[11].

'The RICS is committed to being the publicly recognized authority on all aspects of surveying and the ownership occupation, development and management of property in the UK and to expand its recognition worldwide'[12].

The foundation of RICS Europe in 1993 and of numerous national societies, for example in Germany, France and the Netherlands, has led to a transfer of standards to most countries in Continental Europe.

Accountable to both members and the public, RICS has three main roles:

1 to maintain the highest standards of education and training;
2 to protect consumers through strict regulation of professional standards;
3 to be the leading source of information and independent advice on land, property, construction and associated environmental issues.

Though RICS has not developed a corporate governance standard, it frequently addresses corporate governance issues indirectly by publishing articles in newspapers and journals. However, the Governing Council is currently discussing the creation of governance standards and the issue of ensuring good corporate governance within the institution.

Corporate governance and EPRA

The European Public Real Estate Association is a common interest group, established as a not-for-profit body under Dutch law in October 1999. EPRA's members include the majority of the leading (listed) real estate companies and investment institutions in Europe. The active participation of the members' senior executives ensures EPRA is a genuinely representative forum and policy-making body. The quality of membership is crucial to fulfilling the Association's mission.

The mission statement of EPRA is to promote, develop and represent the European public real estate sector. EPRA's strategy states that 'EPRA will endeavor to establish standards of best practice in accounting, reporting and corporate governance; to provide high-quality information to investors; and to create the framework for debate and decision-making on the issues which determine the future of the sector'[13].

In January 2006, EPRA Best Practices Committee published a set of revised best practice policy recommendations. Its main objective is to make financial statements of public real estate companies in Europe more transparent and comparable across countries. Its recommendations fulfil information requirements of investors and analysts and contribute to increasing the transparency and comparability of listed property companies in Europe.

Corporate governance and NAREIT

The National Association of Real Estate Investment Trusts is the representative voice for US REITs and publicly traded real estate companies worldwide. Members are mainly US Real Estate Investment Trusts (REITs) and other businesses that own, operate and finance income-producing real estate, as well as those firms and individuals who advise and study these businesses[14].

Acting on behalf of over 2000 REITs, real estate companies, investors, industry professionals and academics, NAREIT represents its members' interests in the investment marketplace, in the political arena and in the financial media. Despite all this, there were scandals – for example, Simon Property Group REIT that went down on accounting issues and is now subject to a Mills Corporation bid.

In 2005, NAREIT sponsored a 'Benchmark Survey', conducted by FPL Associates, which covered corporate governance as well as other topics, such as tenant and investor relations. Nevertheless, it has to be pointed out that NAREIT has not yet developed its own corporate governance standards, best practice recommendations or rules of conduct, although NAREIT is representing an industry with a market capitalization of currently more than $ billion[15].

Corporate governance and INREV

The European Association for Investors in Non-listed Real Estate Vehicles is a non-profit association that was founded in September 2002. It aims to improve market liquidity and accessibility of market information and is committed to serving the needs of investors of the non-listed real estate vehicle market. INREV's board of management and its strategy are predominantly influenced by its institutional investor members.

Its overall mission has been defined as follows:

- to increase transparency and accessibility;
- to promote professionalism and best practices;
- to share and spread knowledge.

INREV aims to achieve these goals largely by a number of working committees, currently nine, each with a clearly defined purpose. INREV also intends to create a broad European forum, with a wide membership representing all aspects of the industry[16].

Consultations and surveys carried out among INREV members have indicated that both institutional investors and managers have a keen interest in establishing standards of corporate governance for European non-listed real estate funds. These consultations and surveys revealed that corporate governance has become an important factor in the fund selection process.

In January 2007, INREV has announced the publication of the 'INREV Corporate Governance Principles and Guidelines' paper. The hope is expressed in the foreword 'that this document will serve as a useful basis on which to build and develop standards for good Corporate Governance in the non-listed real estate fund sector over the years ahead. It is the intention of the Corporate Governance Committee that these principles and guidelines are reviewed at regular intervals having regard to market practice, and that a revised document be published when considered appropriate'[17].

Initiative Corporate Governance for the German Real Estate Industry

The 'Initiative Corporate Governance der deutschen Immobilienwirtschaft e.V.' was formed in Autumn 2002. Leading companies in the real estate sector have joined the Initiative as corporate members, whilst many well-known representatives of the sector are also individual members.

The initiative intends to discuss and establish principles of transparent and professional corporate management in the real estate industry.

The Initiative has achieved positive interim results since it was formed more than 2 years ago. Firstly, it has produced and passed the 'Principles of Proper and Fair Management in the Real Estate Industry'[18]. These guidelines place an obligation on members of the sector to give particular consideration to values such as professionalism and transparency. They advise on the avoidance of conflicts of interest and their disclosure. They also place the businesses under an obligation to pay attention to professional skill and independence in selecting auditors and members of corporate bodies.

Secondly, the corporate governance code for real estate companies was passed in 2003 at the members' meeting[19]. The code supplements the more eneral German Corporate Governance Code with precise regulations about issues concerning conflicts of interest, valuation of real estate and greater professionalism for management boards and supervisory boards. This code also serves as a benchmark for closed funds and trust enterprises.

In 2004–05, the initiative focused its work on value management. A top-level working group developed principles and concentrated on the establishment and implementation of a value management system. The initiative anticipates and hopes that these steps will lead to an improvement in sector transparency and will help to restore the confidence of investors and the reputation of the sector which has suffered from recent investigations and accusations.

The interim results of the above initiative are respectable. However, a further development of the established governance standards, and the implementation of these principles on a day-to-day basis, must be seen as an ever-continuing process. The initiative will remain committed to the achievement of good corporate governance in the future for German real estate companies. This should improve the reputation of the German real estate sector on a national and international scale.

European code of business ethics

In October 2006, representatives of the real estate industry came together to form a working group titled 'European Corporate Governance Code'. They decided to establish a round table together with the main European associations, such as EPRA, INREV, EPF, AREF and ULI Europe, in order to align their interests and requirements on corporate governance issues, create a road map and design a European umbrella code for the real estate industry. These efforts will result in more standardized corporate governance guidelines within Europe and will ultimately help to improve transparency in the European real estate industry.

Impact of corporate governance on firm value

From a theoretical and professional perspective, the most important corporate governance issue is whether the capital markets reward it.

To understand the theoretical relationship between corporate governance and firm value, it is necessary to first investigate the fundamentals of corporate valuation. The firm value is determined by discounting future free cash flows with an appropriate opportunity cost of capital reflecting the risks associated with the company being valued. There are many risks, for example, agency costs which are defined as the sum of monitoring expenditures; costs related to the provision of management incentives and losses resulting from value-diminishing investments by corporate management in negative net present value projects[20]. In other words, the higher the agency costs of a particular firm, the higher the inherent risk and the lower the value of that firm. From a theoretical point of view, 'good' corporate governance is expected to reduce agency costs and therefore to have a positive effect on corporate value[21]. It seems quite reasonable that investors are willing to pay a premium for companies with better corporate governance structures in expectation to receive higher dividends in the future[22].

The effect of corporate governance on firm performance has been the subject of a number of empirical studies in academic literature. Most of these studies rely on Tobin's Q as an indicator for firm performance. Tobin's Q represents the relation between market value and replacement costs and serves as a popular valuation measure in financial literature. The underlying concept goes back to Brainard/Tobin (1968) (Figure 12.6).

The studies are characterized by a lack of standardization; they differ in terms of country focus, choice of corporate governance mechanisms, data sources and choice of the statistical model being applied. Three different approaches can be identified for the retrieval of corporate governance data for empirical purposes: self-constructed survey-based corporate governance indices, corporate governance indices and ratings offered by organizations, such as professional corporate governance consultants (e.g. Institutional Shareholder Services, Governance Metrics International) or rating agencies, as well as corporate publications and disclosures.

The majority of the empirical studies examining the relationship between corporate governance and firm performance focuses on single governance mechanisms in isolation, for example, legal norms[23], insider shareholdings[24], institutional shareholdings and blockholdings[25], takeover provisions[26] as well as board size[27] and board structure[28]. Since corporate governance is a highly complex system that is composed of multiple control mechanisms, the above-listed studies are likely to suffer from 'missing' or 'omitted variable bias'. Another strain of empirical work

Authors	Year	Sample	Empirical model	Details
Agrawal *et al.* (USA)	1996	$n = 400$ (USA)	Empirical study using multivariate regression (2SLS)	• Selection of 7 control mechanisms • Positive relationship between control mechanisms and valuation (Abhängigkeit der Mechanismen untereinander)
Black (USA)	2001	$n = 21$ (Rußland)	Empirical study using univariate regression (OLS)	• Application of CG-ranking provided by a Russian investmentbank • Strong positive relationship between CG and valuation of publicly traded companies in Russia
Black *et al.* (USA)	2003	$n = 515$ (Korea)	Empirical study using multivariate regression (3SLS)	• Construction of a broad CG-index (survey-based) • Strong positive relationship between CG and valuation of publicly traded companies in Korea
Gompers *et al.* (USA)	2003	$n = 1.500$ (USA)	Empirical study using multivariate regression (OLS)	• Construction of a CG-index considering 24 governance-rules as proxies for shareholder rights (focus on the defense of hostile takeovers) • Companies with strong shareholder rights feature higher market values
Bauer *et al.* (Netherlands)	2004	$n = 249$ (Europe)	Empirical study using multivariate regression (OLS)	• Application of CG-ranking provided by Deminor • Positive relationship between CG and valuation of companies that are listed in the FTSE Eurotop 300
Drobetz *et al.* (Switzerland)	2004	$n = 91$ (Germany)	Empirical study using multivariate regression (OLS)	• Construction of a broad CG-index following the German Corporate Governance Code (survey-based) • Positive relationship between CG and valuation of publicly traded companies in Germany
Beiner *et al.* (Switzerland)	2006	$n = 235$ (Switzerland)	Empirical study using multivariate regression (3SLS)	• Construction of a broad CG-index (survey-based) • Positive relationship between CG and valuation of publicly traded companies in Switzerland

Figure 12.6   A selection of corporate governance studies in financial literature. *Source*: Author research.

addresses this problem by examining the influence of a wide set of corporate governance mechanisms on the market valuation of exchange-traded companies[29]. Using samples from different countries, like the USA, Korea, Germany and Switzerland, to name just a few, most studies find a positive relationship between control mechanisms and market valuation. Nevertheless, only some of them provide evidence for causality instead of merely an indication.

Comparable studies can be found in real estate literature as opposed to the general finance literature (Figure 12.7).

Some of these studies examine performance effects of single-governance mechanisms, for example, insider shareholdings[30], executive compensation[31], institutional shareholdings[32], external versus internal management[33], board structure[34] and the market for corporate control[35]. Other studies examine the impact of multiple corporate governance mechanisms on the market value of exchange-traded real estate companies[36]. Studies belonging to the latter category are rare and provide inconsistent empirical results. While Hartzell *et al.* (2004) do not find a significant relationship between corporate governance and the valuation of US-Equity REITs using governance data from proxy statements, Bauer *et al.* (2006) do find positive effect of corporate governance on the value of US-REITs using governance data from ISS and GMI. In this context, it has to be pointed out that REITs possess a unique governance setting and therefore provide a special case in the analysis of the impact of corporate governance on firm value. Due to their legal structure, REITs are subject to tighter restrictions on business operations, payout policy and ownership structure. Consequently, there is less need for traditional corporate governance mechanisms[37].

Research agenda for corporate governance in the real estate industry

The discussion on agency conflicts resulting from the separation of ownership and control as well as on governance mechanisms to reduce related agency costs have been subject to scientific literature for a long time. Since Berle/Means (1932), which addressed potential conflicts of interest between management and shareholders of companies, the understanding of corporate governance has improved decisively.

While general finance literature includes numerous research studies on the impact of corporate governance on firm performance across different capital markets around the world, the topic has been often neglected in real estate literature.

With regard to the increasing importance of corporate governance worldwide, comparable research should be initiated for publicly traded

Authors	Year	Sample	Empirical model	Details
Davis and Shelor (USA)	1995	$n = 130$ (USA)	Empirical study using multivariate regression (OLS)	▪ Using data from annual reports ▪ Positive relationship between management compensation and performance (e.g. EPS, total assets/total equity) of real estate companies
Friday and Sirmans (USA)	1998	$n = 135$ (USA)	Empirical study using multivariate regression (OLS)	▪ Higher percentage of external board members (up to 50%) and greater equity-participation by management leads to higher shareholder value (market-to-book ratio) for a sample of US-REITs
Hartzell *et al.* (USA)	2004	$n = 66$ (USA)	Empirical study using multivariate regression (OLS)	▪ Using governance data from proxy-statements ▪ No significant relationship between corporate governance and valuation of US-Equity REITs
Campbell *et al.* (USA)	2005	$n = 53$ (USA)	Event-study	▪ Issuance of convertible securities by UPREITs for the purpose of purchasing real estate from private sellers serves as governance mechanism
Bauer *et al.* (Netherlands)	2006	$n = 134 – 228$ (USA)	Empirical study using multivariate regression (OLS)	▪ Application of governance data provided by Institutional Shareholder Services (ISS) and Governance metrics international (GMI) ▪ Positive relationship between corprate governance and valuation of US-REITs
Eichholtz *et al.* (Netherlands)	2006	$n = 95$ (Global)	Uni- and multivariate regression (OLS) and event-study	▪ Market for external control (hostile takeovers) only has a minor impact on the control of REIT-CEOs ▪ Transparency of the REIT-structure as an explanation for the minor significance of the market for external control as a governance mechanism
Han (USA)	2006	$n = 156$ (USA)	Empirical study using multivariate regression (OLS)	▪ Significant positive relationship between valuation of US-equity REITs and insider ownership ▪ Insider ownership plays an important role in reducing agency problems

☐ Focus on multiple CG-mechanisms
☐ Focus on single CG-mechanisms

Figure 12.7   A selection of corporate governance studies in real estate literature. *Source:* Author research.

real estate companies in countries other than the USA to provide further insight on the impact of corporate governance on the market valuation of respective real estate companies around the world.

In this context, the following research questions might be of particular interest.

- Is there a relationship between firm-specific corporate governance and the market valuation of exchange-traded real estate companies?
- Does 'good' corporate governance imply a higher valuation by the capital market?
- If there is a causal relationship, is it economically relevant for decision makers of respective companies or for investors?
- Is a greater use of particular corporate governance mechanisms positively related to the valuation of exchange-traded real estate companies by the capital market?
- Do country-specific differences exist with respect to the corporate governance quality of publicly traded real estate companies?
- Which consequences can be derived for a corporate governance-guided management strategy in the real estate sector as well as for the investment strategy of real estate investors?

Future real estate research is required to discover answers to these questions. An extensive research project addressing exactly the above-stated issues is currently conducted by the IREBS Institute at the University of Regensburg. The specific subject of this research project is to theoretically and empirically investigate the impact of corporate governance on the valuation of publicly traded real estate companies across major real estate capital markets worldwide, such as the USA, Australia, UK, France and Germany.

Appendices

Appendix 1

Principles of Proper and Fair Management in the Real Estate Economy (Version September 2005)

1 **Professionalism, Transparency and Fairness** in relation to shareholders/ trustees ('investors'), business partners, tenants, staff and the public are the indispensable basis of entrepreneurial activity in the real estate sector, which constitutes an important part of the national economy. Compliance with these principles strengthens confidence in the real estate economy. For this reason, companies – in particular the providers of services – which do not operate real estate business

in the narrower sense also feel bound by these principles; a significant part of the following provisions, therefore, is not applicable to them on a word-for-word basis.

2 Enterprises that work in or for the real estate economy operate their business **in the interests of the investors and/or principals** and are dedicated to the aim of increasing the value of the enterprise/real estate assets.

3 The **management** has the necessary suitability and sufficient experience. It ensures the continuing further education of managers, junior managers and specialists.

4 Expert **supervisory and consultation bodies** improve the decision-making quality in real estate transactions. These bodies are appointed accordingly, and are provided with anticipatory, clear and comprehensive information by the management.

5 An appropriate **valuation of the real estate assets** is undertaken in accordance with recognized valuation methods by qualified, independent experts on the basis of up to date and objective market information. The valuation method and its alteration, and the market values of the real estate portfolios, are explained in a suitable way.

6 Real estate business usually involves a high capital commitment and long-term planning. For this reason, the establishment and continuing further development of an **internal monitoring system and risk management** is indispensable.

7 **Conflicts of interest** between staff, members of the management, supervisory and consultation bodies on the one hand and the real estate enterprise on the other hand, or between the enterprise and the investors, must be avoided or disclosed through suitable regulations.

8 The **audit of the annual accounts** is important for the protection of investors and the establishment of confidence. The criteria of independence and qualification will be strongly emphasized in the selection of the auditors.
   a. The **business model** of the real estate enterprise, the **organizational structure** and the **participation situation** must be clearly shown, and any alterations explained.

9 The **information policy** is characterized by the principles of credibility and equal treatment. Real estate enterprises provide information to institutional and private investors, German and foreign, and other market participants in an objective, clear, comprehensive form and language appropriate to the addressee, as well as in suitable media.

Appendix 2

Corporate Governance in the German Real Estate Economy: Amendments to the German Corporate Governance Code (Version September 2003)

1.i

Preamble for the Real Estate Economy

The German Corporate Governance Code is hereby appropriately supplemented for public limited companies operating real estate business, that are currently listed, or intended for future listing, on the stock exchange ('real estate enterprises'). The supplements also apply to other public limited companies of any sector that

   *hold a significant amount of real estate themselves or through affiliated enterprises, or conclude and implement real estate transactions either directly or through participations ('real estate transactions')

   *or provide services for such transactions (generally 'real estate enterprises').

Application by analogy is also recommended for other forms of enterprise in the real estate business, as far as possible.

The supplements to the principles of corporate management and supervision that are important for enterprises in the real estate business are marked with an 'i' and emphasized in bold type.

The Initiative Corporate Governance der deutschen Immobilienwirtschaft has stressed the necessary supplements at particular points in a clearly emphasized, exemplary fashion, in keeping with the outstanding importance of the real estate sector in the German economy.

3.1.i

The executive board and the supervisory board in the principal companies in groups of companies must carefully monitor the management of the transactions of dependent companies, in particular with regard to real estate activities.

3.3.i

As far as real estate enterprises are concerned, this in particular applies to

   *fundamental alterations of valuation methods

   *the purchase and sale of real estate and project development of the enterprise's own sites above a threshold to be fixed depending on the size of the enterprise.

3.9.i

Real estate transactions between the enterprise and members of the executive board or the supervisory board should be avoided. To the extent to which they are nevertheless concluded, they must be subject to the consent of the supervisory board.

4.2.i

Members of the executive board of companies that operate in the real estate business must have relevant training or sufficient experience. In executive boards of companies whose group companies operate in the real estate business to an extent that can have a considerable influence on the assets situation, the financial situation and the income situation of the controlling enterprise, at least one member of the executive board should have special knowledge or sufficient experience in the real estate business.

4.3.6.i

In case of real estate transactions by the enterprise, even the appearanceof a conflict of interest should be avoided. In every such transaction, the interests of the enterprise alone must be safeguarded. Members of the executive board may under no circumstances derive personal advantages from transactions of the enterprise.

Privately conducted real estate transactions and private commissions regarding such transactions by members of the executive board should be disclosed to the chairman of the supervisory board.

The members of the executive board should ensure compliance with the principles for the avoidance of conflicts of interest, in particular in case of

   *transactions between associated enterprises
   *the purchase and sale of real estate
   *the award of commissions in the real estate sphere.
The supervisory board should establish rules of procedure for individual cases.

5.1.1.i

In case of real estate transactions of considerable importance, the supervisory board should

   *ensure that its members are informed sufficiently well and in good time
   *appropriately regulate the frequency and time budget for meetings in accordance with the transaction volume and the business requirements
   *assist the members in fulfilling their supervisory function more easily.

Banking institutions can establish special rules for rescue bids that may diverge from this.

5.3.2.i

In real estate enterprises, the supervisory board or the audit committee should deal with the valuation of the existing real estate assets. This task can also be transferred to a separate valuation committee.

5.4.1.i
In supervisory boards of companies whose group companies operate in the real estate business to an extent that can have a considerable influence on the assets situation, the financial situation and the income situation of the controlling enterprise, at least one member of the supervisory board should have special knowledge or sufficient experience in the real estate business.
In supervisory boards of real estate companies, a sufficient number of supervisory board members should have such special knowledge or experience.

5.5.1.i
Fig. 4.3.6.i applies by analogy to the members of the supervisory board.

6.1.i
Real estate companies should also publicize real estate transactions without delay if their respective total volume exceeds 5% of the balance sheet value of the sites and buildings that are shown as fixed assets, floating assets and participation assets. This does not apply to rescue bids by banking institutions.

7.1.1.i
Legally recognized valuation methods must be used for the valuation of real estate. These valuation methods, and changes to them, must be explained in the annex to the annual accounts, together with the reasons for them. The business report or the annex should also state the market value (excluding real estate investment assets used by the company itself) and the valuation methods used for its determination, together with any changes made to them. If no market value is stated in relation to the individual real estate asset, the greatest possible transparency should be achieved by stating generally applicable (e.g. DIX) regional and/or use-specific clusters that were assessed on the basis of the individual market values.

7.2.2.i
Contracts with auditors concerning additional consultancy services for real estate companies should be submitted to the supervisory board for consent if the cumulative fees due for these services exceed 50% of the remuneration for the annual audit. Section 114 of the Stock Corporation Act applies by analogy to this extent.

Notes

1. See Jensen (2001), p. 299.
2. See Berle & Means (1932), p. 6f; Jensen & Meckling (1976), p. 308.

3. See Smith (1996), p. 227; Nestor & Thompson (2001), p. 20; Gillan & Starks (2003), p. 3; Becht *et al.* (2002), pp. 11–12; Drobetz *et al.* (2004), p. 268.
4. See Nestor & Thompson (2001), pp. 19–20; Becht *et al.* (2002), pp. 12–13.
5. See Pagano *et al.* (2002), p. 2652.
6. See Becht *et al.* (2002), p. 14.
7. See Agrawal & Chadha (2005), p. 371f.
8. See Agrawal & Chadha (2005), p. 372.
9. See McKinsey & Company (2004), p. 9.
10. See Nestor & Thompson (2001), p. 2; Doidge *et al.* (2004), p. 2; Drobetz *et al.* (2004), p. 268.
11. See www.rics.org, About RICS.
12. RICS Professional Conduct: Rules of Conduct and Disciplinary Procedures, London 2006.
13. www.epra.com, About EPRA.
14. www.nareit.com, About NAREIT.
15. Composite REIT industry market capitalization as of year end 2006, see NAREIT (2007).
16. www.inrev.org, About INREV.
17. See Corporate Governance Principles and Guidelines, INREV 2006, p.3.
18. Appendix 1: Principles of Proper and Fair Management in the Real Estate Economy; see Initiative Corporate Governance der deutschen Immobilienwirtschaft (2005).
19. See Appendix 2: Corporate Governance in the German Real Estate Economy: Amendments to the German Corporate Governance Code, see Initiative Corporate Governance der deutschen Immobilienwirtschaft (2003).
20. See Jensen & Meckling (1976), p. 308.
21. See Lombardo & Pagano (2002), p. 1.
22. See LaPorta *et al.* (2002), p. 1147.
23. See LaPorta *et al.* (2000).
24. See Morck *et al.* (1988); McConnell & Servaes (1990); Loderer & Martin (1997); Cho (1998).
25. See Demsetz & Lehn (1985); Smith (1996).
26. See Gompers *et al.* (2003).
27. See Yermack (1996); Eisenberg *et al.* (1998).
28. See Weisbach (1988); Rosenstein & Wyatt (1990); Hermalin & Weisbach (1991); Rosenstein & Wyatt (1997); Bhagat & Black (2002).
29. See Agrawal & Knoeber (1996); Bauer *et al.* (2004); Drobetz *et al.* (2004); Durnev & Kim (2005); Klapper & Love (2004); Beiner *et al.* (2006); Black *et al.* (2006).
30. See Friday & Sirmans (1998); Friday *et al.* (1999); Han (2006).
31. See Davis & Shelor (1995).
32. See Gosh & Sirmans (2003).
33. See Ambrose & Linneman (2001).
34. See Friday & Sirmans (1998); Gosh & Sirmans (2003).
35. See Campbell *et al.* (2005); Eichholtz & Kok (2006).
36. See Hartzell *et al.* (2004); Bauer *et al.* (2006).
37. See Bauer *et al.* (2006), p. 16.

References

Agrawal, A. & Chadha, S. (2005) Corporate governance and accounting scandals. *Journal of Law and Economics*, *48*, 371–406.

Agrawal, A. & Knoeber, C.R. (1996) Firm performance and mechanisms to control agency problems between managers and shareholders. *Journal of Financial and Quantitative Analysis, 31* (3), 377–397.

Ambrose, B.W. & Linneman, P. (2001) REIT organizational structure and operating characteristics. *Journal of Real Estate Research, 21*, (3), 141–162.

Bauer, R., Guenster, N. & Otten, R. (2004) Empirical evidence on corporate governance in Europe: the effect on stock returns, firm value and performance. *Journal of Asset Management, 5* (2), 91–104.

Bauer, R., Eichholtz, P.M.A. & Kok, N. (2006) Corporate governance and firm valuation: the REIT-effect, Preliminary Working Paper presented at the ERES Conference 2006, Maastricht University, 2006.

Baums, T. (2001) Bericht der Regierungskommission Corporate Governance, Cologne 2001.

Becht, M., Bolton, P. & Röell, A. (2002) Corporate governance and control, NBER Working Paper 9371, 2002.

Beiner, S., Drobetz, W., Schmid, M. & Zimmermann, H. (2006) An integrated framework of corporate governance and firm valuation, Working Paper, University of Basel, 2006.

Berle, A.A. & Means, G.C. (1932) The modern corporation and private property, New York 1932.

Bhagat, S. & Black, B.S. (2002) The non-correlation between board independence and long-term firm performance. *Journal of Corporation Law, 27*, 231–274.

Black, B.S., Jang, H. & Kim, W. (2006) Does corporate governance affect firm value? Evidence from Korea. *Journal of Law, Economics and Organization, 22*, 366–413.

Brainard, W.C. & Tobin, J. (1968) Pitfalls in financial model building. *American Economic Review, 58*, 99–122.

Cadbury, A. (1992) Report of the committee on the financial aspects of corporate governance, London 1992.

Campbell, R.D., Gosh, C. & Sirmans, C.F. (2005) Value creation and governance structure in REIT mergers. *Journal of Real Estate Finance and Economics, 31* (2), 225–239.

Cho, M.H. (1998) Ownership structure, investment, and the corporate value: an empirical analysis. *Journal of Financial Economics, 47*, 103–121.

Davis, B.J. & Shelor, R.M. (1995) Executive compensation and financial performance in the real estate industry. *Journal of Real Estate Research, 10* (2), 141–151.

Demsetz, H. & Lehn, K. (1985) The structure of corporate ownership: causes and consequences. *Journal of Political Economy, 93* (6), 1155–1177.

Doidge, C., Karolyi, G.A. & Stulz, R.M. (2004) Why do countries matter so much for corporate governance? ECGI Working Paper, 2004.

Drobetz, W., Schillhofer, A. & Zimmermann, H. (2004) Corporate governance and expected stock returns: evidence from Germany. *European Financial Management, 10*, 267–293.

Durnev, A. & Kim, E.H. (2005) To steal or not to steal: firm attributes, legal environment and valuation. *Journal of Finance, 60*, 1461–1493.

Eichholtz, P.M.A. & Kok, N. (2006) How does the market for corporate control function for property companies? Working Paper, Maastricht University, 2006.

Eisenberg, T., Sundgren, S. & Wells, M.T. (1998) Larger board size and decreasing firm value in small firms. *Journal of Financial Economics, 48*, 35–54.

Friday, H.S. & Sirmans, G.S. (1998) Board of director monitoring and firm value in REITs. *Journal of Real Estate Research, 16* (3), 411–427.

Friday, H.S., Sirmans, G.S. & Conover, C.M. (1999) Ownership structure and the value of the firm: the case of REITs. *Journal of Real Estate Research, 17* (1), 71–90.

Gillan, S.L. & Starks, L.T. (2003) Corporate governance, corporate ownership, and the role of institutional investors: a global perspective, Working Paper, University of Delaware, 2003.

Gompers, P., Ishii, J. & Metrick, A. (2003) Corporate governance and equity prices. *Quarterly Journal of Economics, 118* (1), 107–155.

Gosh, C. & Sirmans, C.F. (2003) Board independence, ownership structure and performance: evidence from Real Estate Investment Trusts. *Journal of Real Estate Finance and Economics, 26* (2), 287–318.

Han, B. (2006) Insider ownership and firm value: evidence from Real Estate Investment Trusts. *Journal of Real Estate Financial Economics, 32,* 471–493.

Hartzell, J.C., Sun, L. & Titman, S. (2004) The effect of corporate governance on investment: evidence from Real Estate Investment Trusts (REITs), Working Paper, University of Texas at Austin, 2004.

Hermalin, B.E. & Weisbach, M.S. (1991) The effects of board composition and direct incentives on board composition. *Financial Management, 20,* 101–112.

Initiative Corporate Governance der deutschen Immobilienwirtschaft (2003) Corporate Governance in the German Real Estate Economy: Amendments to the German Corporate Governance Code, <http://www.immo-initiative.de/inter-national/kodex/kodex_capital.shtml>, publishing date: 19.09.2003, retrieval date: 20.02.2007.

Initiative Corporate Governance der deutschen Immobilienwirtschaft (2005) Principles of Proper and Fair Management in the Real Estate Economy, <http://www.immo-initiative.de/international/kodex/principles.pdf>, publishing date: 01.09.2005, retrieval date: 20.02.2007.

IVG (2006) IVG Immobilien Annual Report 2005, <http://www.ivg.de/down-load/IVG_GB_2005_Englisch.pdf>, publishing date: 22.03.2006, retrieval date: 14.02.2007.

Jensen, M.C. & Meckling, W.H. (1976) Theory of the firm: managerial behavior, agency costs and ownership structure. *Journal of Financial Economics, 3,* 305–360.

Jensen, M.C. (1986) Agency costs of free cash flows, corporate finance, and takeovers. *American Economic Review, 76* (2), 323–317.

Jensen, M.C. (2001) Value maximization, stakeholder theory and corporate objective function. *European Financial Management, 7,* 297–360.

Klapper, L.F. & Love, I. (2004) Corporate governance, investor protection, and performance in emerging markets. *Journal of Corporate Finance, 10* (5), 703–728.

La Porta, R., Lopez-de-Silanes, F., Shleifer, A. & Vishny, R. (2000) Investor protection and corporate governance. *Journal of Financial Economics, 58,* 3–27.

La Porta, R. *et al.* (2002) Investor protection and corporate valuation. *Journal of Finance, 57,* 1147–1170.

Loderer, C. & Martin, K. (1997) Executive stock ownership and performance – Tracking faint traces. *Journal of Financial Economics, 45,* 223–255.

Lombardo, D. & Pagano, M. (2002) Law and equity markets: a simple model, Working Paper, University of Salerno, 2002.

McConnell, J.J. & Servaes, H. (1990) Additional evidence on equity ownership and corporate value. *Journal of Financial Economics, 27,* 595–612.

McKinsey & Company (2002) Global investor opinion survey, <http://www.mckinsey.com/clientservice/organizationleadership/service/corpgovernance/pdf/GlobalInvestorOpinionSurvey2002.pdf>, publishing date: 01.07.2002, retrieval date: 07.12.2006.

McKinsey & Company (2004) US sets global trend behind governance shake-up, <http://www.mckinsey.com/clientservice/organizationleadership/service/cor-pgovernance/pdf/Wong-US_sets_global_trends_behind_governance_shake-up   _(IFLR)(Sept_2004).pdf>, Erscheinungsdatum: 01.09.2004, Abrufdatum: 07.12.2006.

Morck, R., Shleifer, A. & Vishny, R. (1988) Management ownership and market valuation: an empirical analysis. *Journal of Financial Economics, 20,* 293–315.

NAREIT, National Association of Real Estate Investment Trusts (2007) Historical REIT Industry Market Capitalization: 1972-2006, <http://www.nareit.com/ library/industry/marketcap.cfm>, publishing date: 2007, retrieval date: 20.02.2007.

Nestor, S. & Thompson, J.K. (2001) Corporate governance patterns in OECD economies: is convergence under way?, OECD Working Paper, <http://www.oecd. org/dataoecd/7/10/1931460.pdf>, publishing date: 01.01.2001, retrieval date: 07.12.2006.

OECD, Organisation for Economic Co-operation and Development (1999) OECD principles of corporate governance, Paris 1999.

OECD, Organisation for Economic Co-operation and Development (2003) Financial assets of institutional investors in million US Dollars, OECD statistical database, <http://cs4hq.oecd.org/oecd/eng/TableViewer/Wdsview/dispviewp. asp? ReportId=1880&bReportOnly=True>, publishing date: 25.11.2003, retrieval date: 11.01.2007.

Pagano, M., Röell, A. & Zechner, J. (2002) The geography of equity listings: why do companies list abroad. *Journal of Finance, 57,* 2651–2694.

Rosenstein, S. & Wyatt, J.G. (1990) Outside directors, board independence and shareholder wealth. *Journal of Financial Economics, 26,* 175–191.

Rosenstein, S. & Wyatt, J.G. (1997) Inside directors, board effectiveness and shareholder wealth. *Journal of Financial Economics, 40,* 229–250.

Shleifer, A. & Vishny, R. (1997) A survey of corporate governance. *Journal of Finance, 52,* 737–783.

Smith, M.P. (1996) Shareholder activism by institutional investors: evidence from CalPERS. *Journal of Finance, 51,* 227–252.

Weisbach, M.S. (1988) Outside directors and CEO turnover. *Journal of Financial Economics, 20,* 431–460.

Yermack, D. (1996) Higher market valuation of companies with a small board of directors. *Journal of Financial Economics, 40,* 185–211.

13

The Future of Real Estate Education

Tony Key

Introduction

The task of real estate education is to produce well-rounded entrants into real estate professions. The problem of real estate education has been to decide exactly what is meant by a well-rounded real estate professional. That problem is being intensified by the rapidly changing character of the industry itself, as it is simultaneously expanding into a globalised asset class and blending into mainstream capital and financial markets.

This chapter attempts to meet the challenge of a fast-changing topic through a review of previous work on the topic, through a little new analysis and with a large measure of speculation and personal opinion. It has, fortunately, been saved the groundwork of assembling basic information on global real estate education by a recent and magisterial survey by Schulte (2002), together with the a global snapshot of current educational provision from The Royal Institution of Chartered Surveyors (RICS) directory of courses available at www.rics.org.

Any activity connected with the real estate industry has, first, to take account of a pace of change which comes close to a transformation even in the 5 years since Schulte's study. This review begins with a brief outline of those trends and their implications for the global supply and demand for real estate skills, then moves on to discuss how real estate education is delivered, the core body of knowledge (if any) it is seeking to convey and the style in which it is taught.

The demand for real estate skills

Real estate has a good claim to being the asset class of last decade. Its standing in the investment industry and capital markets is beginning to reflect its share of global wealth, amounting to a massive shift in the way real estate assets are owned, managed and financed. That wave of real estate expansion has both short-term and long-term causes: a surge in investor demand prompted by a flight from equities and search for yield has been coupled to an increase in the supply of investment stock produced by corporate sales and the opening of new markets in transitional and emerging economies.

Rising demand and supply have been eagerly intermediated by global financial conglomerates keen to add real estate to their wholesale and retail investment businesses, and to use cheap debt to refinance real estate assets. To give just one indicator, global investment transactions in commercial real estate have doubled in 3 years, with 42% of deals now across borders (Jones Lang LaSalle, 2007).

The implications for real estate education are obvious. We are experiencing an explosion in global demand for real estate skills, much of it arising in countries where the profession barely existed a decade ago, but on a scale which, to my knowledge, no one has even tried to measure. Figure 13.1 attempts an illustration. It estimates of the total value of investment grade commercial real estate[1] up to 2050 in the four largest emergent economies (the 'BRIC' group, Brazil, Russia, India and China) compared to the G6 group of the current largest economies (France, Germany, Italy, Japan, UK and USA).

On these calculations, the total value of real estate stock in the BRIC group is currently only 6% of the G6 total. But that share will rise to half the G6's by 2030 and overtake the G6 around 2040. While the calculations are speculative, the direction and scale of shift is indisputable.

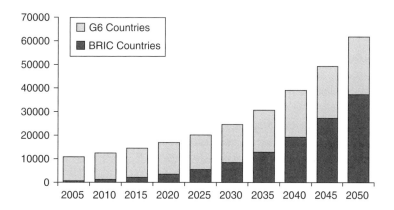

Figure 13.1 Estimated value of investment-grade real estate. *Source*: From EPRA estimates of real estate stock, Goldman Sachs economic projections.

Real estate's borders are not only expanding geographically, they are also merging into neighbouring tracts of the financial industry. From early 1990s, beginning in the USA, real estate has adopted the structures of mainstream finance – REIT securitisations of equity, CMBS securitisations of debt, a flood of investment vehicles structured as private equity and open-ended funds overlaid by funds of funds and most recently embryonic markets in derivatives and Exchange Traded Funds. At an accelerating pace, flows of capital through these structures are marshalled by global financial conglomerates, which have absorbed and overtaken the real estate specialists businesses which once dominated the industry.

Geographical expansion simply increases the demand for traditional core real estate skills in property management and valuation. Integration into wider capital markets has a more ambiguous impact. At first sight, each financial innovation looks like an extension of demand for real estate professionals – at the equities, fixed income and derivatives desks of financial conglomerates, among mortgage lenders and investment bankers, in credit rating agencies and among the army of consultants and journalists who feed the appetite for information that drives mainstream financial markets.

But that trend at the same time puts a question mark over whether the skills needed to work in (say) structured finance or credit default risk in real estate are really a distinct discipline with its own educational and professional requirements. If the basis of analysis has shifted from the esoteric language of valuers to the generic methods of discounted cash flow, from the private market of expert opinion to public markets in equity and debt, does that extended territory belong to real estate professionals who have learned enough finance, or to financial professionals who have learned enough real estate?

How much matching change can we see in the globalisation and sophistication of real estate education? Any answer has to be partial, because the scene can be readily viewed only through the prism of RICS, which stands as the only internationally accepted accrediting body which aims to accommodate a full spread of real estate disciplines within a single career path.

The RICS' degree-level courses already have a fair claim to be international. Close to half of the total current courses in core areas such as valuation and commercial property are now outside the UK (Table 13.1 – which classifies courses by 'specialisms' offered. Some courses offer more than one specialism and are therefore counted under two or more heads). In total, the RICS Directory records 687 undergraduate and postgraduate courses, of which 487 are RICS accredited, of which in turn 174 are outside the UK. For the core real estate specialisms, the top four in Table 13.1, 45–50% of offerings are currently outside the UK.

Table 13.1   RICS directory of property courses.

Course Specialisation[a]	All Courses	RICS-accredited Courses:	In the UK	Overseas
Commercial Property	244	192	99	93
Residential	228	180	91	89
Valuation	218	177	88	89
Quantity Surveying	175	128	70	58
Building Surveying	82	57	44	13
P&D	53	42	38	4
Project Management	52	42	29	13
Geomatics	42	30	21	9
Facilities Management	40	30	17	13
Environmental Engineering	33	21	20	1
Other Land & Buildings[b]	16	12	12	0

Source: RICS course directory at www.rics.org. Downloaded 18 July 2007.
[a]Excludes RICS non-property specialisations in Antiques & Fine Art, Dispute Resolution, Machinery/Business Assets. [b]Comprises Building Control, Management Consultancy, Minerals and Waste Management.

How much programmes outside the RICS umbrella contribute to the supply of real estate skills is very hard to judge. In the USA, in 2003 04, graduates from specialist real estate degrees numbered only 705 at Bachelors level and 423 at Masters level (Institute of Education Science, 2007). Both totals had increased by less than 100 since the early 1990s. A US graduate output of 1100 per year compares with an output from RICS-accredited courses in the UK alone of more than 5000 per year. The apparently huge gulf is, however, in large part a matter of definition, and lies in a radical difference between UK and US approaches to real estate education. This difference also leads us from the volume of real estate education to its organisation, taken up in the next section.

Paradigms for real estate education

One of the features of real estate education most often remarked upon in previous work is an international divergence in approach, which reflects an even more fundamental divergence in the organisation the real estate profession(s). Schulte *et al.* (2005) identifies the 'surveying approach' of the UK and Commonwealth countries, the 'investment and finance approach' in the USA and an 'interdisciplinary approach' in Continental Europe.

On the UK model, real estate (or 'surveying') is an integrated profession (or perhaps more accurately a cluster of linked professions) overseen by the RICS and embracing disciplines from geomatics and quantity surveying through valuation to commercial property, and taking in some non–real estate valuation areas such as the valuation of business machinery, antiques and fine arts. So, RICS qualification is achieved via a total of 17 'faculties', which are in turn built up from 160 specialisms. Full professional qualification has been, since the 1980s, been predominantly via graduate entry from an RICS-accredited university-level course, followed by different tracks in on-the-job experience (French & Palmer, 2002).

The US model is very different. Real estate brokers, appraisers, construction managers, investment managers all have different professional bodies, and varying routes to qualification. Previous literature on the USA generally takes real estate education to refer to Masters courses run in Schools of Business, where real estate is seen largely as a sub-branch of business and finance. Below Masters level, real estate options may be provided in Bachelors of Commerce degrees, but the education and training of brokers and appraisers is regarded as a branch of technical training. Accordingly, a large part of what in the UK is treated as core real estate education has been little discussed in the US academic literature. Webb and Smith (2002) estimate that around 200 public and private universities offer real estate classes within Bachelors courses, while around 30 universities offer specialist Masters degrees in real estate or MBAs with a real estate specialisation.

For the rest of the world, the only identifiable bloc is a 'British Commonwealth' group, where specialist real estate education has evolved along the UK model, though latterly with a tilt towards the US model. Within the Commonwealth countries, however, there are notable exceptions such as India where no college-level courses in real estate existed until very recently.

Outside these blocs, university-level real estate education, and in many cases the organisation of real estate as a distinct profession, is mostly a recent development, dating back to the 1990s. Traditionally, the core real estate professions of brokerage and valuation have been entered through vocational training rather than university courses, or as adjuncts to university courses in construction, civil engineering or law. Specialist real estate programmes at undergraduate or postgraduate level have either been added in recent years, or have yet to emerge.

But these traditional blocs are changing and merging. Major changes in the UK model flow from 1998, when the President of the RICS Richard Lay's 'Agenda for Change' called for 'a radical shake up of the syllabus, with greater emphasis put on business and economic issues' leading to 'a truly transferable qualification, which is not wholly property specific' (Lay, 1998).

These goals have been carried through in a new system of RICS course accreditation, based on a 'strong partnership between RICS and a limited number of centres of academic excellence throughout the world'. In essence, the RICS no longer seeks to prescribe in detail the syllabus followed in accredited degrees, substituting overall quality standards and a 'market test' recruitment from courses into the real estate industry. Thus, RICS Partners are required to meet four key threshold standards, specifying the pre-entry attainment level for undergraduate (but not postgraduate) entrants, the research and teaching quality of the institution and the recruitment of graduates into relevant employment. University partnerships have been the basis of RICS accreditation in the UK since 2001, but are still in the process of being extended to other countries.

Some aspects of the Partnership system have been controversial. In its early years, a number of UK courses were deaccredited, and doubts were raised that student numbers could be maintained with the higher entry standards, particularly in the construction and quantity surveying areas (Wilkinson & Hoxley, 2005). Judged by the raw numbers, however, the Partnership system looks like a resounding success. Starters on RICS-accredited courses in the UK had fallen by more than 40% over the 7 years to 1999, to less than 3000 (Ellis & Wood, 2006). Student recruitment has rebounded to over 8000 by 2006, about 50% above its early 1990s peak. While many other factors have contributed to the growth – not least a very healthy industry demand – at the very least, the new system has not, as some feared, constrained entry into the profession.

Within the totals, there has also been a marked change in the composition of the student intake. In 2000, less than 500 of the 3400 UK entrants to RICS-accredited courses were starting postgraduate courses. By 2006, the number of postgraduate entrants had multiplied 10-fold to 4500, against a rise of 26% in undergraduate entrants to 3700. Masters degrees have, in a very short space of time, become the dominant entry route in the UK. And there has been a proliferation not only in the number of postgraduate courses, but also in the range of specialisms they offer. In 2000, 17 UK institutions were offering a total of 24 different RICS-accredited postgraduate courses (documented in French & Palmer, 2002). By 2007, 45 institutions were offering no less than 183 different postgraduate courses. In 2000, individual universities generally offered one or two postgraduate courses with either broad general titles (like Land Management) or narrow technical specialisms (Geographic Information Systems, Housing Policy and Practice). Today's postgraduate courses still mostly carry general labels (Quantity Surveying, Facilities Management, Planning and Development, Real Estate) but also show a flourishing of new specialisms such as Urban Regeneration, Sustainable Construction, Satellite Positioning Technology and Conservation of Historic Buildings.

In contrast to this proliferation of Masters courses, the number and range of UK undergraduate courses accredited by the RICS have gone in the opposite direction, from a total of more than 50 institutions offering 130 separate courses in 2000 to 39 institutions and 124 courses in 2007.

A few institutions, indeed, may appear to have adopted the US model in its entirety, relocating their real estate programmes into Business Schools (as at Aberdeen, City University and Reading), or establishing real estate courses labelled as MBAs (at Aberdeen, Sheffield Hallam, College of Estate Management).

Part of the apparent contrast between UK and US real estate education has been because academic discussion of the latter has largely ignored training for brokers and appraisers, which is largely delivered through technical and vocational courses, overseen by state regulation (in the case of appraisers, overseen by the federal Appraisal Foundation) and a number of professional bodies. The largest are National Association of Realtors (NAR, which with 1.3 million members claims to be the largest professional association in the world) and the Appraisal Institute (AI, with 22 000 members). For comparison, the RICS global membership is 136 000.

The NAR is predominantly concerned with residential brokerage, which is the one major area of real estate mostly outside the RICS umbrella in the UK. For appraisers, however, entry conditions can be seen as shifting towards the UK model of graduate entry. Thus, the Appraisal Foundation will, from 2008, raise higher educational prerequisites for Certified Residential and Certified General Appraisers to Associate or Bachelors college degrees respectively. The graduate entry requirement is followed by requirements for specialist courses (at least 200 classroom hours for the Certified Appraiser level), and work experience (at least 2000 hours). The US requirement for postgraduate learning is, in required content and duration, close to the RICS requirement for an accredited postgraduate degree and work experience.

Overall, the historic differences between the UK and US models of real estate education have perhaps been exaggerated by an emphasis on university-level courses, and in the USA primarily on postgraduate courses. A marked shift in the UK model towards general first degrees and succeeded by specialist real estate Masters degrees, and a shift in the US appraiser qualifications towards graduate entry and prescribed classroom training means the two systems have a lot more in common. That leaves countries where real estate education is still taking shape with a flexible choice from a broad palette.

A point on which there are still differences, however, is that the UK model takes real estate as a wide, and increasingly varied, cluster of specialisms running from building and construction through to finance and investment, with branches off into planning and environmental management, all overseen by the RICS. This structure may be better equipped to preserve real estate as a self-aware professional grouping from encroachment by other professions such as banking and finance. But it also makes it increasingly difficult to define what, if any, core body of skills and expertise defines a real estate professional.

A real estate body of knowledge

Some authors set a very high hurdle for the 'requisite knowledge for making effective decisions concerning property involvements in the global context of the 21st century' (Roulac, 2002). Roulac sees real estate outcomes as 'a synthesis of theory, history, content, context, process, methodology'. This perspective ropes in no less than 48 'fundamental disciplines for real estate involvement', running from accounting to urban land economics, adding along the way humanities, history of science, science and sociology alongside more predictable headings like land economics, construction management and investment.

Roulac leaves his list as a conceptual device, with no rendering into a manageable educational syllabus. Schulte (2002) takes a more practical view, visualising a 'House of Real Estate Economics', which sits on an interdisciplinary foundation of economics, law, spatial planning, architecture, engineering and business administration. Drawn out of these disciplines, Schulte identifies 12 primary subject areas within a generic area he terms real estate economics, most of them with titles readily recognisable to anyone familiar with the syllabuses of most university real estate courses: Project Development, Facilities Management, Appraisal and Portfolio Management.

Table 13.2 follows the set of headings from Schulte (2002), reorganised in a schema which loosely groups them by their relationship to the creation and management of physical assets, through the analysis of markets in which they sit to the way in which they are financed.

It is hoped that this is a reasonable general framework which covers the bulk of university-level real estate courses. Specialisations by property type – commercial, residential, rural, regeneration, corporate etc. – could of course be accommodated as a third dimension to the table, with different weightings of the generic subject headings.

Table 13.2 A real estate body of knowledge.

Creation	Management	Analysis	Investment and Finance
Land surveying, Geomatics	Building surveying	Valuation and development appraisal	Asset pricing
Construction management	Property management	Market analysis and forecasting	Portfolio construction
Quantity surveying	Facilities management	Spatial economics	Debt finance
	Leasing, landlord and tenant	Public policy and planning	Corporate finance
			Equity and debt investment

It might well be highly desirable that a 'rounded real estate professional' has a working knowledge of all the topics listed in Table 13.2. But
it is clearly impossible to treat all of them in any depth within a standard
undergraduate course, and still less within the increasingly common confines of a 1- or 2-year Masters course.

Table 13.2 should therefore be taken as a real estate 'body of knowledge'
in the wide sense of the term, the sum total of all knowledge that constitutes the expertise of a profession, rather than the narrow sense of the
expertise expected of individual members of the profession.

In the UK, there has been little general discussion of what constitutes an
appropriate body of real estate knowledge. This may well be because the
RICS oversees all strands of the profession, from the physical to the financial, and defines different sets of competencies required for final qualification by 17 different 'pathways'. Different pathways represent very distinct
specialisms within the broad profession. For example, out of around 20
competencies required for each of the Facilities Management and Finance
and Investment pathways, there are only two which are required for both.

Some parts of the US system are even more fully specified than the RICS
pathways. Thus, appraisers require a licence from State boards, working to minimum requirements laid down by the Appraisal Foundation.
Membership of a professional body is not mandatory, but the leading body,
the Appraisal Institute, formally defines a body of knowledge covered
by its own education programmes and examinations (nine examinations
in valuation techniques, plus two in professional practice and business
ethics).

Although there may well be lively debate within the RICS and the
Appraisal Institute on the competencies required, the open debate among
academics about the real estate body of knowledge has mostly been generated around the US Masters-level courses which are not determined by
the entry requirements of any professional body. There was enough unease
about what real estate students should know for the American Real Estate
Society (ARES) to establish a Body of Knowledge Committee in 1990.
Disappointingly, its conclusion was that 'the study of real estate has not
evolved through the detailed debate necessary to achieve consensus among
educators about a common body of knowledge' (Epley, 1996). This may in
part reflect a long-standing split between adherents of a broad urban economics and land use approach to real estate education, as advocated by
Graaskamp (1977) versus a finance approach taught in business schools, in
the ascendancy since the 1960s (Webb & Smith, 2002).

Efforts by US academics to define a body of real estate knowledge have,
nonetheless, continued, through surveys of employers to determine what
skills are required, or surveys of academics to determine what skills are
taught. Weeks and Finch (2003) report a survey of curriculum content

at US collegiate business schools offering real estate courses as a major (40 cases) or concentration within a more general programme (27 cases). Manning and Epley (2006) attempt to match up the competencies regarded as important by employers with those taught in real estate Masters courses. Black and Rabianski (2003) is the most wide ranging exercise of this type, reporting a survey of 275 real estate academics and working professionals across 23 countries. Galuppo and Worzala (2004) appear to be the only authors who have used surveys of their peer groups and working professionals as an input to designing actual degree programmes.

Despite this substantial effort, the academic studies cited above do not lead to any real closure on what constitutes a core body of knowledge. This may reflect problems of methodology. The survey samples are often small and self-selecting, and responses are based on varying classifications of real estate topics, with categories such as 'Real Estate Economics' or 'Risk and Return Analysis', for which the precise meaning appears open to subjective interpretation. Black and Rabianski (2003) conclude that 'there is no consensus on what constitutes a body of knowledge in real estate based on this survey', a failure which they attribute to the different interest groups – say appraisal versus market analysis versus finance and investment – represented among the respondents. Perhaps because their work was focussed on the practical definition of academic programmes, however, Galuppo and Worzala (2003) conclude with a more succinct listing of nine topics regarded as most important in Graduate Real Estate programmes from their survey of US professionals (Table 13.3). At least to this observer, this looks very much like the palette from which many UK Masters courses in real estate – with labels permutated from Real Estate, Investment, Finance, Economics – have been blended. It is a set of topics which it is possible to cover within the confines of a specialist one Masters programme.

Whether there is a definable body of knowledge for real estate therefore seem to end up largely as a matter of definition. If, like Roulac, we take real estate as the crossroads of economics, space, history and technology, or like the RICS, we take it as a cluster of professions linked to land and buildings, the body of knowledge can only mean the sum of knowledge across all

Table 13.3 Important topics in a Graduate Real Estate programme.

Real estate investment	Real estate economics
Project analysis (DCF, NPV)	Capital markets
Real estate finance and lending	Real estate law
Real estate markets	Development of real estate
Valuation of real estate	Planning and land use controls

Source: Galuppo and Worzala (2003).

members of the profession, not the knowledge available to each individual member. This may look a lot more fragmented and messier than, for example, The Chartered Financial Analyst Institute's candidate body of knowledge for investment professionals, which runs to 37 closely typed pages.

But, for practical purposes, an educational programme for a particular type of real estate professional can be quite tightly defined by one of the RICS' 17 pathways, or by the Appraisal Foundation's four levels of qualification. Even for less tightly specified specialisms such as real estate finance, sitting on the fluid boundary between real estate and general finance, there appears to be a large measure of common ground in the structure of courses.

On this view, a fragmented body of knowledge is not at the end of the day a big problem for real estate educators. It may be more of an institutional problem for a professional body like the RICS, which has taken on the task of setting global standards for the education of the full range of real estate professions. Already, only around half of graduates from RICS-accredited degrees continue through work experience to full RICS membership. Many graduate entrants into fund management or banking – and even some entrants into London firms of chartered surveyors – are proceeding to professional qualifications such as Chartered Financial Analysts. If, quite apart from the RICS's institutional interests, it is desirable to retain control of standards and professional identity among real estate specialists in these areas, it might be achieved by cross-recognition of qualifications with other professional bodies.

The methods of real estate education

The final aspect of the delivery of real estate education dealt with here concerns the style rather than the content of teaching, and whether that style is well-matched to the needs of students and their ultimate employers. This question in large part resolves to a well-worn contrast between the emphasis on problem solving, personal skills and group-working characteristic of business courses, or the more traditional conveying of a set of specific professional techniques and text-based learning.

On this score, some of the thin evidence on employer attitudes to real estate education makes dismal reading. A recent survey of 150 European real estate employers, conducted for the Urban Land Institute, reported that academic training in property ranked 12th out of a list of 12 skills and attributes most valued in employees. The most valued attributes were proactiveness, entrepreneurialism, the ability to learn quickly, analytical skills, oral communication and business judgement (Equinox Partners, 2003). This matched the low rating given to real estate education in an earlier survey of US employers (Equinox Partners, 2002). These surveys are, however, sketchily analysed and appear to relate to the recruitment of employees at all levels, rather than the recruitment of graduate entrants where specific education is likely to be more highly prized.

More rigorous assessments of how consumers – students and employers – rate real estate education are very rare. Butler *et al.* (1998) suggest that the US employers rate a range of 'soft' skills including communications, problem solving, negotiations and team building as extremely important. Newell and Acheampong (2002) report a fair level of satisfaction with property degrees among Australian students, attributed to their success in getting jobs, but report ratings for teaching quality below those in related disciplines. Callanan and McCarthy (2003) suggest that New Zealand employers wanted more practical skills, which might be created by more input into courses from the property industry.

These findings are consonant with trends in business education which put a higher value on generalised transferable skills such as verbal communication, problem solving, report writing, team working than on technical knowledge and academic learning (Mintzberg & Gosling, 2002). In the real estate field, several authors have set out an agenda for education which take these messages on board, recommending teaching styles based on self-learning, more use of real-world case studies and interaction with industry through internships and projects (Butler *et al.*, 1998; Manning & Roulac, 2001).

How far and how fast real estate is adopting these alleged 'best practice' methods of education with closer industry linkages has not been registered in the literature. Impressionistically, it is safe to suggest that for US business schools they are now considered to be the standard, and that the majority of real estate educators in other countries would like to follow in the same direction – not least as a way of keeping up with industry practice, which is often outstripping academic texts. Matching US best practice in this area could be accelerated by a commitment from individual firms and real estate trade bodies to support real estate education (not least through generous funding) which matches that in the USA.

In several important respects, it is possible to read recent years as a story of convergence in the global practice of real estate education, which blends elements of both the US and UK paradigms. There are other counts, however, on which real estate education is still a long from globalisation in (say) finance or economics which is achieved by the production of core texts which are equally relevant and useful in all countries. As Schulte *et al.* (2005) point out, real estate academics have been very willing to recognise the globalisation of the industry through adding 'European' or 'International' markets modules to their programmes, and by fostering cross-border exchanges of various types, running from joint degree programmes, staff and student exchanges to summer schools and field trips. In the research arena, there is even more intensive cross-fertilisation between countries through international co-authorships, conferences and journals.

But, as those readers who work in classrooms populated with graduate students from several continents will know, there are still no 'real estate principles' texts which are international in character in the way that there are international texts in other quite specialist fields such as urban economics. The most comprehensive one-volume text on valuation, finance and investment from the UK is Brown and Matysiak's 'Real Estate Investment', (Brown & Matysiak, 2000) while that from the USA is Geltner and Miller's 'Commercial Real Estate Investment' (Geltner & Miller, 2001). While both are admirable, the contents of the two books are deeply rooted in their respective traditions – a lot on UK methods of freehold and leasehold valuation from the former, much more on debt financing and CMBS in the latter. Both books rely exclusively on examples and illustrative data drawn exclusively from their home countries.

Though there are textbooks on the topic of international real estate (Adair *et al.*, 1996; Seabrook *et al.*, 2004), they have been concerned with describing differences in institutional and market structure, rather than extracting fundamental common principles. This is clearly an area where education is falling behind practice among the global firms of valuers, fund managers and bankers who are dealing every day with the adaptation of international best practice to local conditions.

It is fairly easy to envisage the production of a global principles text on real estate finance and investment, which is an adaptation of standard techniques such as discounted cash flow, and general theories such as modern portfolio theory and capital asset pricing model. Texts which distil general principles from the more varied international practice in conventional valuation methods, in landlord and tenant law, will be harder to produce, but even more valuable.

Further progress and integration in the style of real estate teaching, in the textbooks and case studies through which it is conveyed, could be advanced by more research and discussion on international real estate education. With the notable exception of Schulte *et al.* (2005), academic debate on the topic has been largely confined to the USA. Discussion in the USA has also been fostered by the existence of the specialist Journal of Real Estate Practice and Education. While there would perhaps not be enough material to fill a UK or international equivalent of that journal, occasional editions of some of the mainstream research journals dedicated to educational issues would be a valuable stimulant.

The future of real estate education

This attempt to cover a wide-ranging and fast-changing topic within the confines of a single chapter has no doubt meant that many of the issues touched on have been poorly resolved, and other important topics ignored. But if forced to the ultimate compression of a single-word summary of the state of real estate education, I would pick 'coping'.

A period of remarkable expansion of the real estate industry – in multiple senses of its size, geographical extent and overlap with other disciplines – has been accommodated without any obvious sense crisis in the supply of skills. That is not meant to deny that the market for real estate graduates has not been very tight, or that a further huge expansion of provision in emerging markets is not urgently required. A tight supply of skills has also meant that territory which real estate professionals might regard as rightfully theirs is being colonised by generalists in finance, investment and consulting.

A second keyword for the trend in real estate education is 'convergence'. Some debate over paradigms of delivery, over the body of knowledge for real estate education, is an inevitable and ongoing consequence of the lack of a universally accepted global accrediting body, frictions between strands within the cluster of real estate professions and its blurred boundaries with other disciplines. But the fact that real estate is by nature less coherent than parallel professions has not, at the end of the day, prevented the evolution of a *de facto* international model. At the risk of an accusation of home bias, the 'UK Mk II' model represented by the RICS' adoption, as a standard entry route, of general first degrees followed by Masters course serving pathways into a cluster of real estate specialisms seems to be a reasonable pragmatic solution, and one which bridges across previous international divergences.

Lest this seem complacent, it is happily acknowledged that on many points there is a woeful lack of evidence on the adequacy of real estate education in either scale or content. Even if it is headed in the right direction, there is much which could be done to smooth its path.

First is some basic manpower planning. In well-established real estate markets, some periodic indicators of the scale of demand for real estate graduates, the pressure points in supply and the match of graduate skills to employer needs would help university providers design courses which meet those needs. For emerging markets, scoping the likely path of demand on the basis of expected growth of real estate stocks and the rate at which the management and financing of those stocks converges with that in mature markets would focus attention on their massive future demand for real estate professionals, and in many countries how poorly it is being met. Any exercise along these lines will no doubt highlight one major issue that has not been covered in this chapter – how the supply of real estate educators can be expected to match the growth in demand for real estate education.

Second is the production of teaching materials which match up to the globalisation, increased sophistication and speed of change in the real estate industry. Here the onus is on academic authors to produce real estate texts which emphasise the common standards of international best practice without ignoring how they interface with the idiosyncrasies of national markets. But real estate businesses, given to calling for high-quality graduates with skills on a par with other branches of finance, could further that objective by a more systematic effort to provide the case studies, internships and funding which match firms in those other branches of finance.

So, to sum up, the future of real estate education is undoubtedly an expansion in numbers and a shift in geographical focus towards what are currently termed emerging markets. For those elements of the real estate body of knowledge which blend into other disciplines – most obviously finance and investment, but including planning, environmental management and other neighbouring fields – it seems to me that qualification via general first degrees followed by a specialist real estate Masters is already a *de facto* international standard and likely to be the primary mode of expansion.

Note

1.   Stocks of commercial real estate are estimated by a formula based on GDP and GDP per capita (taken from Hughes and Arissen, 2005) applied to long-range economic projections from Wilson and Purushothaman (2003).

References

Adair, A., Downie, M.L., McGreal, S. & Vos, G. (1996) *European Valuation Practice: Theory and Techniques.* E & FN Spon, 337 pp.

Black, R. & Rabianski, J. (2003) Defining the real estate body of knowledge: a survey approach. *Journal of Real Estate Practice and Education,* 6 (1).

Brown, G.R. & Matysiak, G.A. (2000) *Real Estate Investment: A Capital Market Approach.* FT Prentice Hall, Harlow.

Butler, J., Gunterman, K. & Wolverton, M. (1998) Integrating the real estate curriculum. *Journal of Real Estate Practice and Education,* 1 (1).

Callanan, J. & McCarthy, I. (2003) Property education in New Zealand: industry requirements and student perceptions. *Journal of Real Estate Practice and Education,* 6 (1).

Ellis, R. & Wood, G. (2006) *The Future of Surveying Education in Universities,* RICS.

Epley, D. (1996) The current body of knowledge paradigms used in real estate education and issues in need of further research. *Journal of Real Estate Research,* 12 (2).

Equinox Partners, Real estate - the human capital factor. 2002 and 2003 from www.equinoxsearch.com

French, N. & Palmer, S. (2002) Great Britain in Schulte (2002) op cit, 149:159.

Galuppo, L. & Worzala, W. (2004) A study into the important elements of a Masters Degree in real estate. *Journal of Real Estate Practice and Education,* 7 (1).

Geltner, D. & Miller, M. (2001) Commercial real estate analysis and investments. South-Western College Publishing Co.

Graaskamp, J.A. (1977) The failure of the universities to teach the real estate process as an interdisciplinary art form. Urban Land Institute.

Hughes, F. & Arissen, J. (2005) *Global Real Estate Securities – where do they fit into the broader market?* European Public Real Estate Association.

Institute of Education Sciences (2007) *Digest of Education Statistics*, Table 252.

Jones Lang LaSalle (2007) Global Capital Markets Bulletin from www.jonelanglasalle. co.uk [accessed on June 2007]

Lay, R. (1998) *The agenda for change: 1998 Presidential address.* RICS, London.

Manning, C. & Epley, D. (2006) Do real estate faculty teach the skills and competencies needed by corporate real estate executives? *Journal of Real Estate Practice and Education, 9* (1).

Manning, C. & Roulac, S. (2001) Where can real estate faculty add the most value at universities in the future? *Journal of Real Estate Practice and Education, 4* (1).

Mintzberg, H. & Gosling, J.R. (2002) Reality programming for MBAs. *Strategy and Business, 26* (1), 28–31.

Newell, G. & Acheampong, P. (2002) *The Quality Of Property Education In Australia.* Paper presented to the Pacific Rim Real Estate Society Conference, Christchurch, January 2002.

Roulac, S. (2002) Requisite Knowledge for Effective Property Involvements. United States in Schulte (2002) op cit 3:19.

Schulte, K-W (ed.) (2002) *Real Estate Education Throughout the World: Past, Present and Future.* Research Issues in Real Estate (7). Kluwer Academic Publishers, Boston.

Schulte, K-W. Schulte-Daxbök, G. Holzmann, G. & Wiffler, M. (2005) *Internationalisation of Real Estate Education.* Paper presented at FIG Working Week, Cairo, Egypt, April 2005.

Seabrook *et al.* (2004) *International Real Estate.* Blackwell, Oxford.

Webb, J. & Smith, H. (2002) United States in Schulte (2002) op cit 320:330.

Weeks, H.S. & Finch, J.H. (2003) An analysis of real estate curriculum requirements at AACSB international-accredited institutions. *Journal of Real Estate Practice and Education, 6* (2), 257–268.

Wilkinson, S. & Hoxley, M. (2005) The impact of the 2001 RICS education reforms on building surveying. In: Queensland University of Technology Research Week International Conference, Brisbane, Australia, 4–8 July 2005, pp. 1222–1223.

Wilson, D. & Purushothaman, R. (2003) *Dreaming With BRICs: The Path to 2050,* Goldman Sachs Economics Paper No: 99.

Index